Praise for *Discovering Speech, Words, and Mind*

"The study of speech – its articulation, perception and linguistic organization – has been enormously influential in cognitive science. Now, Byrd and Mintz offer a lucid and appealing introduction to the theoretical themes and empirical practices that move the field. In exposing the role of speech in language, their treatment of the important topics is impressive: both challenging and engaging!"

Robert Remez, Columbia University and Barnard College

"It's wonderful to have an authoritative introduction to speech production and perception, presented in the context of recent research in linguistics, psychology, and neuroscience."

Mark Liberman, University of Pennsylvania

"While there are several textbooks that offer an introduction to cognitive science, this one is unique in integrating a comprehensive introduction to speech articulation and acoustics into the study of language and mind, and providing a concise, fundamental introduction to the methodological assumptions behind work in this field. The writing is engaging, and it manages to explain complex concepts without oversimplifying them."

Louis Goldstein, University of Southern California

Discovering Speech, Words, and Mind

Dani Byrd
and
Toben H. Mintz

 website at www.discoveringspeech.wiley.com

WILEY-BLACKWELL

A John Wiley & Sons, Ltd., Publication

This edition first published 2010
© 2010 Dani Byrd and Toben H. Mintz

Blackwell Publishing was acquired by John Wiley & Sons in February 2007. Blackwell's publishing program has been merged with Wiley's global Scientific, Technical, and Medical business to form Wiley-Blackwell.

Registered Office
John Wiley & Sons Ltd, The Atrium, Southern Gate, Chichester, West Sussex, PO19 8SQ, United Kingdom

Editorial Offices
350 Main Street, Malden, MA 02148-5020, USA
9600 Garsington Road, Oxford, OX4 2DQ, UK
The Atrium, Southern Gate, Chichester, West Sussex, PO19 8SQ, UK

For details of our global editorial offices, for customer services, and for information about how to apply for permission to reuse the copyright material in this book please see our website at www.wiley.com/wiley-blackwell.

The right of Dani Byrd and Toben H. Mintz to be identified as the authors of this work has been asserted in accordance with the UK Copyright, Designs and Patents Act 1988.

Library of Congress Cataloging-in-Publication Data
Byrd, Dani.
  Discovering speech, words, and mind / Dani Byrd and Toben H. Mintz.
    p. cm.
  Includes bibliographical references and index.
  ISBN 978-1-4051-5798-8 (hardcover : alk. paper) – ISBN 978-1-4051-5799-5
(pbk.   ) 1. Oral communication. 2. Speech. 3. Speech perception.
4. Language and languages. I. Mintz, Toben H. II. Title.
  P95.B97 2010
  302.2'242–dc22
                                                                    2009039198

A catalogue record for this book is available from the British Library.

Set in 11/13pt Palatino by Graphicraft Limited, Hong Kong

1   2010

This book is dedicated to
James Byrd, who didn't live to see it,
and
Benjamin and Anna Siegel

Contents

Ⓦ Accompanying web material can be found at
www.discoveringspeech.wiley.com

Acknowledgments

There are many people who have helped us. All errors are of course our own. We thank Sophie Ambrose, William Badecker, Freddie Bell-Berti, Hagit Borer, Susie Choi, Sandy Disner, Oliver Foellmer, Teruhiko Fukaya, Louis Goldstein, Ernest Greene, Roberto Mayoral Hernandez, Yu-Chi Huang, Aaron Jacobs, Keith Johnson, Elsi Kaiser, Abigail Kaun, David Li, Frank Manis, Michal Martinez, Franc Marušič, Tatjana Marvin, Emi Mukai, Emily Nava, Laura Siegel, Linda Siegel, Reid Swanson, Jean-Roger Vergnaud, Rachel Walker, Hao Wang, Kie Zuraw, and the Bread and Porridge restaurant in Santa Monica. And a special thanks to Barry Schein and Maryellen MacDonald who conceived the course we've so enjoyed teaching.

Chapter 1

Human Language as a Scientific Phenomenon

Section 1: The Specialness of Language

What Is Special About Language

Language is our most important and universal communication medium. As humans, we rely on our capacity to communicate with one another and to "speak our mind." However, we almost never stop to consider that these abilities are made possible by three facts: we can move our bodies in highly skilled ways; these skilled movements create physical changes in the environment that our senses can apprehend; our brains allow the development and use of a complex system of structuring information for expression to other individuals. As scientists, it is fascinating to turn a scientific eye and scientific tools to studying each of these aspects of language. One reason for this fascination is precisely because our language feats are accomplished with ease and no real awareness on our part of their intricate and structured nature. Throughout this book, we will investigate both the nature of language and our human linguistic abilities.

All healthy humans, and only humans, are born capable of using language, and people acquire these abilities simply through exposure without any overt instruction. You may have to take lessons to learn to play the clarinet, but no children need "do this–don't do that" lessons to learn their first language. Children gain this ability simply through their normal course of development and interaction with other speakers of a language, just as infants learn visual depth perception or toddlers learn to walk.

Language's capacity for transmitting information is unrivaled. We've all heard the expression "a picture is worth a thousand words." But while humans can transmit information to one another through facial expression or visual constructions or touch or even smell, none of these can transmit the enormous amount of detail and specificity that is possible with the use of language. Language can also be tremendously evocative – a poem or story or conversation with a boyfriend or parent can move one to tears, hysterical laughter, an intense insight, or a visceral opinion. Not only does language succeed remarkably in transmitting information from one individual to another at a particular time, it permits the continuity of culture over time through oral, written, and now digital recording of knowledge.

For the scientist newly come to the study of language (perhaps like yourself), an objective quantitative and experimental approach to investigating language can prove challenging for exactly the same reasons that make language an interesting object of study: namely, most people – other than your rare linguist or psychologist – simply don't think much about speaking language. Certainly all of us – even language scientists – learn and use language effortlessly. So as *scientists* of language, we will need to become objectively aware of aspects of language that we normally pay no attention to. To dissect its properties as scientists will require us to suspend the preconceptions or biases we may have about how people speak and also require us to be willing to learn about tools scientists use to investigate human behavior – physical measures of the world and human behavior, techniques for experimentation, and critical analysis of data.

The Speech Chain

Let's consider an extremely simple exchange of information through language. Suppose you are at a party (and are over the legal drinking age) and further suppose that the party has run out of beer. It might occur to you that more beer is needed. Seeing as how friends, however close, do not in fact have ESP, in order to express this desire for more beer, you will need to formulate a message and speak it. In addition to knowing the **proposition** or idea that you wish to express, you will now need to select and combine words to express this thought – in English these words might be *we*, *need*, *more*, and *beer*. However, the particular language you speak, in addition to determining the sounds used to form each word (and even how many words are needed) also determines how these words are to be combined. A linguist would call sensible combinations – *we need more beer* – **grammatical** and term nonsensible combinations – *more need beer we* – **ungrammatical**. (This is a specialized use of the term grammatical having nothing to do with the schoolroom rules.) Now, mind you, a thirsty partygoer is nowhere near finished yet. Having selected the words and put them into a sensible combination, our partygoer must convey them to someone, preferably someone having money, at the party. To do this, the partygoer will have to move his or her mouth or **vocal tract** in intricate fashion using the vocal folds, tongue, jaw, nasal port, and lips. Each word

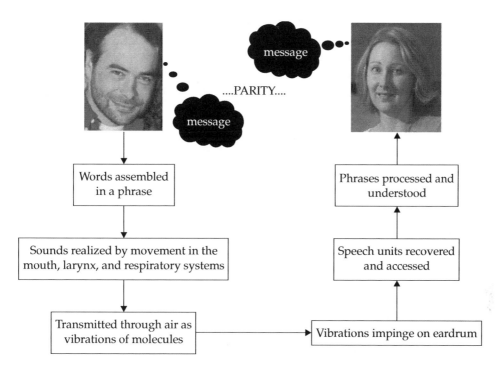

Figure 1.1   The speech chain

is associated with a set of complexly organized movements that cause sound waves to propagate or travel through the air. If the partygoer has been paying attention to where his or her friends are at the party, these sound waves will come into contact with the eardrum of a nearby listener. The listener's brain will respond to the nerve signals created in the inner ear by activating the words in their mind that are consistent with the physical acoustic signal that they just encountered. From these words, the listener will be able to reconstruct the intended message. When the listener recovers the message, and the speaker's intended message matches the one received by the listener, we say that **parity** has been achieved. This is a primary goal in communication.

How can such a complex behavior be so intuitive? The human brain has an inborn or innate capacity for language development and use. This means that it has neural structures whose functionality is, or becomes, specialized for language. Just as humans have evolved to have upright gait, stereoscopic vision, and fine manual manipulation abilities, they have evolved to use language. In addition to the specialization of the human brain, these evolutionary adaptations have also included anatomical and functional characteristics of the vocal tract and auditory system.

It's important to realize that while we have been drawing a picture of *spoken* language, the brain and body can demonstrate the same important properties with language in another modality, namely *signed* language. Language does not necessitate the use of the vocal tract, sound, and the auditory system; it merely requires that humans act in the environment so as to create a structured, information-carrying signal that other humans can perceive well and with parity. Just like spoken languages, signed language also requires movement of the body in a highly skilled way; these skilled movements create physical changes in the environment that our senses can apprehend (reflection of light off the body sensed by the retina), and our brains allow the development and use of a complex system of structuring information in signed languages. In fact, there is a strong correspondence between the parts of brain that process spoken language through vision (i.e., during reading) and the parts of the brain that process signed language (necessarily via vision).

Language Knowledge

What kinds of scientists study this phenomenon of language? The answer is, fortunately, many different kinds of scientists: linguists, psychologists, physiologists, physicists, physicians, engineers, computer scientists, speech-language pathologists, and educators, for example. In this text, we will use bits of information from a variety of scientific arenas to consider the questions of what knowledge is acquired when a child learns language, how this learning is accomplished, and how speaking and understanding take place.

Linguists describe and/or model what people (often subconsciously) *know* that allows them to speak their language. One piece of knowledge that this includes is the set of sounds used in their language and precisely how to articulate and coordinate them. It's clear that people become highly skilled at making a particular set of sounds or vocal tract actions because when we are confronted with a sound or sound-sequence that's not in our own language – such as the sound at the end of *Bach* or at the end of *Favre* – we often substitute other sounds or combinations – you've heard these pronounced, no doubt, as [bak] or [farv]. (We will be using square brackets in this book to indicate sound pronunciation, known as **transcription**.)

Another type of knowledge that humans have about their language is the connection between a certain sound pattern and its specific word meaning. Like the particular sounds in one's language, the meaning of myriad sound sequences – words – must be learned: the sounds "eegl" means a predatory bird in English and the same sequence of sounds means a hedgehog in German. Humans must learn the mapping between sound and meaning that exists in the particular language(s) they are learning, because a child comes into the world prepared to learn *any* human language. Lastly, a person must know how words may be combined with one another in ordered structures and what those combinatorial structures mean. So in English, objects follow verbs, but in Navajo, Japanese, Basque, and Hopi, they precede them. In addition to needing to learn all of this – and apparently doing it with amazing grace and speed by the early years of life – a language learner will also need to learn the appropriate patterns of interaction among participants in a conversation or discourse. We use the term **linguistic competence** to refer to all the myriad patterns that a language user knows that allow for the production and comprehension of language. A person's linguistic competence is the idealized body of knowledge of the structures, sequences, and organizations that may or may not occur in his or her language and their relation to meaning. When linguists want to refer to this body of specialized knowledge, they use the term **grammar**. The term grammar does not mean to a linguist what it means to a grade school English teacher. For a linguist, "grammar" is used to mean a theoretical or formal description of linguistic competence or certain aspects of competence.

Languages Change

One preconception we might have about language is that it exists in some pristine form in the minds of a particularly prestigious speaker or group of speakers. In fact, different forms of a language occur in a variety of socio-economic and geographic groups. And every instantiation of language in the mind of any individual is equally valid and worthy of scientific study. Language also changes with each generation of speakers. You don't speak in the same way as your parents and grandparents; nor will your children use the same form of language that you use. Some of these changes found in a particular generation are ephemeral or short-lived. Will the once derogative term "geek" leave the language in the next generation, or perhaps become a positive term for a technologically sophisticated person? Some changes to a language will persist and become incorporated into the more widely spoken language. Believe it or not, the term "email" was once actually limited to academics and technophiles. The fact that language is always changing means that your linguistic competence will be different than that of your parents and children.

You can no doubt think of examples of geographic differences in vocabulary – "pop" versus "soda," "fountain" versus "bubbler." Can you think of pronunciation variants around the United States? In the West, where the authors of this book live, the words *cot* and *caught* are generally pronounced the same; however, in the Northeast, they have different vowels. Likewise *pull* and *pool* and *which* and *witch* are often homophonous in the West, but certainly not elsewhere. Generation-related variation in pronunciation can be harder to pin down, but we find that most undergraduates pronounce "The End" with the "the" rhyming with "duh" not with "dee." However, most older folks prefer the other pronunciation for the article when it occurs before a word starting with a vowel. A language change currently in progress relates to the grammaticality (used in the *linguistic* sense, *not* the prescriptivist middle-school sense) of using the word "fun" as an adjective, in addition to its standard use as a noun. Anyone is perfectly likely to use *fun* as a noun ("I had a lot of fun at the party"); in addition, many of those people, though not all, will also be comfortable saying "It was a really fun party," with an adverb modifying *fun*. However, the older generation of speakers would not say, "It was the funnest party I've been to this year," while younger folks will find this adjectival use (note the –est adjectival suffix) perfectly acceptable. Another youthful example of a standard noun being called into use as an adjective as language changes is "dope," meaning (we gather, since we are too old to find ourselves using this) "cool" or "hip." A case of an adjective being used as a noun is the currently popular phrase "my bad." As you can see, language is constantly in flux across groups of people and even to some degree in individuals over their lifetime. As psycholinguists we examine the competence of any particular individual speaker, at some point in time. We investigate the knowledge that that speaker has that allows him or her to speak and understand.

So What is Language Anyway?

We have stated that all and only humans use language. Animals do use communication systems, some rather sophisticated. These systems, however, do not exhibit all the hallmark properties shown by language. We will want to consider what are the characteristics common to all communication systems and what characteristics might be exhibited by language alone. These characteristics were generally enumerated by a linguist named Charles Hockett in the 1960s and have been presented over the past half century in various versions. Here are the properties we think are important for you to know.

All communication systems, by definition, must have a means of transmitting a message. Humans generally use a vocal-auditory **mode** for their language, but a manual-visual mode is also possible, as can be found in signed languages. No human language, however, incorporates whistles, foot stamps, or claps (though other nonlanguage types of human communication may use these). Some animals use a hormonal-olfactory chemical mode of transmission to communicate group recognition, alarm, sex, territory, or aggression information. For example, moths convey sexual information via pheromones, while cockroaches convey aggression, and hyenas convey territory marking. Also, the signals of all communication systems, again by definition, must be **meaningful**; they are not random or nonsensical. The signaling in a communication system also serves a useful function for the animal in its environment, that is, it is **ecological**. It may aid in finding food or finding a mate or protecting offspring, for example.

Two other properties of communication systems have to do specifically with the relation between individual communicators. Some animal communication systems, including human language, must be learned through **interaction** with other individuals sharing that communication system. All babies can and will learn whatever language (or languages) they are sufficiently exposed to in childhood through interaction, regardless of the language spoken by the biological parents who contributed their DNA. In humans all aspects of the language system require exposure to other individuals to develop successfully, even though the ability to learn language is an innate genetic endowment. In some other species, such as in

> The mosquito species that carries yellow fever communicates mating availability by an acoustic matching of the sound created by its wingbeats. While the male wingbeat sound is normally higher in pitch than the females, when near one another these mosquitoes signal mating availability by converging to an even higher tone that is an overtone or harmonic of these two frequencies. Thus the **mode** could be said to be wingbeat-auditory (though their auditory system is rather different than a mammal's); the signal is **meaningful** and **ecological** in that it conveys information about an important activity for the animal in its environment – the opportunity for reproduction.

some birds, certain aspects of the communication system are learned while other parts are genetically coded. In yet other species, such as some insects, all communication is encoded directly in the genetics, so deviations, modifications, or innovations to the system by the creature simply are not possible. Humans, and a number of sophisticated animal communicators, also exhibit **reciprocity** in their communications, meaning that any particular individual can both create a communicative signal and understand such a signal. I can speak an utterance to communicate a message and also I can understand such an utterance if someone else speaks it to me. Some animal communicators may only send one type of signal, for example, indicating their sex, and another individual may only be able to receive that signal. A female organism in such a system can perceive the "I am male" signal but can't send it, and vice versa. Such a communication system does not exhibit the feature of reciprocity.

Some communication systems, including human language, have the property of **arbitrariness**. This means that the form of the signal (e.g., a word form) is not required to be related to (e.g., sound like) the thing it represents. In fact, it rarely does (which is to say that onomatopoeia is the exception, not the rule, and even onomatopoetic words vary arbitrarily from language to language). Many animal communication systems use iconic signals and therefore do not exhibit the property of arbitrariness. Honey bees use movements that indicate the direction to a food source by effectively "pointing" to it; distance to the food is also related directly to the speed of the bee's dance; and this appears to be an innate, unlearned, behavior of honey bees. We humans, however, must learn the words of our particular language; there is nothing that requires that some particular sequence of sounds have some particular meaning, as we saw with the *eagle/hedgehog* example earlier. Further, the allowed patterns found in a particular language for how words may be combined is also arbitrary and language-specific. There is nothing in the environment that requires that an adjective precede or follow the noun it modifies; different languages make an arbitrary choice.

Scientists studying language have arrived at further features that, linguists would argue, distinguish human language from all other forms of natural communication. The first unique feature of language is that messages are generated from recombinable parts – this is the property of **compositionality**. The recombinable parts that compose messages are called the language's **discrete units** and crucially the patterns of recombination are meaningful; they encode meaning differences. Messages in human language are communicated by phrases composed of words. Compositionality also applies at the level of words. Words are composed of combinations of sounds or vocal tract actions that individually do not have any meaning of their own. There are a limited set of speech units in any particular language that can be recombined to form meaningful words. Messages communicated by nonhuman animals generally do not show compositionality. Nonhuman animals use signals that cannot be broken down into parts that the animal can recombine to make new or alternate messages. The signal communicating the message is, if modulated at all, modulated in a continuous way – say for example, in loudness or strength or rate. It is true that scientists have argued about the existence of compositionality in animal communication from time to time, but overall naturally occurring animal communication systems appear to lack compositionality.

Another particular property of human language is that it incorporates the possibility of communicating about objects, events, and emotion that are not in our immediate environment – a dream you had last year, a graduation ceremony you hope to participate in next year, or the surface of Neptune. Linguists have called this language property **displacement** because messages can concern items displaced in space and time. Messages are not necessarily driven by stimuli present in the animal's – human's – environs. Human language even allows us to talk about things that patently don't exist, like a dessert you've never had but imagine tasting or the wedding you called off. It is reasonable to attribute this ability to the complexity of human cognition, but even acknowledging that, human language still provides the means for communicating about the past, the future, and counterfactual situations.

Human language also has the potential to express an infinity of messages – it is an **open-ended** system. There are infinitely many sentences possible in a language, and new words can always be made up and added to a language when there is a use for them; indeed, this happens all the time. This may seem an obvious property of human language, but it has an important implication that you may not have thought of. The fact that all human languages are **open-ended** means that humans cannot learn their language by memorizing a set of possible messages. Other animals appear to learn (or innately be genetically provided with) a fixed set of messages that they use to communicate. Unlike these other animals, you will always be able to say something new that you have never said before and even that you have never heard said before. Try it for fun right now: think up a sentence that you believe you have never, ever said and never, ever heard before. It's not even a very hard challenge for us humans. For other animals, such a communication is not possible.

What makes possible this productive capacity of human language? Linguists sometimes use the term **generative** to describe language's combined properties of **compositionality** and **open-endedness**. Language is **generative** because it is based on a systematic relation of meaning and sound created by body actions. Meaning is of course internal; for meaning to become accessible between a speaker and listener – between a language producer and perceiver – it must be transmitted in the environment. By this, we simply mean that humans do not have ESP! Remember the speech chain we looked at above? This transmission is done by combining units of production (which we will discuss at length in later chapters) that can be recovered and decoded by the listener.

Linguists are interested in understanding the cognitive units used as the building blocks of human language and the system of relations among units of different sorts. An important system in language is its **syntax**. Syntax is the system of how words may be arranged in an utterance to convey meaningful relations among them. Consider, for example, the sentences:

Toby gave the book to Dani.
Dani gave the book to Toby.

The syntax of English determines that in the first sentence it was Toby who did the giving and that what he gave was a book and the person to whom he gave it was Dani. The second sentence specifies a different set of relations between Dani and Toby. Syntax refers to the structuring of units of meaning (for now, words) in sequence via structural (hierarchical)

Table 1.1 Properties of Communication Systems

Meaningfulness	*All communication systems*
Ecological validity	
Reciprocity	*Some communication systems*
Learned through interaction	
Arbitrariness	
Compositionality	*Viewed as properties particular to human language*
Displacement	
Open-endedness	
Duality of patterning	

organization or relations between words. (We will discuss the notion of hierarchical organization in later chapters.)

Words are meaningful units and are part of an expandable set. But words also are composed of cognitive units. Linguists call the system that governs the organization of units composing words **phonology**. Phonology structures a relatively small set of units that is *not* expandable. In English, for example, the sounds composing "top" can be rearranged to form "opt" or "pot" (though not "pto" or "otp"), but a speaker of English could not wake up one morning and decide that a brand new sound, let's write it <!>, could be used to form words in English. In any particular language, words, new or old, must draw from a stable, small set of nonmeaningful units called **phonological units**. *So in human language the meaningful messages (both sentences and words) are infinite in variety by virtue of the fact that words are produced from a system of combining a finite set of meaningless units.* Linguists, since Hockett in the 1960s, have described this hallmark property of language as **duality of patterning**.

What Scientists of Language – Including Linguists – Don't Do (at Least for a Living)

Scientists who study language are not interested in prescriptive grammar, that is, rules that some authority decrees ought to be followed in speaking and/or writing a language – things like "don't end a sentence with a preposition" and "don't split an infinitive" and "don't say *ain't*." (Notice how often the folks who apparently hold these positions of authority come up with rules starting with "don't.") Many of these rules in fact come from historical idiosyncrasies of a language. Prescriptivist views of language are often motivated sociologically, as nonstandard dialects of a language are often held in poor regard. Because of this, using these dialects can inhibit upward socioeconomic mobility of these speakers, and learning and implementing prescriptive grammatical rules might help to increase this mobility. This does not mean that pejorative judgments about nonstandard dialects are linguistically or scientifically valid. The idea that one dialect is *intrinsically better* than another is simply false. For a scientist of language, every person's own system of speaking his or her language is a legitimate and valuable object of scientific study. Scholarly linguists are not interested in prescriptive rules that suggest that a particular way of speaking is good or bad or right or wrong. Ⓦ

> Throughout this book, you will see a Ⓦ symbol at various locations. This indicates that there is accompanying material to be found on the book's website, www.discoveringspeech.wiley.com

Summary

Chapter 1, Section 1

1   Wherever humans exist, language exists.
2   All languages continually undergo change.
3   The relation between sounds and meanings are arbitrary in language.
4   All languages use a finite set of discrete sounds that are combined to form words; these words form a potentially infinite set.
5   Words themselves can be combined in systematic and meaningful ways to produce sentences.
6   All languages are equally complex, expressive, and valuable for study as examples of specialization of the human cognitive system.

Section 2: The Study of Language as a Cognitive Science

Section 1 of this chapter introduced the notion that speakers of a language have specific pieces of **linguistic knowledge** about how their language works, and about how language in general works, which we called **linguistic competence**. The study of language as a cognitive science is, to a large degree, the scientific study of linguistic competence: what is the nature of the knowledge that allows us to produce and understand language, and how does this knowledge develop in young children? Section 2 begins to explore how linguistic competence can be studied scientifically. But first, we want to consider additional examples of the kind of linguistic knowledge a speaker of a language has, and we introduce additional concepts for thinking about linguistic knowledge.

The Nature of Linguistic Knowledge

As we said earlier, the kind of knowledge at issue here is not the rules of grammar that you may have been drilled in when in elementary school. Rather, we are talking about the kind of knowledge that you – or any language user – has by virtue of having learned a language natively, which means as a young child. As an example, consider the following exercise devised by the linguist Morris Halle, to demonstrate the knowledge that English speakers have about English words. In all likelihood, none of the words in (1) are familiar to you; in fact, some may seem downright bizarre. Now, suppose you were asked to select the words that *could* be a word of English; which would you choose?

(1)   ptak, mgla, thole, vlas, hlad, flitch, plast, dnom, sram, rtut

In all likelihood, you chose the items *thole*, *flitch*, and *plast*. Moreover, virtually all English speakers when asked that question would come up with the same answer. Speakers of a language apparently make the same judgments about words they've never heard or seen before! The only way they could do this is if all the speakers of a language rely on some common pieces of knowledge about how their language is structured. In this case, you were making a judgment based on the consonant sequences that can occur at the beginning of real English words. For example, English words cannot begin with a "d" sound followed by an "n" sound, although that "dn" consonant sequence is perfectly fine *within* a word, as in the word *sadness*. (Note that we are talking about *sound* sequences, not *letter* sequences or spelling – this exercise would work equally well if you only heard the words pronounced without seeing them.)

Having chosen *thole*, *flitch*, and *plast*, consider the following questions: if those words were singular nouns, how would you make them plural nouns? If they were verbs, how would you put them in the past tense? In thinking about the answer, don't worry about how you would *spell* the resulting word, but focus on how you would *say* them – in fact, try saying them out loud right now.

You probably answered the first question with "thole-z," "plast-s," and "flitch-ez," and the second question with "thole-d," "plast-ed," and "flitch-t." As before, you undoubtedly had no trouble doing this, and you probably did it quickly and without much effort. Now notice what you did: although in each case you formed a plural out of a singular, the *sounds* you used to do so were different. Why were they different? And why would all native speakers of English come up with the same answer? Remember, these are words you've never heard before!

The answer to both questions is that you were relying on your linguistic knowledge of forming the plural and past tense in English. In fact, modifying the sounds you use to produce the plural marker is something you do all the time in English. You may not have noticed it before now, but when you form the plural of English words, the sounds you use for the plural depend on the sounds in the word, in particular, the sound right before the plural marker: the plural of *cat* is pronounced "cat-s," but the plural of *dog* is pronounced "dog-z," and the plural of *maze* is pronounced "maze-ez." This is knowledge that you have by virtue of being an English speaker, and it's knowledge you brought to bear on the task of pluralizing words you've never seen before – and virtually all English speakers would behave as you did.

The knowledge you relied on in this exercise is the kind of linguistic knowledge we explore in this book. There are three critical features of this kind of knowledge: first, it is **implicit**. By this we mean that it is not (necessarily) knowledge that you are consciously aware of, or could explain to someone. Until reading this chapter, you probably weren't aware of the different sounds you used in forming the plural or past tense. And we haven't yet discussed in any detail the factors that actually determine what plural or past tense sound you produce in particular circumstances. Yet, despite having no **explicit** understanding of these factors, you and all English speakers consistently produce the same patterns of behavior with respect to these linguistic activities. In this sense, the knowledge you are using is implicit.

A second, and related, characteristic of linguistic knowledge is that it is **automatic**. We can produce words and form sentences from sequences of words without giving it much thought. Likewise, we can't help interpreting the language that we hear spoken around us. In short, we don't have to make a conscious effort to put our linguistic knowledge to use; it happens automatically. Contrast this with other skills such as solving a long division problem. It takes more than simply seeing the problem written on the page to solve it – the answer doesn't just pop out at us. Rather, we have to consciously apply the *explicit* rules we learned for solving such problems. This is different than how we speak and understand in our native language.

This brings us to our third important feature of linguistic knowledge: it is **untaught**. We use this term to refer to the fact that linguistic knowledge is not explicitly taught to children (as long division is), yet children end up acquiring the knowledge nevertheless, in some cases very early in their life. In some sense, this feature arises from linguistic knowledge being implicit; one can't explicitly teach implicit knowledge. However, just because it isn't explicitly taught, we are not suggesting that linguistic knowledge isn't *learned*. Clearly there are many things speakers have to learn about their language. As we saw from our exercise, speakers learn what sequences of sounds are permissible at the beginnings of words in their language. However, although *mgla*, *dnom*, and others, are not potential English words, they are possible words in other languages, such as

Russian, and speakers of those languages would respond differently when asked to choose possible words from (1). More broadly, speakers learn what speech sounds their language uses, what the words are, what they mean, how their language orders subjects and verbs within a sentence, and so on. The crucial point is that much of that knowledge is acquired by children without instruction; merely being immersed in an environment where a language is spoken is sufficient for a child to learn it.

These three characteristics of linguistic knowledge make it an interesting challenge to study. We can't simply ask people to introspect, or introspect ourselves, on the underpinnings of linguistic knowledge – its implicit, automatic, and untaught nature makes it inaccessible to this kind of study. What we can do is study the effects of linguistic knowledge, both by studying the patterns present in the utterances language users produce, and by studying the behavior of language users in controlled experiments. In addition, recent technological advances make it possible to measure activity-dependent changes in the brain during language processing, adding yet another tool. Below, we introduce a framework from **cognitive science** for approaching the scientific study of language. We touch on the kind of discovery that is possible by behavioral observation and experimentation, as well as some of the challenges in inferring knowledge from behavior.

Studying Linguistic Knowledge Scientifically: The Framework of Cognitive Science

Cognitive science encompasses an interdisciplinary approach to the study of intelligence, in the broadest terms, whether in humans, other species, or collections of organisms or entities. Linguistics and cognitive psychology are both part of the cognitive sciences, as these disciplines are interested in understanding specific kinds of human intelligence. Another important discipline is computer science, because most cognitive scientists view intelligence behavior within individuals as involving **computations**. One influence of computer science on cognitive science is in terms of the kinds of formal distinctions it makes. For instance, in computer science, a distinction is often made between **data** and **procedures**. Procedures are the operations a computer program performs, like addition, multiplication, and so on. Data are the entities that the procedures manipulate: numbers, words, images, and so on. A computer program is roughly a specification of data and procedures, as well as a specification of which procedures operate on which data entities, and when, to perform some function(s). Cognitive scientists often make a similar distinction in studying the human mind – the distinction between **mental representations** and **mental processes**. We said earlier that the study of language as a cognitive science is the study of linguistic competence, or linguistic knowledge, so we can be a little more specific now, and divide this into the study of the mental representations underlying linguistic knowledge and the mental process underlying linguistic knowledge (we'll sometimes use the terms **representations** and **processes** in what follows). Essentially, the processes operate on the representations.

In the interests of full disclosure, we make one further comment on the words listed in (1). The words we identified as possible English words – *thole, plast,* and *flitch* – in fact *are* part of English! A thole is a pin used to hold an oar in place on a boat, and a flitch is a side of cured meat, or a section of a log. While not a word on its own, "plast" is an ending in many English words (e.g., cytoplast), and carries the meaning of cell or organized particle.

This distinction emphasizes the fact that what we know as speakers of a language is not only facts about the language (e.g., its sounds, its words, the words' meanings, etc.), but also how to cognitively manipulate those entities in the act of speaking and understanding: how to generate a sentence from a set of words, how to apply grammatical operations to a word (e.g., making it plural, putting it in the past tense, etc.). The distinction also provides a framework for thinking about how to investigate the nature of linguistic knowledge, because we see that there are, broadly speaking, two different kinds of knowledge that we need to study: the *what* and the *how*.

How can one study linguistic knowledge? If we want to find out what mental representations and processes are involved in language use, what are we really looking for? If we could watch the brain in action as it processes language, would we expect to be able to "see" the representations of sounds, of words, of meanings? What would these representations look like? The computer analogy is again useful. Suppose we want to understand the way a piece of software works, say, a program that checks for spelling errors in a document. Somewhere in the computer there must be some representation of the words that the computer "knows" how to spell. Surely we don't expect to be able to see the words by opening up the computer and looking inside, or even opening up the microprocessors – the computer's "brain" – and looking inside. The words as we know them don't exist visually in the computer, yet there is a coded representation of them – in the case of digital computers, coded as voltages in semiconductor memories or flux states on magnetic disks.

In the human brain as well, words must be represented somewhere. And, as in the computer analogy, we should not expect to be able to "see" the words inside the brain in any obvious sense. Rather, we should expect that the words are represented in some special code in the neural circuitry of the brain, just as words are represented in a special code in the electronic circuitry of the computer. However, while we understand how computers represent words (because humans designed them), we know relatively little about how the *neural* hardware codes anything as complex as language. Does this mean that we cannot learn anything about linguistic knowledge in the brains of language users? Fortunately, it does not; there are methods of discovering the representations and process of language in the brain that don't require understanding how neural circuits code words or other units of language. Let's again turn to an example with computers to understand how we can learn about knowledge without a physical characterization of how knowledge is coded in a medium (brain or computer). (Though the physical details of knowledge and learning are also of great interest to scientists.)

Returning to our spelling-checker program, we could ask whether the program looks up a word alphabetically to see if a word is correctly spelled; in other words, does it go through all the As and Bs before getting to the Cs and checking whether "carr" is a correctly spelled word? If we don't know the details of how the computer codes letters and words, how could we test this? We might construct an experiment whereby we give the program words that start with different letters at various positions in the alphabet and measure how long (using a super accurate timer) it takes to render a decision about the spelling of the word. If the time taken is correlated with the position in an alphabetized list, then we have some evidence that is at least consistent with an alphabetical organization of the words. Furthermore, such a correlation would tend to argue against alternative plausible organizations of words, for example by length, or by frequency of use.

It's a good place to note here that although we discussed the problem just mentioned as a question of representation (how the words were organized), we could also think about it as a question of processes (how the words were searched). Suppose we found evidence for alphabetization in the experiment above, does that mean that there is a physical alphabetical list in the computer's memory – one that spatially organizes "car" before "card," and so on? Maybe, maybe not; we wouldn't know from just this experiment. It could be that the physical representation of words in the computer's memory is more random, but the *procedure* that searches through the memory processes alphabetically. What we would know is that **functionally**, the words are stored alphabetically. This means that when the word representations are accessed by the spell-checking process, alphabetic position plays a role in how quickly the process is completed. For many questions in cognitive science, including questions of linguistic knowledge, understanding the **functional** characteristics of representations and processes is a fundamental goal of the research. A functional description of a cognitive system defines what the important components are, and how they are organized and interact. This kind of analysis can be extremely revealing about the nature of cognitive mechanisms and representations, without providing details about how the brain (or other computing device) physically supports them.

Let's step back briefly and consider some of the concepts that were implicit in the preceding discussion. We made the important distinction between understanding how a system worked at a functional level, and how the hardware of the system – the computer or the brain – actually encoded representations and carried out the processes. Within a functional level of analysis, we made an additional distinction between the broader goal of a procedure – for example, analyzing whether a word a user typed is misspelled or not – and how the procedure actually caries out the goal – for example, organizes the words it knows alphabetically, or by word length, or by frequency of use in the language. The importance of these distinctions in cognitive science was emphasized by David Marr, a neuroscientist who studied visual processing. Marr labeled the three levels we just discussed with the following terms:

- **Computational level** – This is the level of analysis pertaining to a broad description of a system. Addition and multiplication are terms that describe aspects of what calculators and computers (and humans) do, at a computational level. "Checking a word's spelling" is also describing a function of a system at a computational level. Notice that these are broad, rather abstract conceptual descriptions that don't describe detailed steps in a process.
- **Algorithmic level** – This level describes specific ways in which a system carries out functions, describing the organization of representations – for example, whether a list of words is organized alphabetically, by word length, or by word frequency in our example above – and the specific steps in processing the representations, much like a flowchart does. The distinction between computational and algorithmic levels is important, as a given computation could, in principle, be carried out by many different algorithms. As we saw, one can devise experiments to test the degree to which the behavior of a system is compatible with various algorithms, and rule out some on the basis of the experiments' outcomes. Together, the computational and algorithmic levels provide an account of the functional properties of a system.
- **Implementational level** – This level describes how a computational medium (e.g., a digital computer, the human brain) implements an algorithm. In a computer, it refers to how digital circuitry encodes binary representations (the 0s and 1s that are the fundamental representational units in computers), and how the various components of the computer – the memory, processor, keyboard, and so on – are connected. In the brain, it refers to neural coding and neural circuitry, as well as the connections between the sense organs and the brain. Note that any algorithm could, in principle, be supported by many different implementations.

In a nutshell, the computational level provides a description of *what* the system does, the algorithmic level addresses the question of *how* the system carries out its functions, while the implementational level describes *what tools or equipment* the system uses.

Notice we can learn about one level without knowing a lot about lower levels. For instance, in our spell-checker example, we didn't have to know about how letters and words were coded in computer circuitry to devise an experiment that could reveal how the known words were organized and searched. Likewise, we don't have to know about neural codes to learn about the representations and processes underlying language use. Indeed, what scientists can learn from studying the computational and algorithmic aspects of linguistic knowledge may ultimately inform our understanding of their implementation in the brain. This is because theories at the functional levels provide a framework for interpreting phenomena at the implementational level. Without such a framework, the organization and function of neural circuits would be virtually impossible to interpret. It would be like trying to understand what voltage fluctuations in computer memory meant, when you have no information about what the computer is doing, what problem it's solving, and so on. It would be like trying to figure out how an automobile engine worked without knowing anything about the "goal" of the engine (e.g., to convert the energy in liquid fuel into kinetic energy to move the car).

We have been discussing the implementation level mostly in connection with the brain, but it's important to note that, for language, other parts of the body are involved in this level of analysis. In particular, the vocal tract and the ear are crucial components of the implementation of language in the spoken modality, just as the hands, and the eye are for the implementation of language in the signed modality. It's also important to realize that, just as a functional understanding of a cognitive system provides a framework for analyzing the implementational level, understanding the implementational level, in turn, constrains the kinds of algorithms one might propose. For example, as we will see in later chapters, properties of the human vocal tract and the fact that in speaking we produce sounds in a coordinated manner affect the way adjacent sounds influence each other – for example, a "k" sound is physically produced differently depending on the sounds occurring before and after it. This is an effect of the implementation of human speech, but the result in the acoustic signal requires listeners to work with this variability if they are to recover the intended message. Therefore, we might expect that part of the algorithms and computations of speech perception are specialized to deal with these consequences of facts about implementational level: facts about how speech is implemented in speakers influences the kinds of computational processes we expect to find in perceivers.

The Complex Relationship Between Behaviors and Underlying Mental Representations

The study of behavior can reveal a great deal about the functional organization of human knowledge, or knowledge in any species. However, scientists must also be aware of factors outside of the brain that could lead to systematic patterns in behavior. In some cases, what appear to be interesting or "clever" properties of an organism's knowledge turn out to be otherwise. One example is the honeycomb that bees construct to store honey and rear offspring. Mathematically, the hexagonal lattice structure is the optimal construction for storing liquid using the least amount of wall space – an excellent efficiency since producing the wax that makes the honeycomb walls consumes a great deal of honey. The intricate structure would seem to suggest that the honeybees have some sort of blueprint or representation of the honeycomb pattern in their brains, honed by evolution. How else could they construct the honeycombs so well?

While there is some debate on the precise mechanism of the honeycomb formation, on a number of accounts the hexagonal cells are an **emergent** property of a collection of bees building the comb at once, rather than the result of a master plan inside a bee's brain. One intriguing theory is that the hexagons are formed as the warmed up wax flows like a liquid around the bees building the honeycomb. A bee is roughly cylindrical, so many bees working in close quarters produces an array of closely packed cylinders, which would look like an array of circles in two dimensions (see Figure 1.2). Because of the geometry of closely packed circles, any given bee is making contact with six other bees around it. As the bees in this configuration produce wax for the comb, they produce a great deal of heat,

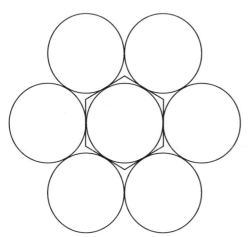

Figure 1.2 Circles represent honeybees. The hexagon depicts the resulting form of the flowing wax, which is subject to forces from the central and surrounding bees

and the wax becomes malleable and liquid, and flows around the cylindrical bees. The forces on the wax from the central bee and the bees surrounding it shape the wax into a hexagonal form. Thus it is the physics of the bees' formation and the wax that results in an array of hexagonal cells. In fact, this mechanism is related to the very physical phenomenon that makes hexagons an efficient shape for storing liquid in separate compartments. So, according to this theory, it is physical phenomena that makes the ideal hexagonal configuration, not a clever design represented in honeybee cognition.

On the other hand, sometimes apparently sophisticated intelligent behavior is indeed more directly linked to the mental representations and processes of the organism exhibiting the behavior. For example, rats can learn to navigate through mazes when rewarded with food at the end of the maze. At first, they may make many wrong turns and take a long time to get to the end. But after a number of tries at learning the same maze, they end up taking only a path that takes them to the food. The rats internalize some sort of representation of their trajectory through space that allows them to "solve" the maze. What is the nature of that representation?

Many psychologists at the beginning of the twentieth century believed that rats were simply remembering motor sequences – the movements of their limbs as they traversed the maze and made turns at choice points. Sequences that led to a reward were reinforced, and those that did not were inhibited. On this view, just as the honeybee has no representation of the hexagonal cells it will build, the rat has no real representation of the space it traverses, only the steps (literally) it needs to take to get to the food at the end. But through a variety of experiments, scientists discovered that rats build up rather sophisticated spatial representations of the location of the food with respect to the start of the maze, and that these representations are more like maps than representations of motor sequences.

In one such experiment, rats were initially trained on a simple maze that included an alley to a circular table and a continuation on the opposite side of the table (Figure 1.3.i). That path continued on a series of turns, with food at the end. The trajectory along the path was often in a direction away from or tangential to the food. After rats learned to traverse the path quickly, the maze was modified so that the exit path from the circular table was blocked, and over a dozen additional paths were added at intervals around the table (Figure 1.3.ii). Rats initially tried to proceed through the original maze arm, but found it blocked. They returned to the circular table, and after exploring the entrances to the newly added paths, almost unanimously chose the path that pointed directly to the location of the food (which they could not see). They could not have used memory of motor sequences to traverse the new path, as the sequences were completely different from the ones in the original maze. However, if the rats had built a representation of the location of the food relative to their

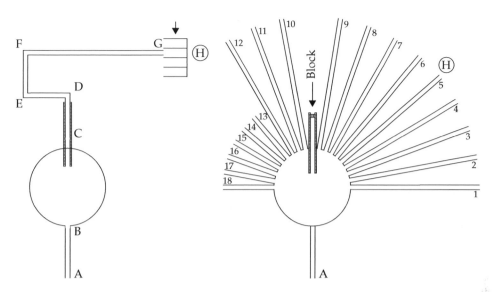

Figure 1.3 (Left) Rats learned to navigate from start (A) to food (G). (Right) Rats would traverse path (5), in direction of the unseen food, when their usual passage was blocked.

Note. Images copyright © 1992/1946 by the American Psychological Association. Reproduced with permission. The official citation that should be used in referencing this material is Tolman, E.C., Ritchie, B.F., Kalish, D. (1946). Studies in spatial learning. I. Orientation and the short-cut. *Journal of Experimental Psychology, 36,* 13–24. The use of APA information does not imply endorsement by APA.

starting location, they could then choose a path that would lead directly to that location. Numerous experiments involving different techniques followed this one and converged on the idea that rats have some sort of mental map that they use in navigating through space.

In summary, in some cases an organism's intelligent behavior is linked to mechanisms in the brain. In others, explanations for apparently sophisticated or intelligent behavior lie outside the brain. Understanding the physical world in which organisms exhibit a behavior can be extremely important in forming theories about the cognitive underpinnings of that behavior.

Are we like bees or like rats?

We've just seen how an organism's behaviors that on the surface seem to draw on complex knowledge could result from constraints outside of its brain. Could such constraints be involved in our behavior in our earlier example involving plural and past tense formation? Maybe we're always trying to produce an "s" sound, but perhaps something about the physical mechanisms of speech require that the "s" is produced as a "z" when it follows the "l" in *thole*, but not when it follows the "t" in *plast*. This would be important for our understanding of linguistic knowledge, because in that case we would then be more like bees, whose intricate hexagons do not exist in their minds, rather than the rats with their mental representations of space.

We can rule out the alternative explanation just offered if we can show that there are words in English (or any language, for that matter) in which "s" sounds can follow "l" sounds. In fact, there are many English words where this happens, as in *pulse* – we don't say "pulz"! So, for better or for worse, we seem to be more like rats than bees when it comes to this piece of linguistic knowledge. But just because we ruled out one alternative hypothesis doesn't mean that there aren't others we should consider. As scientists, we want to analyze all plausible alternatives. So far, the best explanation for the systematic patterns we observed in our previous examples is that speakers rely on implicit, automatic, and untaught linguistic knowledge when producing words.

Summary

Chapter 1, Section 2

1   Linguistic knowledge is implicit, automatic, and untaught.
2   Linguistic knowledge is supported by mental representations and mental processes.
3   A cognitive system can be analyzed at the computational level, the algorithmic level, and the implementational level. Analysis at the first two levels constitute a functional analysis of the system.
4   A functional understanding of a cognitive system can be very informative, and needn't require a detailed understanding of the implementational level, though it may be informed by such an understanding.
5   Intelligent behavior is not always due to models of the behavior in the mind of the organism. Sometimes external factors blindly constrain behavior in seemingly intelligent ways.

Chapter 2
Speaking, Sound, and Hearing

Section 1: Speaking and Transcribing

One area of scientific investigation in linguistics is called **phonetics**. Phoneticians study how the sounds of human language are produced by speakers, what the acoustic characteristics of these sounds are, and how humans perceive and recognize these events. In addition to the linguist's interest in understanding human speech, other scientists are also interested in aspects of speech. Clinicians might be concerned with speech therapy for children or brain-injured adults. They also deal with a range of other concerns to do with the voices of patients with laryngeal cancers or singers and others with delicate or damaged voices. Educators have an interest in foreign language teaching, reading pedagogy, or musical and theatrical training. Engineers, on the other hand, may be involved in designing computers that can synthesize speech or recognize language spoken to them by humans. Other engineers may work on coding speech in ways that can be efficiently transmitted over networks. All of these various professionals have a stake in understanding the production, acoustic, and perception properties of human speech.

We will start with an overview of the general qualities of the vocal tract movements that produce speech. Then we will move to a more detailed examination of the anatomy of the human vocal tract and how particular movements are used to produce consonant and vowel sounds. A practical goal in this chapter will be to learn to use a system of written **transcription** to record the speech sounds that American English speakers produce.

Speaking requires complex, coordinated movements of a number of anatomical organs. These include the respiratory system, the larynx and the vocal folds it houses, the port that opens the passage from the rear of the mouth to the nose, the lips, the jaw, and the tongue extending from the mouth into the throat. All the complicated content of language – the concepts, messages, emotions – are communicated by these choreographed movements of the vocal tract. These movements must be conducted in just the right way in both space and time in order for the speaker's message to be communicated successfully. As scientists, we are interested in the question of which aspects of these body movements encode the linguistic information about the message being conveyed. In the simplest terms, the answer to this question is that informationally critical aspects of these movements are: (1) which part of the vocal tract is moving, (2) with what magnitude and (3) at what location, and (4) what is the relative coordination or timing among the various movements. Because these speech movements are the linguistic building blocks of words, they are sometimes given the special name of **gestures**. Gestures are speech tasks (such as closing the lips or widely separating the vocal folds) that are executed by the vocal tract and coordinated with one another to create speech.

The movements of the tongue, lips, laryngeal apparatus, and nasal port are not movements that abruptly start and then stop. On the contrary, when you are talking, parts of your vocal tract are in continuous motion. When you talk, you do not make one movement and then stop and then make the next and then stop – just as when you walk, you do not stop between each step. So, because the movements are responsible for the production of the acoustic signal that is the speech we hear, this means that the speech we hear is also continuous. Just like the movements, the acoustic speech signal is not composed of sounds separated by "spaces" or silences. It is continuously changing as the speech movements are being made. Because so much of our lives in a literate society has been spent dealing with speech recorded as letters and text in which spaces do separate letters and words, it can be extremely difficult to understand that spoken language simply does not have this characteristic. Figure 2.1 shows the sound wave for the sentence "Lena wanted a medicine for malaria." A waveform is a record

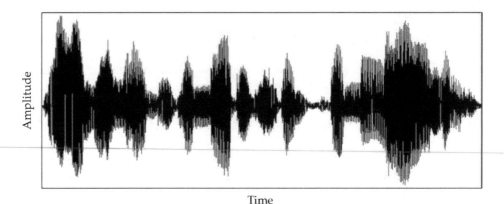

Figure 2.1   Waveform of "Lena wanted a medicine for malaria".

of the back-and-forth movements of the membrane inside a microphone caused by air pressure fluctuations that the talker produces; these movements are similar to those that the eardrum of a listener would undergo. In saying this sentence, along with the vibrations sound created by the vocal folds, the lips and tongue front and tongue rear are all moving continuously. Because speech is produced continuously, the acoustic sound signal does not have silent (flat line) intervals between speech sounds or between words. You can see that this phrase is made up of relatively loud and relatively soft sounds but never regular chunks of silence or "space"; there are no silences (flat zero-amplitude separations) delimiting the various speech sounds or words. Ⓦ (As we will see, certain sounds in language do cause very brief silences in the speech signal as one part of the vocal tract closes against another, but these silences are not indications of gaps such as that between printed letters and words.) Not only are the movements continuous but they overlap or co-occur with one another in time. That is, the movement(s) or gestures(s) used to make one sound are co-occurring in time with the gestures being used to make the sounds somewhat before and after it. This property of speech production is called **coarticulation**. This means that at any moment in the acoustic speech stream, information is being transmitted about multiple sounds and even multiple words. So, although we write, perceive, and (to a degree) cognitively process speech linearly – one sound followed by another – the actual sensory signal our ear encounters is not composed of discretely separated bits. This is an amazing aspect of our linguistic abilities, but on further thought one can see that it is a very useful one. The fact that speech can encode and transmit information about multiple linguistic events in parallel means that the speech signal is a very efficient and optimized way of encoding and sending information between individuals. This property of speech has been called **parallel transmission**.

Overview of the Vocal Tract

The vocal tract can be viewed as a tube or airway with air entering at one end – from the lungs – and leaving from the other – the lips and nose. As the air leaves, it creates pressure fluctuations radiating from the mouth that are heard as sound waves.

However, just moving air smoothly, for example as you do when you exhale, does not in and of itself generate much noise. There are several ways to generate noise that can be used for speech, but the primary one we will be concerned with and the one which is dominantly used in all human languages is the vibration of the vocal folds. The vocal folds are two delicate mucosal membranes housed inside the protective larynx cartilage (called the thyroid cartilage). They are not moved open and closed

Think about blowing a "raspberry" with your lips – do you see how your lips rapidly separate and come back together without you using muscles to move them. As long as they are positioned loosely together and airflow is sufficient, the lips vibrate. This is similar to how vocal folds vibrate.

by muscles but rather, when positioned loosely near each other, they are repeatedly and quickly made to open and close by being blown apart by air from the lungs and then sucked back together again. This happens approximately 80 to 300 times per second. This rate is typically somewhat slower for men than women and relates directly to the perceived pitch of the voice. Many speech sounds – such as all vowels in English – use this as their noise-generating vocal tract event. You can probably hear and feel the differences between sounds occurring with and without vocal fold vibration by placing your fingertips on your larynx and thinking about the tickling feeling in the following pairs: feel the tickle on your tongue tip and fingertips for [voiced] zzzzz but not for [voiceless] sssss; feel the tickle on your lower lip and fingertips for [voiced] vvvvv but not for [voiceless] fffff.

Each opening and closing of the vocal folds "taps" like a little hammer on the column of air that is in the vocal tract tube, creating noise. The vocal tract tube downstream from the vocal folds shapes or **filters** this noise (as well as noise created in other ways in the vocal tract). The vocal tract tube is not a hard, stiff tube, however. It is a malleable and deformable tube composed of many soft and moveable structures. This allows the tube to be squeezed and maneuvered into many intricate shapes. It is these squeezings or **constriction gestures** along the vocal tract tube that we will want to characterize as information-encoding body movements in speech. Constrictions can occur from very low in the pharynx (right above the larynx) in the throat, in the back of the mouth, the front of the mouth, or at the lips. Because it is critical to sound creation, we will want to be able to identify both the active moving **articulators** and the passive articulatory locations at which the articulators create constrictions. These are labeled in Figure 2.2.

Classifying English Consonants and Vowels

We've seen that many sounds occur with the vocal folds vibrating; however, others lack this property. We say that sounds having vocal fold vibration are **voiced** sounds, and we call the process of vocal fold vibration during speech **voicing**. Other sounds that do not use vocal fold vibration are said to be **voiceless**. This is one dimension of classification that linguists use in describing the sounds of human languages.

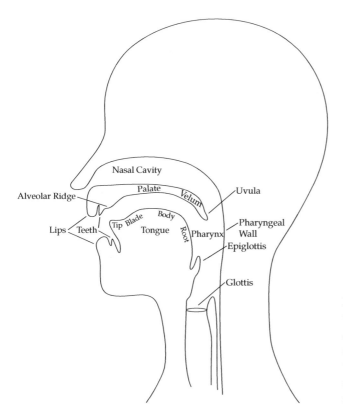

Figure 2.2 The human vocal tract: this is an actual tracing of one of the authors' vocal tract with important speech-functional structures labeled.

Linguists use descriptions of the **place of articulation** of a constriction and its **manner of articulation** to classify the consonant sounds in the world's languages. **Place** refers to the location in the vocal tract at which a constriction is made, and **manner** is roughly the type or degree of constriction. (Vowels, which all involve tongue deformations that are generally less tight or narrow constrictions than consonants, are described slightly differently, as we will see.) We call sounds involving both lips **bilabial** (e.g., the first sound in "*b*at"); while we refer to sounds in which the lower lip comes up to meet the top teeth as **labiodental** (as in "*v*at"). The tongue tip can also protrude to the dental area, either behind the upper front teeth or between the upper and lower front teeth. We call sounds with this place of articulation **dental** or **interdental** (as in "*th*at"). (In English, regions and individuals can differ in which they use; Western US speakers often produce interdentals rather than dentals, i.e., the tongue tip can actually be seen in these articulations.) There is a hard gum-covered area behind your front teeth – in some people it is more prominent than in others – we call this the **alveolar ridge** and refer to sounds made with tongue tip constrictions in this location as **alveolar**. If you continue to slide your tongue (or finger) up back from the alveolar ridge you will rise into the vault of the hard palate – again, this area is higher and more vaulted in some people than others. Sounds made with constrictions in this region are called **palatal** (as in "*you*"). Moving backward you may gag slightly if you touch the soft area far back in the roof of the mouth. This is called the soft palate or **velum**. When the tongue body makes constrictions in this area, the resulting sounds are called **velar** sounds (as in the final sound in "si*ng*"). The velum or soft palate is also moveable. When it lowers or moves downward sufficiently, this opens up an air passageway into the nose. Sounds made with the velum in this lowered posture are called **nasals**, but these sounds also simultaneously use some posture of the tongue or lips; so a nasal sound must (in English) be bilabial, alveolar, or velar in its **place of articulation**. One cannot reach farther back down the throat or **pharynx** (at least not safely and comfortably), but the tongue does in fact continue far down and is moveable in the front-back direction in the pharynx. We call sounds made with constrictions in this area of the vocal tract **pharyngeal sounds**; in English these are largely limited to the production of certain vowels and the "r" sound, during which the tongue rear moves towards the back pharyngeal wall. Finally, the space between the vocal folds is also a possible location to shape the airway, albeit at its very bottom. We call this space the **glottis**. Sounds made by manipulating this space to be very open or tightly closed (rather than in the default loosely together position for voicing) are called **glottal** sounds.

Table 2.1 shows a list of places of constriction used in English, shown as columns, and symbols for sounds made at these places. Ⓦ (We will learn the terms naming the rows shortly.) When linguists want to refer to a particular speech sound, they adopt the practice of placing that sound in square brackets; so the first sound in "sheen" is **transcribed** as [ʃ]. The whole word would be transcribed [ʃin]. You will notice that a transcription symbol stands for a single sound – it is not a letter, as letters in English

Table 2.1   IPA Chart for English Consonants

Manner of articulation	*Bilabial*		*Labiodental*		*(Inter)Dental*		*Alveolar*		*Palatal*		*Velar*		*Glottal*
Stop	p	b					t	d			k	g	ʔ
Fricative			f	v	θ	ð	s	z	ʃ	ʒ			h
Affricate									tʃ	dʒ			
Nasal		m						n				ŋ	
Lateral liquid								l					
Retroflex liquid								r					
Glide	w̥	w								y			

bear only a very rough and historical relation to the sounds in words. We will go through several examples demonstrating further that transcription is not spelling later.

In actuality, some sounds such as [l], [r], and [w] have more than one place of articulation, even though they appear in only a single cell on the chart. For [w], we generally will use both of its places in its description calling it labiovelar, but for [l] and [r] (for brevity and historical reasons), we will generally only refer to them by a single place of articulation – alveolar.

You may remember that in addition to describing a sound as voiced or voiceless and describing its place of articulation, linguists also include **manner** of articulation in classifying a sound. Manner roughly refers to what *kind* of constriction is being made – how much air is able to get through the constriction, does the air flow down the center or sides of the tongue, and is there air flowing through the nose. Linguists use what we like to call the "Starbucks" system of description; that is, just like ordering at Starbucks where one always gives size (grande), milk (nonfat), and drink (latte) in a particular order, consonant sound classifications are always given in the order voicing–place–manner.

When the constriction completely blocks the airflow, the sound is referred to as a **stop**, because the air is momentarily stopped. During this brief part of the constriction when the active articulator such as the tongue or lips is forming a complete seal at some part of the vocal tract, the only sound that can radiate is voicing vibrations that are heard through the walls of the vocal tract. Try plugging your nose and closing your lips and making a sound. You will only be able to make a brief quiet murmur. For voiceless sounds, the interval of complete stop closure is a brief completely silent interval, as they have no vocal fold vibration and no air escaping the vocal tract. Because air is still building up behind a stop constriction as it moves up from the lungs, the air is released in a sudden extremely short burst or popping sound when the active articulator separates from the passive and releases the stop occlusion. For instance, try saying "toe" slowly. You should notice a slight burst as your tongue tip releases the closure into the vowel.

Sounds that have a slight vocal tract opening that allow air to escape in a noisy and turbulent way are called **fricative** sounds. These are sounds like [ʃ, z, f, v, θ, ð]. Fricatives, as we have seen, can occur both with and without voicing. Remember your own experiment above with [sssss] and [zzzzz]. Human languages also make use of sounds that are initiated with a stop closure and then are released into a narrow constriction. Acoustically, these are a silent or near silent (if voiced) interval, followed by a noisy release interval. These are called **affricates**. In English, there are two – [tʃ] and [dʒ]. The transcription we use annotates both the stop and fricative portions. (Some other textbooks just use the fricative symbol with a haček – the diacritic mark (ˇ) – above it.) If you say them slowly,

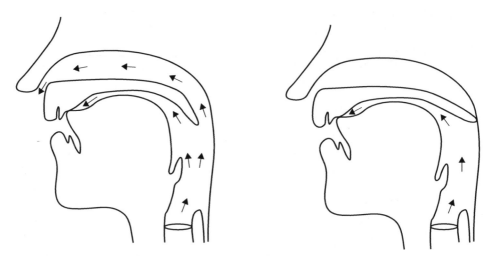

Figure 2.3   An alveolar nasal stop [n] (left) and an oral alveolar stop [t/d] (right). Observe that in both the oral and nasal stop the airflow is blocked at the oral closure (at the alveolar ridge). However, in the nasal stop, the air can flow out through the nasal cavity due to the lowered velum.

for example in the word "hat<u>ch</u>," you should be able to hear (and/or feel) these two separate intervals. You might notice that after the vowel when you start forming the affricate, you make a closure, much like you do when making a [t], and then when you release that closure you might feel and hear turbulent noise created, much like in [ʃ]. In English, affricates are limited to tongue tip sounds, but in other languages other affricates occur; for example, the [pf] of German "pferd" [meaning horse].

The next manner, **nasal**, is a bit different from the others because it demands a complete closure *in the mouth* accompanied by an opening or lowering of the soft palate or velum that allows air to escape through the nose. Because the velum is lowered, air escapes through the nose rather than building up behind an oral (or mouth) constriction. A comparison of the airflow of an alveolar nasal and an oral alveolar stop is shown in Figure 2.3. In English, there are three nasals [m, n, ŋ], which are all voiced. Note that [ŋ] is the sound, for example, at the end of "ing." In fact, [ŋ] is limited to occurring at the end of syllables in English; it's fun to try to practice saying this same sound at the beginning of a word. Can you say "ing" [ɪŋ] backward? (The small capital "ɪ" is the symbol for a short i sound.) Remember that there should be no perceptible "g" sound or release, only the nasal [ŋɪ] sequence.

Following nasals in the classification system are **liquids**; in liquids the air flows smoothly through the constriction(s). In English, we have two, both involving the tongue tip and both with vocal fold vibration or voicing. In the first of these – [l], the tongue stretches at its front and rear, giving it a very narrow profile. This causes air to escape the mouth down the sides of the tongue rather than its center. For this reason, this sound [l] is called a lateral liquid. The acoustics of this sound are somewhat different at the beginning of a word like "lee" than at the end of a word like "all." Perhaps if you say these slowly, you will be able to hear the difference, but many Americans find this rather hard to hear. The differences arise because at the beginnings of words the forward and backward stretching is rather synchronous, while at the end of words, the backing of the tongue occurs much earlier, making it audible during the preceding vowel. You can hear the results of this in listening for the vowel difference in the words "leap" and "peal" (try saying them slowly). When a consonant has the property of lateral air flow, the term **lateral** must be included in its description, if this term is not present, the sound is assumed to have central airflow as most sounds do. Starbucks-style, the term "lateral" is specified after voicing and place and before manner; so the English [l] is described as a "voiced, alveolar, lateral, liquid." The other liquid in English is [r]. This is an articulatory complicated sound that is learned late by children (have you heard children saying "wabbit" instead of "rabbit"?). This American-type [r] is found in only very few languages. It does not involve a severe constriction (like a stop or fricative) but rather involves (typically) three less severe constrictions – one in the pharynx, one in the mouth either with the rear of the tongue or with raising the tongue tip upward, and one with protruding the lips. The first two constrictions are difficult to feel (though you can try sticking a toothpick in your mouth during [rrrr] and feeling if it touches your raised tongue tip) but you should be able to feel (or see in a mirror) the lip protrusion with your fingers during, for example, comparing the word "ray" and "hay."

Lastly, along the consonant classification system, we find **glides**. These are the least constricted consonant such that air flows smoothly through the constriction(s). In English, we have a glide that involves raising the tongue body high into the palate and we will transcribe this using [y]. The other involves both retracting the tongue rear and protruding the lips – [w]. Interestingly, these consonants are little different than the vowels in "ee" and "oo." Sometimes you will see the term **approximant** used as a convenient cover term for vowels, glides, nasals, and laterals. You can see a schematic showing the relation between constriction degree and airflow in Figure 2.4.

Contrast

When linguists desire to describe the sounds of a language, they are generally interested in the sounds that **contrast**. The term **contrast** is an important linguistic concept. It refers to the *potential* of a sound to change

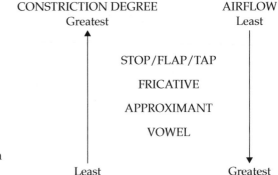

Figure 2.4   Schema showing the relation between constriction degree and airflow.

the meaning of the word. Two sounds contrast if and only if changing one sound to the other has the potential to change the meaning of a word. So [k] and [b] contrast in English because "cat" [kæt] and "bat" [bæt] are words that mean two different things. It is important to understand that not every *potential* word demonstrating a contrast might be a real word in a language. So [k] and [d] also contrast even though "dat" is not a word; there are of course other words that demonstrate that the minimal change from [k] to [d] can change meaning in English – "come" versus "dumb," for example. Each language has its own system of contrast and its own set of sounds that form that system of contrast. Sounds in this set for any given language are called its **phonemes**. The contrasting consonants of English are shown in Table 2.2.

All languages have vowels and consonants. Vowels are formed by wider constrictions than consonants and always involve the tongue body or rear. All languages have voiced vowels with oral (through the mouth) airflow, though some languages also have voiceless vowels or vowels with nasal as well as oral airflow. Vowels are generally the loudest and longest parts of words. Figure 2.5 shows a composite of three MRI images of the position of the tongue in the vowels [ɑ], [i], and [u].

Historically, vowels have been described by a different classification system in terms of their acoustic rather than articulatory properties. We will learn more about the nature of these acoustic properties and how to quantify them in the next chapter. For now, we merely present the three dimensions of classification. The two primary dimensions of classification are **high–mid–low** and **front–central–back**. Although it would be easy to think that these refer to tongue position, in actuality, they only relate to it rather loosely. If a vowel involves protrusion of the lips, it is said to be **round**. In English, as in many languages, the nonlow back vowels (those in the upper right quadrant of the classificatory vowel space) are *round*. It is possible for front vowels to be round, as we will see in the vowel systems of other languages. The vowel chart for English is given

Table 2.2   Contrasting consonants in English

Phoneme	Initial	Final
[p]	pie	
[t]	tie	
[k]	kye	
[b]	by	
[d]	dye	
[g]	guy	
[m]	my	
[n]	nigh	
[ŋ]		ring
[f]	fie	
[v]	vie	
[θ]	thigh	
[ð]	thy	
[s]	sigh	
[z]	zoo	
[ʃ]	shy	
[ʒ]	genre	
[tʃ]	chai	
[dʒ]	jive	
[l]	lie	
[r]	rye	
[w]	why	
[h]	hi	
[y]	you	

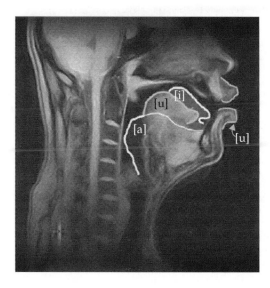

Figure 2.5   MRI image of vowels [ɑ], [i] and [u]. By Mark Tiede, adapted and used by permission. Ⓦ

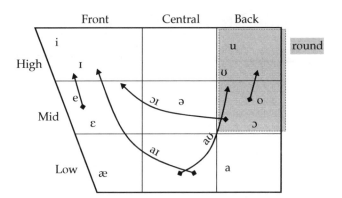

Figure 2.6   A vowel chart for American English.

in Figure 2.6. ⓦ Note that rounding is not specified by the placement of a phonetic symbol on the chart, but rather by the symbol itself (though rounded vowels are typically shown on the right when there is a round–unround pair in the same quadrant). Finally, there are vowels whose quality changes quite a bit from the beginning of the vowel sound to the end of the vowel sound. These are called **diphthongs**, and they are written with two symbols indicating roughly where the vowel sound starts and where it ends; on the vowel chart in Figure 2.6 this change in quality is shown with an arrow. Vowels whose quality is relatively steady are called **monophthongs**.

Linguists prefer this plane of classification for vowels so that subtle differences in vowel sounds can be captured by small changes in placement in the vowel chart. Sometimes a language may have two vowels in the same general area of the vowel chart. For example, English has two vowels that are both high, front, and unrounded: [i] and [ɪ]. In such cases, further differences between the vowels must be described. In the case of this specific example in English (as well as the English pairs [e] [ɛ], [u] [ʊ], and [o] [ɔ]), the second member of the pair is shorter in duration, somewhat less toward the edges of the vowel space, and may not end a syllable in English words. We refer to this group as "lax" and to their longer more peripheral counterparts as "tense." It is very important to remember that these (somewhat unfortunate) terms have *nothing* to do with the muscular behavior of the tongue, but rather refer to these jointly varying properties of duration, peripherality, and word distribution.

The English vowel contrasts are given in Table 2.3.

Transcribing English Consonants and Vowels

When linguists wish to provide an objective record of an actual or potential pronunciation of a word, they cannot depend on any particular language's spelling system, as systems used for creating text in a language

Table 2.3 Some possible vowel contrasts for English

Monophthongs		
	[i]	heed
	[ɪ]	hid
	[e]	hayed
	[ɛ]	head
	[ae]	had
	[u]	who'd
	[ʊ]	hood
	[o]	hoed
	[ɔ]	hawed
	[a]	hod
	[ə]	hud
Diphthongs	[aɪ]	hide
	[ɔɪ]	ahoy
	[au]	how

may be only very loosely related to pronunciation. Furthermore, the exact *details* of an individual's spoken form of a word can be expected to differ from occasion to occasion, from context to context (e.g., the adjacent words), and from person to person. A means of objectively characterizing the detailed sounds used in speech *from any language* has long been viewed as a necessity by linguists. Transcription – in particular the **International Phonetic Alphabet (IPA)** – serves this purpose. Ideally, someone who has never heard a particular spoken utterance should be able to recreate it with reasonable accuracy given knowledge of its **phonetic transcription**.

The standard system to write a language, for those languages that have such systems (not all do), is called an **orthography**. Orthographic symbols may be alphabetic, syllable-based, or of other types. But orthographic symbols can have little relation to pronunciation, and orthographic systems that might once have had a closer relation to pronunciation may now diverge grossly from pronunciation as the language has changed over time. Let's consider some examples that demonstrate that orthography does not allow for a consistent and transparent record of pronunciation.

First, the same sound may be associated with many spellings both within and across languages. Within English, for example, the sound [i] can be orthographically spelled: m<u>ee</u>t, m<u>ea</u>t, m<u>e</u>te, gr<u>ie</u>f, rec<u>ei</u>pt, pet<u>i</u>te, S<u>ey</u>mour. And different languages may use different spellings for the same sound as well; consider the palatal glide, which is spelled "y" in English, "hi" or "ll" in Spanish ("hielo," "llama"), and "j" in German ("ja"). Next, consider that the same spelling can be associated with many different sounds both within and across languages. In English for example, orthographic "ou"

We note here that we have made two choices in this text to help the introductory student. Whereas strict IPA phonetic transcription uses [ɹ] for English "r" and reserves [r] for a Spanish-type trill sound, and uses [j] for English "y" and reserves [y] for a front, rounded vowel, we have made these two simplifications for this elementary presentation since the alternative symbols can be challenging for new students to remember. Your instructor may prefer that you use the stricter symbols, and certainly those symbols are correct if you (or your instructor) choose to use them.

is associated with different sounds in: "bough," "through," "tough," "dough," and "cough." Across languages with alphabetic orthographies, for example, the spelling "j" is associated with the affricate [dʒ] in English "Joe," a fricative in Spanish ("José"), and glide in German "Johann."

The International Phonetic Alphabet (IPA) was established in 1888 utilizing the principle of having a different symbol for each contrastive sound observed to occur in human language. The same symbol is used for that sound in every language in which it occurs. The IPA is a phonetic tool for supplying symbols that are a shorthand phonetic description, capturing voicing, place, and manner, for example, for consonants. It is *not* meant to denote or represent the cognitive linguistic units in language. (In Chapter 7 we will discuss possible cognitive building blocks for words.)

The symbols are based on the Roman alphabet but include many additional symbols. A complete IPA chart of symbols is given in the Appendix. The same symbol is used in transcribing phonetically comparable sounds in different languages or produced by different speakers, but this does not necessarily imply that the sounds are acoustically identical, only that they have important phonetic properties in common. An IPA transcription is intended to minimally denote differences between contrasting sounds in a language ("pin" [pɪn] versus "bin" [bɪn]), but when desired by the linguist, further detail of a particular instance of pronunciation can also be recorded – consider "miss" [mɪs] versus the fluent phrase "miss you" [mɪʃyu].

Practicalities of Transcription

In a linguistics class, even an elementary one, a student will almost certainly be asked to practice doing phonetic transcription. Here is some practical advice for doing phonetic transcription:

1   Place your transcription in square brackets. This distinguishes it from orthographic text. No capitalization is used (though the IPA specifies

a small-capital Roman letter for some specific sounds). Spaces between words are often not used but for lengthy stretches of speech, may be used for ease of reading the transcription.

2   Decide how many sounds are present, then choose their appropriate symbols. There's no requirement that this be done left-to-right; some sounds may be easier for you to identify than others, and you may wish to transcribe those first.

3   *Listen* to yourself (or your partner if you are transcribing someone else's speech) *out loud* before deciding on how to transcribe your pronunciation. Then read your transcription back out loud to check it.

4   No c, q, or x should appear in your transcription of English. (In fact these are IPA symbols for sounds occurring in other languages.) Also be on the lookout for . . . sh . . . , . . . th . . . , and . . . ch . . . sequences in your transcriptions, as these sound sequences (not letter sequences) do not occur within words transcribed in English – for example "ship" is transcribed [ʃɪp] not [shɪp]. *Concentrate on ignoring spelling!*

5   Especially for consonants, pay attention to what your mouth is doing. Where do you feel contact of an active and passive articulator along the vocal tract? You can even use your finger or a mirror to check on what your lips and tongue tip might be doing to identify labials, labiodentals, (inter)dentals, or rounded vowels.

6   If you are asked to transcribe your own speech, assume that your instructor is interested in how you say a particular word or utterance, *not* how you or anyone else *think* it should be said or how someone else might say it (unless you are specifically asked to transcribe the speech of someone else.) (If your English is very nonfluent, most instructors will allow you to transcribe a partner whose sounds might be more likely to reflect the English sounds we have learned here.)

Let's work through some example transcription. First, let's look at some cases in which multiple orthographic letters are associated with a single sound and, therefore, a single IPA symbol. Try saying the words slowly to appreciate how the transcription (typical of many though not all American English speakers) was arrived at.

Multiple letters, one sound

<u>ph</u>antom	[fæntəm]
<u>sh</u>ould	[ʃʊd]
si<u>ng</u>	[sɪŋ]
<u>ch</u>oose	[tʃuz]

Next, observe some words in which single orthographic letters are associated with multiple sounds and, therefore, multiple IPA symbols.

One letter, two sounds

extra   [ɛkstrə]
fume   [fyum]

Here are some words in which a particular orthographic letter is associated with different sounds and, therefore, different IPA symbols.

Same letter, different sound

thing   [θɪŋ]
then   [ðɛn]
excuse (noun)   [ɛkskyus]
excuse (verb)   [ɛkskyuz]

This distinction can be challenging to hear at first as the sounds [θ] and [ð] only differ in voicing, not in place or manner. Saying them slowly and extending them can help you feel the absence or presence of voicing vibration as the air moves between your tongue tip and teeth. Next, there are orthographic sequences that include a letter that denotes no sound at all.

Letter, but no sound

whole   [hol]
hole   [hol]

And there are sounds that are associated with no letters in orthography – in particular, the glottal stop – a complete closing of the vocal folds followed by a release burst of this stop closure. The sound transcribed with the symbol [ʔ] occurs throughout English before vowels that are the first sound in a phrase (and sometimes when a word starting with a vowel occurs in other contexts in an utterance). It also can occur sometimes with or in place of a word-final stop, especially [t], and in certain dialects in places where other dialects would produce [t] between vowels.

Sounds with no letters – glottal stop

uh-oh   [ʔəʔo]
button   [bəʔn] or [bətʔn]

There is also a symbol that you may see or use in transcribing English (and some other languages like Spanish) that denotes a very short voiced closure made with the tongue tip – more or less a very short [d] sound. This sound is called a tap or a flap and is transcribed [ɾ]. This sound occurs in words like the following, often when the preceding syllable bears a stronger stress than the following syllable, though flaps can also occur between words:

Flaps

butter	[bəɾr]
knitting	[nɪɾɪŋ]
hit ahead	[hɪɾəhɛd]

Vowels can be very challenging to transcribe accurately. This is partly because English has so many of them (many languages only have five), partly because regions of the US differ in their vowels, and partly because both the orthography and introspection are quite unhelpful. Comparing the word you wish to transcribe with the examples in the chart above will be helpful. It is also helpful to realize that vowels occurring in syllables that are not stressed at all, like the third vowel in "Los Angeles" are usually the schwa vowel [ə]. Vowels also tend to sound quite different when an [r] follows them. Finally, many orthographic vowels are not associated with any sounds. Consider the following particular examples where a consonant forms a syllable of its own without any vocalic interval. In English, this can occur with nasals [m], [n], [ŋ] and liquids [l], [r].

Silent orthographic vowels

battle	[bædl]
her	[hr]

Sometimes the presence or absence of a vowel in a syllable might vary depending on how fast someone is speaking. Remember that the transcriber's job is to record what is heard on any given occasion. Figure 2.7 presents two different instances of the word "hidden." In the first, a schwa vowel is present in the second syllable; in the second, it is not. Ⓦ

> There are two excellent practice transcription exercises that you can try at Ⓦ:
> *http://sail.usc.edu/~lgoldste/ General_Phonetics/Listening/ Outer%20Yuccan/Outer_Yuccan. html*
> *http://sail.usc.edu/~lgoldste/ General_Phonetics/Listening/ English/English_Transcription. html*

An Introduction to Waveforms, VOT, and Three Diacritics

The IPA offers us a tool for a symbolic description of speech. It is *qualitative* rather than *quantitative*, since the acoustic and durational properties of a sound are not captured in an IPA transcription. It relies on the human ear and brain to interpret the signal one is hearing and assign a categorization – an IPA symbol – to it. Because the mind plays a role in categorizing the sounds, the IPA transcription can be said to be abstract to a degree. In contrast, scientists will also want to consider representations of speech that are quantitative. One of the most common quantitative

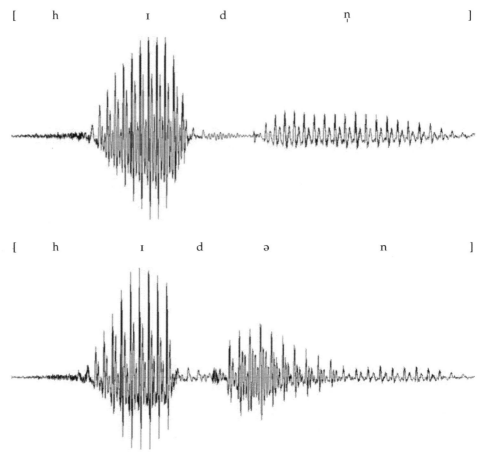

Figure 2.7 (Bottom) Waveform of "hidden," pronounced with a schwa in the final syllable [hɪdən]; (Top) Waveform of "hidden" without a schwa in the final syllable [hɪdn].

Quantitative refers to being able to be measured, calculated, computed, or in some way enumerated in terms of amount or degree. Qualitative refers to providing a description or classification of general size or magnitude, appearance, or other perceptual properties, either relative or absolute.

representations used in studying the speech signal is the speech **waveform**. A waveform graphically and numerically records air pressure fluctuations over time or, in the case of audible air pressure fluctuations, the *sound wave*. Time is shown on the horizontal or x axis, and **amplitude** or sound pressure level of the fluctuations (related to loudness) is shown on the vertical or y axis. A sample waveform is shown in Figure 2.8.

Waveform representations are particularly helpful for examining two acoustic

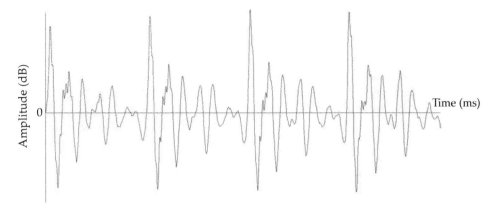

Figure 2.8 A waveform display of a short (approximately 40 ms) voiced speech sound wave.

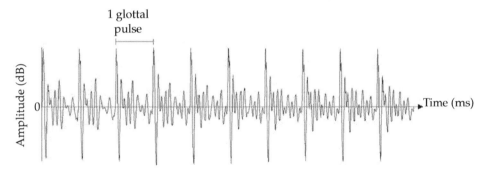

Figure 2.9 Waveform of about 85 ms of the vowel [a] (each "glottal pulse" is one cycle of opening and closing of the vocal folds).

properties of a sound: its duration and the presence of regular or **periodic** vibrations. In speech, regular or periodic vibrations are created by the voicing behavior of the vocal folds. During intervals of speech that have the vocal folds vibrating – or are **voiced** – regular repeating pressure fluctuations are seen in the microphone signal captured for a sound wave (or on your eardrum). Figure 2.9 shows an example of a speech waveform for a sustained vowel; each repeating vibration is due to one cycle of opening/closing of the vocal folds. Ten cycles are shown here for a total of about 85 ms.

If the mouth is closed during a portion of the speech signal, the loudness is greatly reduced. If there is no voicing, the waveform interval during a closure or **stop** may be basically silent. If there is voicing during a closure, small-amplitude periodic vibrations are present in the waveform. If the velum is lowered during a closure, as for a nasal consonant,

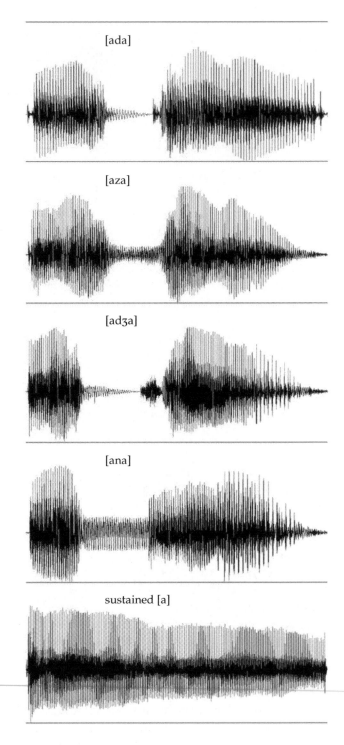

Figure 2.10
Waveforms of a stop,
fricative, affricate,
nasal, and vowel.

the periodic vibrations created by the vocal folds will be somewhat larger as greater signal amplitude is possible since air is leaving the vocal tract through the nose. During fricative sounds, which you will recall have turbulent airflow through a narrow constriction, noisy irregular fluctuations are evident in the waveform. Figure 2.10 shows sample waveforms for different types of **manner**.

We will discuss quantitative representations of speech sounds further in the next chapter. However, there are first three more IPA symbols that we would like to alert you to. Waveforms of the speech signal will be helpful in demonstrating these.

As an exercise, print figure 2.10, and for the first four panels, draw lines where you would separate the first vowel from the following consonant and the start of the last vowel. As an added challenge, in panel one, draw a line where the closure release for the [d] occurs, and in panel three, draw a line between the stop and fricative phases of the affricate. Lastly, why do you think the waveform for the nasal consonant is louder than that for a stop, though not as loud as the waveform for a vowel? Ⓦ

Nasalization, Devoicing, and VOT and Aspiration

There are certain very regular variations in pronunciation related to the timing or **coordination** of two articulatory movements that you will want to be aware of. These are recorded in transcription using additional superscript or subscript symbols called diacritics. The IPA has many diacritics of many sorts that modify symbols or provide greater detail; we will learn only three here.

We know that creating a nasal consonant requires two articulatory maneuvers. It requires the creation of a closure in the mouth somewhere at or in front of the velum, and it requires the lowering of the velum to allow air to flow out of the nose. In principle, one could imagine that the velum might lower at the same time as the oral closure is made or that either one might occur before the other. In fact, all three timings are found in languages of the world. However, in English two of the timings are used in a very regular or **systematic** way.

When a nasal is the consonant at the beginning of a syllable, the two movements are roughly synchronous. However, when the nasal is at the end of a syllable after the vowel, velum lowering for that nasal consonant occurs early relative to the oral closure for that consonant. This means that the velum is going down and air is exiting out the nose during the preceding vowel, as well as during the oral closure for the nasal itself. You can see these two organizations schematically in Figure 2.11.

When we encounter a situation like this – when a sound that in another context would not have nasal airflow has nasal airflow in some particular context – we say that that sound is **nasalized**. So in the word "ham,"

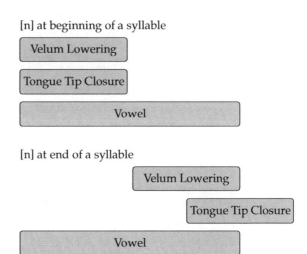

Figure 2.11 Vowel-[n] timing in syllable initial and final positions.

Simple waveform recording and editing software can be used to record yourself onto your computer; we suggest Audacity, which can be downloaded at *audacity.sourceforge.net*. Ⓦ

the vowel [æ] is nasalized (i.e., has nasal airflow). The IPA provides a diacritic symbol for nasalization; it is written with a ˜ over the sound – so "ham" would be transcribed [hæ̃m]. Nasalization causes a change in the acoustic quality of the sound, though most English speakers find this challenging to hear since it is not **contrastive**; it does not change a word's meaning. However, if a thorough IPA transcription is desired, transcription of nasalization is necessary. Consider the pair "daddy" and "Danny" – the first vowels in these words in fact sounds quite different because in "Danny" the velum is already lowering and allowing nasal airflow. You can try recording these yourself; then simply select each [æ] vowel in turn and listen to them; you will hear a dramatic difference.

The next type of systematic variation that interests us also involves the coordination of two articulatory events – in this case the release of a stop closure before a vowel and the initiation of voicing. These two events are in principle independent, and one could imagine them taking place synchronously or with either one occurring before the other. In fact, languages exhibit all three possible timing arrangements to form contrasting categories. Some languages may only have one arrangement, while others may have two or all three of the possible arrangements. The time from the release of a stop closure to the onset of voicing is called **voice onset time** or **VOT** and is one of the most-studied acoustic properties of language.

Although languages use a wide range of actual durations of voice onset time, the three general categories of coordination are given three names:

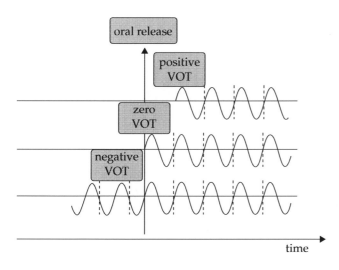

Figure 2.12 Voice Onset Time schematic: Positive VOT, Zero VOT, and Negative VOT. The flat line indicates no voicing and the wavy line indicates voicing.

- Positive VOT: vibration starts after stop release
- Zero VOT: onset of vibration coincides with stop release
- Negative VOT: vibration starts during closure, before the stop release.

Figure 2.12 shows these arrangements graphically.

In situations of positive VOT, there is an interval after the pressure built up behind the stop closure has been released but before there is voicing. During this interval, air is rushing through the nonvibrating glottis creating a light [h]-like noise or puff of air. This interval is called the stop's **aspiration**. Voiceless stops in English ([p], [t], [k]) are **aspirated** before a vowel in the same word. The raised [ʰ] diacritic is used to indicate aspiration.

| "pat" | [pʰæt] |
| "account" | [əkʰaʊnt] |

A waveform such as that in Figure 2.13 is very handy for observing this aspiration interval since one can see the release burst of the stop, the noisy irregular period of aspiration, followed by the initiation of periodic vibration indicating voicing.

There is an important systematic exception to this generalization, however. A voiceless stop is not aspirated when it occurs in a same-syllable consonant cluster with [s]. So the [p] in "pie" is aspirated [pʰaɪ]), but the [p] in "spy" is *not* [spʰaɪ], but [spaɪ]. This can be clearly seen in a waveform (Figure 2.14).

The reason this occurs is that while both the [s] and the stop are voice-less, that voicelessness is achieved for both by only a single opening or separation of the vocal folds. That single laryngeal opening is coordinated

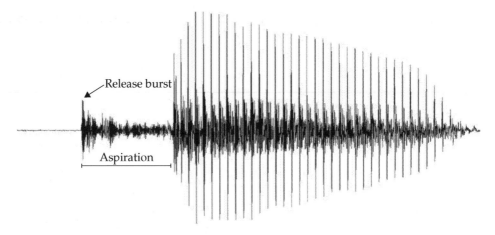

Figure 2.13   Waveform showing aspiration in [kʰa].

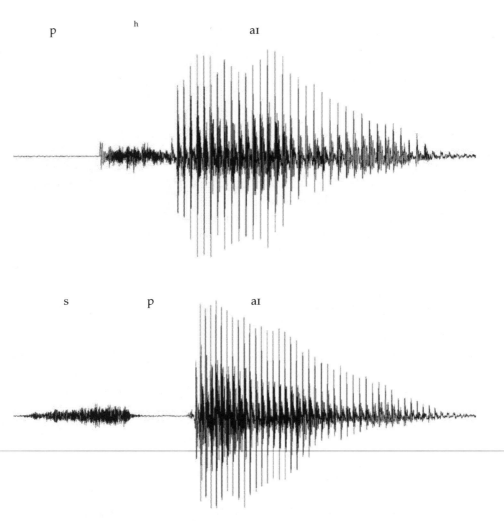

Figure 2.14   (Top) Waveform of "pie" [pʰaɪ], (Bottom) Waveform of "spy" [spaɪ].

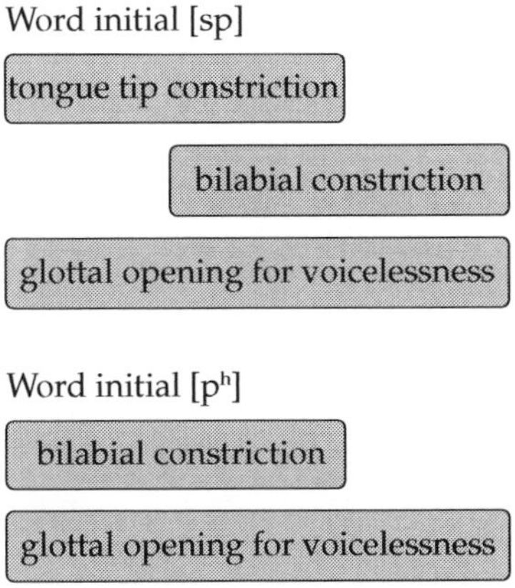

Word initial [sp]

| tongue tip constriction |
| bilabial constriction |
| glottal opening for voicelessness |

Word initial [pʰ]

| bilabial constriction |
| glottal opening for voicelessness |

Figure 2.15 Schema of timing of oral and glottal actions in [sp] and [p] in word initial position.

such that it is "centered" within the entire voiceless sequence rather than occurring late relative to the stop closure, as would occur if the stop closure was not part of a cluster with [s]. This means that while the articulatory maneuver for voicelessness is still present it does not lag late relative to the stop, thereby an aspiration interval does not occur. This can be seen schematically in Figure 2.15.

The final diacritic we consider also relates to the timing of oral (meaning, in the mouth) and glottal (at the larynx) events. When a sound that in most contexts occurs with voicing occurs in a particular context without voicing, it is said to be **devoiced**. The diacritic [̥] is used under the IPA symbol to indicate **devoicing**. Devoicing occurs systematically in several contexts in English, so the diacritic has a number of uses. One circumstance of devoicing is when consonants or short schwa vowels occur after a voiceless stop. Effectively this places the consonant or schwa during the positive VOT lag or aspiration interval when the vocal folds are apart letting air through without vibrating. However, since a consonant constriction is in place in the vocal tract at that moment, the voiceless aspiration airflow occurs during that second consonant:

> "pry"   [pr̥aɪ]
> "potato"   [pə̥tʰeɪdo]

The third situation for English in which a sound that is often voiced may be

Some dialects of English in the North East US have a voiceless [w] sound; words written orthographically with an initial "wh" are likely to have this pronunciation. Thus, in these dialects, "witch" and "which" contrast in their pronunciation. This could be written with the voiceless diacritic or with a separate symbol for a voiceless labiovelar glide: [ʍ].

witch   [wɪtʃ]
which   [w̥ɪtʃ]
which   [ʍɪtʃ]

The contexts when [b, d, g] are fully voiced versus partly voiced versus voiceless unaspirated are actually quite complex in English and even subject to some variation from individual to individual.

unvoiced is for the stops we've been transcribing as [b, d, g]. (In order to understand when this happens, we will need to refer to "stress"; for now, you can just understand the term "stressed" to refer to being the strongest, loudest, longest syllable of a word.) When one of these [b, d, g] stops occurs in certain contexts – for example, before a stressed vowel or as a word-initial

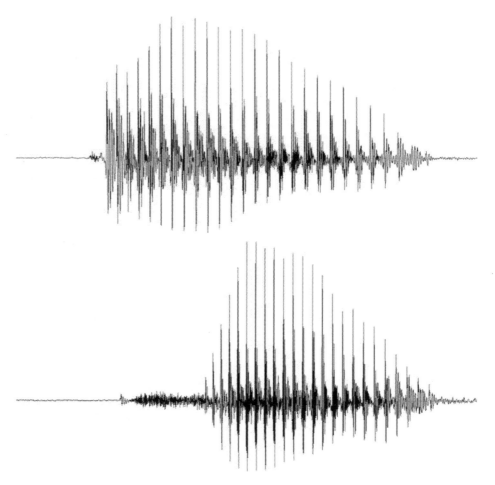

Figure 2.16   (top) waveform of "bad" [b̥æd]; (bottom) waveform of "pad" [pʰæd]. (See figure 2.10 for an example of a voiced production of a stop between vowels.) Can you align the sounds in the transcription with the appropriate intervals in each waveform by drawing lines separating and labeling each portion of the waveform? Where is the oral release? Where does vowel voicing begin?

stop before a vowel or after a voiceless consonant – it shows a near-zero VOT, meaning that voicing begins near the time of stop release; it does not have a negative lag VOT (voicing through stop closure) as it does in many other circumstances and as would be suggested by our earlier description of these sounds as voiced (nor does it have a positive lag VOT, i.e., aspiration). In these circumstances, the stop is described as **voiceless, unaspirated**.

"bad boy"	[b̥ædbɔɪ]	
"pit bull"	[pʰɪtb̥l̩]	([pʰɪʔb̥l̩])

This means that in fact words like "bad" and "pad" are *not* necessarily differentiated by voicing in English (both may start with a voiceless closure) but by aspiration. This is evident in the waveforms in Figure 2.16.

As with all the diacritics, when the regular or *systematic* pattern of variation is acknowledged among those working with the transcription, the diacritic may be viewed as superfluous, but when a detailed transcription is desired, diacritics are used.

Thus, with the introduction of these diacritics, we can frame an interesting question. If voiceless stops are unaspirated after [s] *and* voiced stops are devoiced at the beginning of an utterance, what, if anything, is the phonetic difference between the stops in "s<u>p</u>ay" and "<u>b</u>ay"? (Answer in footnote*)

Another way to put this is: If you remove the [s] from "spay" and then listen to the result, what will you hear? You should try this on your own using waveform editing software. You should be sure that you can provide an answer *and* an explanation to this question before concluding this chapter's work on phonetics.

Playing with speech sound waves on your own

You can download a free, cross-platform waveform editor at *audacity.sourceforge.net*. After you set up your computer to record sound from its own microphone or an external microphone (like a USB microphone), you will be able to open Audacity and make recordings of yourself. Record into separate files the phrases: "a nap," "a bat," "a pat," a pad," and "spat." How long in milliseconds is the [n] in "nap?" How does that measurement compare to the [b] closure interval? The [p] closure interval? Next, measure the vowel in "pat" and "pad." Which one is longer? If you try other syllables ending in voiceless and voiced consonants, you will see that this is a very robust pattern in English. Finally, highlight the [s] in "spat" and delete it. Then play the remaining word. What do you hear? Why?

---

* Nothing

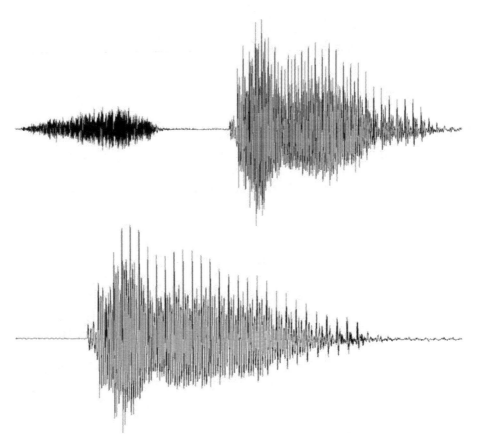

Figure 2.17   (top) Waveform of "spay"; (bottom) Waveform of "bay".

Summary of Topics

Chapter 2, Section 1

1   Vocal tract anatomy
2   Voicing, place of articulation, and manner of articulation
3   The IPA and IPA consonant and vowel charts
4   Phonetic transcription of English using the IPA and why transcription is not spelling
5   Voice onset time (VOT)
6   Diacritics: nasalization, devoicing, aspiration
7   The patterning of aspiration and voicing in English stop consonants.

Section 2: The Sound of Speech

In this section of Chapter 2 we want to develop a grasp of how speech is created by combining the generation of sound energy – usually by vibration of the vocal folds – with shaping of that sound energy by movements of the vocal tract. To do that, we need to consider the *acoustic* properties of sound created by vocal fold vibration and then examine how these acoustic characteristics are shaped as a consequence of the geometry of the vocal tract tube above the larynx. This will help us understand the acoustic properties of spoken language – particularly its vowels.

Starting at the Beginning: Describing a Sound Wave

Have you thought about the basic question of what is sound? Sound, put simply, is changes or fluctuations in air pressure that can be heard. In the real world, the patterns of air pressure changes that we encounter are generally quite complicated. Let's start with a consideration of very simple sound (which is in fact unlikely to occur naturally). That will help us define some terms.

The sound waveform shown in Figure 2.18 varies in its magnitude over time. It does this in a cyclic or **periodic** way, which means that it has a pattern that repeats over time. (In fact, the waveform shown here is a sine wave.) The term **amplitude** is used to describe the extent of variation from normal air pressure, plotted as the zero line or midpoint. Higher amplitude sounds have more acoustic energy. With regard to how sounds are perceived, sounds having higher amplitude (i.e., greater magnitude air pressure fluctuations) are perceived as being louder than those with lower amplitude. Also shown in Figure 2.18 is another important measurable aspect of this sound signal. For a periodic or cyclic signal like this one,

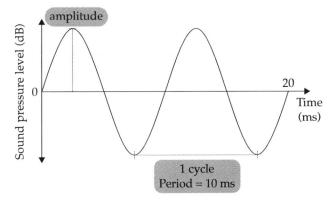

Figure 2.18   100 Hz sine wave.

the property of **period** is an important aspect of the signal. The period is the time taken for one cycle or repetition of the signal's repeating pattern. It is expressed in seconds per [one] cycle (or, more often for speech, milliseconds for one cycle).[†] Thus period is a measure of time. A simple arithmetic manipulation of the period value yields the signal's **frequency**, which is the inverse of period.

So the frequency is a repeating signal's cycles per [one] second; sometimes abbreviated **cps** ("cycles per second"), but more often this unit is referred to as Hertz, abbreviated Hz.

$$period = \frac{1}{frequency} \text{ because seconds per cycle} = \frac{1}{cycles/second}$$

In Figure 2.18, you should be able to observe the period of the signal and then, from that information, figure out its frequency (the answer is in the footnote for you to check yourself.[‡] Feel free to use a calculator if you like, though it's not necessary).

For a simple sound like a sine wave, a sound having a higher frequency is perceived as being higher in pitch than one with a lower frequency. It's important to understand that amplitude, period, and frequency are *physical* properties of a signal that can be measured. However, loudness and pitch are *perceptual* properties that have to do with how the brain interprets the signals it is presented with. Physical and perceptual properties are, of course, often closely related, but they are not identical.

Describing Complex Sounds

In the real world, sounds are rarely as simple as a sine wave. However, we still use amplitude and frequency (or period) for describing more complex sounds. A complex periodic sound will actually have multiple repeating patterns in its waveform; some repeating at faster rates and some taking longer to repeat their cycles. It is the slowest – the longest period/lowest frequency – repeating pattern in a complex periodic sound that governs the signal's perceived pitch. This lowest frequency is called a signal's **fundamental frequency**. The shorthand **F0** (pronounced "F zero") is often used in speech research to refer to fundamental frequency. All complex periodic sounds or waves can be mathematically analyzed as being composed of multiple single-frequency sounds/waves, such as a series of sine waves. There is a famous mathematical statement of this known

---

[†]   1 second = 1000 milliseconds [abbreviated ms]
[‡]   Period = .01 ms; Frequency = 100 Hz.

as *Fourier's theorem.* Fourier's theorem states that any periodic signal is composed of the summation (or *superposition*) of multiple sine waves with particular amplitudes and with particular relative temporal alignment (phases). Fourier's theorem by extension implies that we can *decompose* complex periodic sounds into simple components. An example of this is shown in Figure 2.19 where a complex wave is generated from a 100 Hz component and a 200 Hz component. The component frequencies that compose the complex sound are called **harmonics** of

Jean Baptiste Joseph Fourier (1768–1830) was a French mathematician who studied heat dissipation; these were the types of waves he was interested in, not sound in particular. In addition to his findings on the decomposition of complex periodic waves, he is also credited with discovery of the greenhouse effect.

that fundamental frequency. The frequencies of a signal's harmonics are integer multiples (×2, ×3, ×4 . . .) of its fundamental frequency. Thus the second harmonic is 2 × F0; the third harmonic is 3 × F0; and so on.

Many different ways of looking at sound have been developed and each can be useful for asking and answering different types of questions. The type of display we looked at in Figure 2.17 is called a waveform. You cannot tell simply by looking at a complex waveform what its component frequencies or harmonics are. A computer is generally used to implement algorithms based on Fourier's theorem to find a complex signal's harmonics. A different type of display – called a **power spectrum** – is useful for showing the frequency composition or **spectrum** of a sound. A power spectrum plots frequency on the *x* or horizontal axis and amplitude on the *y* or

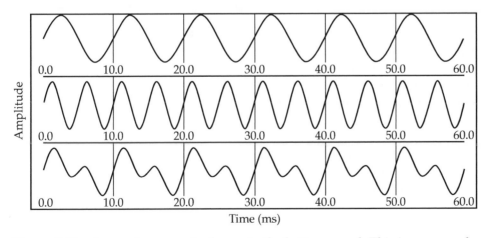

Figure 2.19 A complex wave is shown in the bottom panel. This is composed of the summation of the two sine waves in the top two panels – top 100 Hz, middle 200 Hz. [adapted by permission from Louis Goldstein].

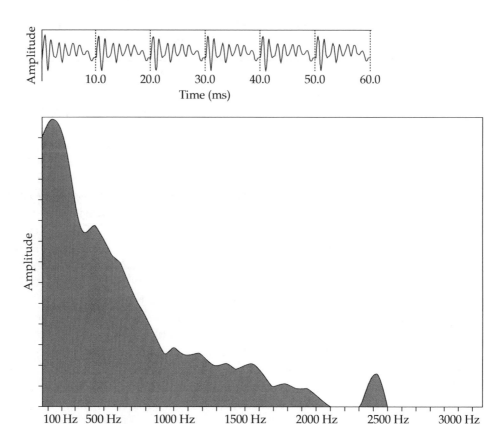

Figure 2.20   A complex waveform and its power spectrum [waveform adapted by permission from Louis Goldstein].

vertical axis. Sometimes the harmonics are shown as a series of discrete lines, and sometimes the frequency composition of a complex sound is shown as a smoothly varying frequency function. Figure 2.20 shows a complex waveform with a fundamental frequency of 100 Hz and a power spectrum showing its composition.

Voicing: The Main Sound Source in Speech

Now we are at last ready to return to speech. When the vocal folds are repeatedly blown open and sucked closed, the vibration sound that is created is a complex, periodic signal. It is complex because it is not a single-frequency (sinusoidal) wave, and it is periodic because a repeating pattern is created by each open–close cycle of the vocal folds. A sample waveform of a noise created by vocal fold vibration is shown in Figure 2.21.

Figure 2.21 Glottal source waveform [adapted by permission from Louis Goldstein].

As a complex sound, the voicing sound source has a fundamental frequency (F0) and harmonics. The fundamental frequency is by definition the lowest frequency component of the complex signal – for voicing, this is the rate or frequency of vocal fold vibration. One cycle of vocal fold vibration is one opening and one closing of the vocal folds. We know that in periodic signals perceived pitch is related to the signal's fundamental frequency. So the fundamental frequency (F0) of a voice will be closely related to the perceived pitch of that voice. It shouldn't be surprising to realize that the fundamental frequency of men's voices, with their generally thicker and slower vibrating vocal folds, tends to be lower than that of women's voices, which tend to have thinner and more quickly vibrating vocal folds. (But these are just generalizations; there is overlap in the population between the F0s seen in men's and women's voices.)

The voicing sound source has harmonics that are integer multiples of the fundamental frequency. So, if the rate of vocal fold vibration is:

F0 = 100 Hz, then harmonics = 200 Hz, 300 Hz, 400 Hz, 500 Hz . . .
F0 = 250 Hz, then harmonics = 500 Hz, 750 Hz, 1000 Hz, 1250 Hz . . .

Notice that a voice with a higher fundamental frequency has more sparsely spaced harmonics than one with a lower fundamental frequency. The lower F0 voice will have more densely packed harmonics. We will return to the implications of this fact below.

The range of fundamental frequencies found in human voices is roughly 60 to 500 Hz, but in adult males a typical F0 might be 120 Hz; in a female voice a typical F0 might be 225 Hz, and in a child it might be 265 Hz. It is critical to understand that variation in fundamental frequency in speech is *not* due to the overall bigness or tallness of a person; it is due to the structure of the larynx and vocal folds *only*. There are many tall men, for example, who don't have a deep, bass voice.

Other sound sources in speech

In addition to voicing, it is possible to generate noise or sources of sound in a few other ways in the vocal tract during speech. A fricative consonant creates noise by the turbulent airflow generated when air is forced

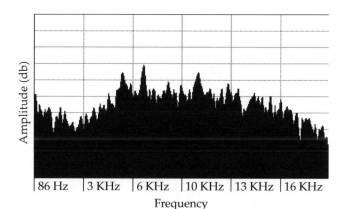

Figure 2.22 Power spectrum for fricative [s].

through a narrow constriction, sometimes directed against the teeth as an obstacle. Unlike the voicing source, this acoustic energy is generated in the mouth, not at the larynx. But it is still a sound source. It is not, however, periodic (though it can be combined with voicing, which is). The noise generated by a fricative constriction has no regular repeating pattern. The air pressure fluctuations that are created are turbulent, basically chaotic or random. A power spectrum of this type of sound would show energy spread throughout a range of frequencies – see Figure 2.22. It does not have harmonic structure.

Occasionally other sound sources occur in speech, such as the transient bursts of noise created when a stop constriction is opened, but we will concentrate on the main sound source in speech – the voicing source – and look next at how the harmonic structure of this source is shaped by the vocal tract.

Source-filter model

To produce spoken language, three separate components interact:

1 A **source** of acoustic energy, primarily generated by voicing, which yields a complex, periodic sound with harmonic structure;
2 A **filter** determined by the shape of the vocal tract that adjusts the strength of the different frequency components found in the source(s); and
3 A **medium** through which the signal travels – usually air.

We've now seen what the acoustic properties of the voicing source are. If the sound source simply came directly out of the mouth, there would be only one kind of sound in speech – a sort of buzzing noise that could only vary in pitch. But we know that the vowels of speech have all sorts of very different qualities. How do all these different sounds arise from a single noise-generating device housed inside the larynx?

Once sound is generated by the vocal folds in the larynx, the sound is shaped by passing through cavities or chambers of particular shapes and sizes. These shapes allow certain frequency regions to come through and emerge strongly in the output speech, while not allowing others to do so. For this reason, the device shaping the sound – namely the vocal tract – can be thought of as a **filter**. It may be useful to know the words **amplifies**, which means strengthens, and **attenuates**, which means weakens, to describe the effects of the vocal tract filter on the harmonic frequency components of the source. The vocal tract filter can amplify or attenuate the harmonic components of the voicing source.

The general process of a filter acting on a noise source can be seen for many musical instruments, such as reed and brass instruments where the musician makes the sound source at the mouthpiece and simultaneously shapes and reshapes the filter by fingering (or sliding, in the case of a trombone).

So how does this shaping take place in a vocal tract? The size and shape of the airspace in the vocal tract can be altered by various maneuvers:

1 Creating constrictions in the mouth and pharynx;
2 Lowering the soft palate/velum to allow air into the nasal cavities;
3 Changing the length of the vocal tract by: (a) extending the lips, (b) lowering/raising the larynx.

Resonance and formants

To understand how a particular shape of the vocal tract acts as a filter, we must now grasp the property of **resonance**. All natural objects have particular frequencies at which they "like" to vibrate – wave periods that fit well within their particular structure. When energy at a variety of frequencies is fed into an object, that object will respond to or be **excited** to certain of those frequencies – the ones that match its inherent **resonant or natural frequencies** – and it will filter or damp out those that are not good matches. (You might hear either the term **resonant frequency** or equivalently the term **natural frequency**.)

If you have ever blown over a bottle or beat on a drum, you have experienced acoustic resonance. The bottle or drum

It is due to the existence of resonant frequencies that soldiers are trained not to march in formation over bridges in field assignments. This prohibition prevents the chance that the high-energy frequency of the mass marching could match a resonant or natural frequency of the bridge. If that were to happen, a less-than-robust bridge might begin to shimmy at the frequency and possibly collapse – something the soldiers would most definitely like to avoid.

has an internal airspace that is excited at its natural frequencies. These are the frequencies that you hear when you blow over the bottle or beat the drum. Similarly, at any particular moment in time, your vocal tract is an airspace with resonant frequencies. If you are sitting quietly, there is no energy being put into the vocal tract, but the vocal tract's resonant frequencies still exist even though they are not being excited. When voicing source energy is put into the vocal tract, harmonics that are near the resonant frequencies are passed along and appear in the output speech strongly. We call these strong frequencies in speech by a special name: **formants**. (Actually in speech, the term formants is often used rather informally to refer both to the natural resonant frequencies of a particular vocal tract speech and to the bands of strong frequency energy that are observable in the output speech.)

For understanding speech acoustics, we are generally interested in the three lowest frequency formants, generally referred to as the first three formants or **F1**, **F2**, and **F3**. For adult vowels, a very rough rule of thumb is that one of these formants is likely to occur per each 1000 Hz interval.

> At higher regions of the frequency range (say above 4000 Hz), there is simply not a lot of energy in speech sounds that only have a voicing sound source. Fricatives, however, do exhibit high frequency energy, so linguists may consider frequencies up to 10,000 Hz when they are studying both consonants and vowels.

> Spectrograms used to be made by a special machine called a spectrograph but now they are generated by signal processing packages on computers.

Previously we have seen two types of quantitative displays of speech: the waveform and the power spectrum. The power spectrum display shows the frequency composition by plotting frequency on the *x* or horizontal axis and amplitude on the *y* or vertical axis. In speech acoustics and speech perception research, there is another very familiar type of display that also reflects the frequency composition of sound. But it does more – it also incorporates time. This is important because one of the hallmark and requisite properties of speech is that it is a signal that it is highly time-varying. You might wonder how one would display *three* parameters – amplitude, frequency, and time. The **spectrogram** display does this by plotting time on the *x*-axis, frequency on the *y*-axis, and amplitude in terms of darkness (either in greyscale or sometimes using a color scale). You can imagine a spectrogram being created by stacking multiple spectrums at successive times side by side and rotating them and plotting from right to left; we've tried to suggest this in Figure 2.23.

Table 2.4 helps summarize the three types of acoustic displays that we've talked about.

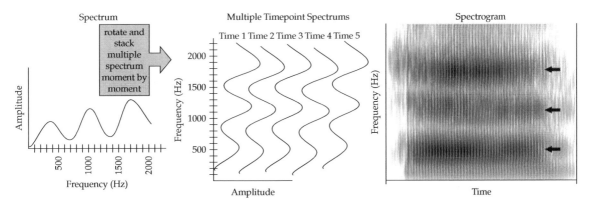

Figure 2.23 A schema showing how a spectrogram is built up from multiple time-slices of power spectra.

Table 2.4 Three types of acoustic display

Display type	x-axis horizontal	y-axis vertical	Greyscale/color
Waveform	Time	Amplitude	
Power spectrum	Frequency	Amplitude	
Spectrogram	Time	Frequency	Amplitude

In addition to the fact that time is plotted, one reason that spectrograms are very useful is that formant frequencies are quite evident as dark (high amplitude) bands – recall that **formants** are the strong resonant frequencies of the vocal tract. In the spectrogram in Figure 2.24 we can observe three strong formants as dark bands.

We will be using spectrograms with some regularity in our exploration of the science of spoken language. In the spectrogram in Figure 2.25 we can observe strong formants as dark bands. The bands' locations move slightly over time because this is a spectrogram of [aiaiai], in which the vocal tract changes shape during the syllable, thus causing the resonant frequency values to change.

The independence of the source and the filter

Figure 2.26 gives us a schematized power spectrum representation showing the properties of a voicing source, the properties of a vocal tract filter, and the resulting output when the two encounter one another.

In this text, we are not going to try to untangle the details of the mathematical relations between particular shapes and what their natural

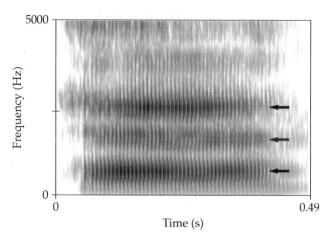

Figure 2.24   A spectrogram of the sounds [hɛ], as in the beginning of the word "head". The dark horizontal bands identified with the arrows are areas of high amplitude at the formant frequencies of the vowel. (The thin vertical striations are individual glottal pulses indicating voicing.)

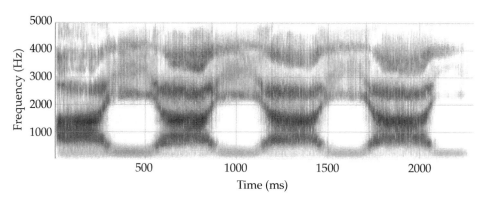

Figure 2.25   Spectrogram of [aiaiai] showing the formants moving over time as the resonance cavities for change from one vowel to the other.

frequencies are. (Speech scientists devote much sweat to this difficult topic!) But there is one basic relationship that we should be aware of, since the vocal tract can in a simplified way be understood as a tube. When a tube is long, it has lower resonant frequencies than when it is short. Thus, *all else being equal,* a longer vocal tract (with a particular shape) will yield speech with lower formants than a shorter vocal tract (with that same shape) will (hint: you can remember "long:low").

One of the most important concepts to grasp in this chapter is the **independence of the source and the filter**. A person's vocal folds might vibrate at any particular fundamental frequency. The size and shape of that

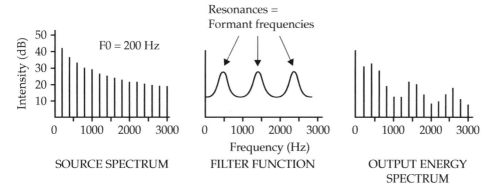

Figure 2.26   Source-filter diagram [adapted by permission from Louis Goldstein].

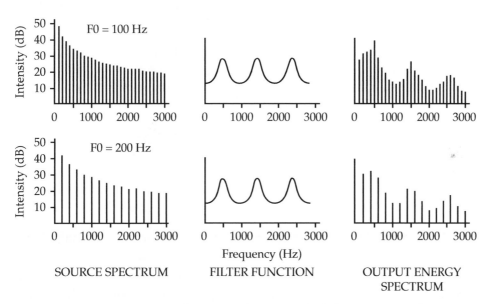

Figure 2.27   A comparison of two vocal tracts with different sources but the same resonant frequencies [adapted by permission from Louis Goldstein].

person's vocal tract is independent of the rate of the vocal fold vibration. The output speech is the consequence of the combination of the particular source and the particular vocal tract filter at a given moment in time.

For example, the same vocal tract "attached" to two different laryngeal sources – one with a low F0 (more male-like) and one with a high F0 (more female-like) will result in different output acoustics. This is shown in Figure 2.27. In particular, recall that a high F0 has relatively widely spaced harmonics (because they are each multiples of a bigger number). This means that there is a greater likelihood in the case of a high F0 that there may not be a harmonic right in the neighborhood of a particular resonant frequency. If this happens, we will not be able to observe that formant as precisely in the output. The *same* vocal tract filter with a lower F0, and thus more densely packed harmonics, is more likely to happen to have a harmonic (and therefore acoustic energy) right in the neighborhood of a formant, exciting it strongly. Both of these vocal tracts have the same resonant frequencies, but the output speech will differ, obviously in perceived pitch, but also more subtly in other acoustic details, because of how the independent sources and the filter combine.

While men *tend* to have both more slowly vibrating vocal folds (so lower F0s) and longer vocal tracts (so lower formants), and women *tend* to have both more quickly vibrating vocal folds (so higher F0s) and shorter vocal tracts (so higher formants), *these tendencies may not be true for any particular individual*. At extremes, one can imagine the speech of Popeye as an example of speech from someone with a low F0 and a short vocal tract; and the speech of Julia Child, who was over six foot tall, as an example of speech from someone with a high F0 and a long vocal tract. Both produced very distinctive and recognizable speech, perhaps in part because of these unusual combinations of source and filter qualities.

Returning to Understanding the Vowel Plane

Every time the vocal tract moves and its air cavities change shape, the result is that the resonant frequencies or formants change. Contrasting vowels, which have different vocal tract shapes, consequently differ from one another in their formant frequencies. You will remember that we described vowels by placing them on a continuous two-dimensional plane, describing those dimensions in terms of "height" and "backness." These terms do not reflect directly tongue position. Rather they reflect linguists' perception of the first formant, as captured in the "height" dimension, and of the second formant, as captured in the "front–back" dimension. The first formant (F1) has an *inverse* relationship with height. The higher the vowel on the vowel chart the lower its F1. The second formant (F2) is high for front vowels and lower for back vowels. Finally, we noted that vowels may need to add rounding or lip protrusion to their description. Because pushing out the lips acts to lengthen the vocal tract tube, it lowers all the formant frequencies. Thus we see that the system that linguists have developed for classifying vowels using the International Phonetic Alphabet critically reflects vowel differentiation in terms of the first three formant frequencies (i.e., the three lowest formant frequencies). Examples of the vowel placement in terms of F1 and F2 frequencies are shown in Figure 2.28.

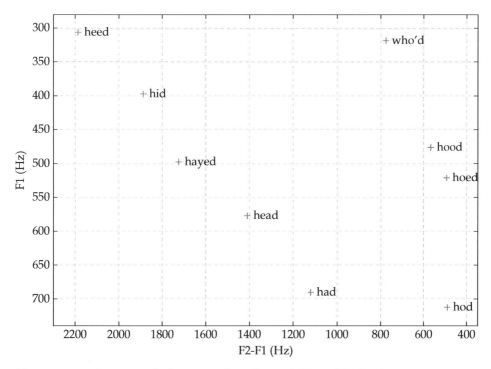

Figure 2.28 An example formant plot of vowel F1 and F2-F1 formant frequencies in these words. [adapted by permission from Louis Goldstein]

You should recognize that the vowel space for each individual will be different, depending on the person's dialect and vocal tract. For example, in Figure 2.29 you can see a different vowel space plot for a speaker from Southern California.

Thus we can see that formant frequencies are an example of a vital acoustic characteristic of speech that allows a listener to identify the actions that have been performed by a speaker. It is because there

Note that sometimes the x-axis of the vowel plane is plotted in terms of F2 frequency and sometimes in terms of the frequency difference between F2 and F1. Both types of displays give suitable descriptions of the vowel space.

is a lawful physical relationship between the properties of the moving vocal tract, both at and above the larynx, and the consequences of those movements in the physical world that speech perception is possible. It is the human ability to connect our perception of acoustic events in the physical world with linguistic actions of ourselves and other individuals – a cognitive action–perception link – that allows for the robust and rich system of human spoken language communication.

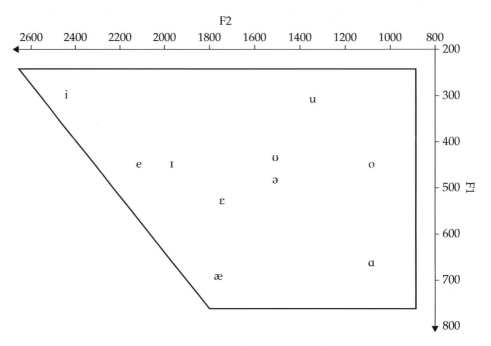

Figure 2.29   An example vowel space for a speaker from Southern California.

Terms to Know

Key terms for Section 2 are:

amplitude	period
filter	power spectrum
frequency	resonance
Fourier's theorem	source
formants	spectrogram
fundamental frequency (F0)	waveform
harmonics	

A key concept for Section 2 is the independence of source and filter.

Section 3: Hearing

In Section 1 of this chapter we investigated how the human body moves to produce speech, and in Section 2 we began our understanding of the properties of the speech sound wave and introduced the source-filter concept to explain how the creation of speech acoustics occurs. In the speech chain, the process of human hearing or **audition** is subsequent to speech production and acoustics. In Section 3 we will outline the structures of the human ear and how they allow for the sensation of hearing.

The Anatomy of the Ear

Structurally the ear can be considered in three sections: the outer ear, the middle ear, and the inner ear. These are shown in Figure 2.30.

The exterior section of the **outer ear** is the cone-shaped soft skin and cartilage that you see on the outside of your head. This is your **pinna**. The pinna's specialized shape serves to focus soundwaves, directing them to the more interior structures of the ear. The second part of the outer ear is the auditory canal. In adults, the auditory canal is about 2.5 mm long. It is the passageway to the eardrum and acts to protect the eardrum from particulates, damage, and injury.

The pinna and auditory canal in combination amplify (increase the energy in) soundwaves. This amplification is particularly strong for frequencies found in human speech. Because of the details of how this sound amplification occurs, and because we have one ear on each side of our head, the outer ear is also useful in helping us determine where a sound is coming from. This process is called **sound localization**.

The separation between the outer and **middle ear** (Figure 2.31) is the eardrum, whose technical name is the **tympanic membrane**. This membrane separates the auditory canal from an air-filled cavity behind the tympanic membrane. The tympanic membrane is exquisitely sensitive to very tiny air pressure fluctuations.

Interior to the tympanic membrane in the middle ear cavity is a chain of three small bones or **ossicles** – the smallest bones in the human body. These bones provide a crucial series of levers that convert the motion of the large tympanic membrane into mechanical energy. Because of their shapes they are named the hammer, anvil, and stirrup or are called by their Latin names the **malleus, incus**, and **stapes**. The first of these, the

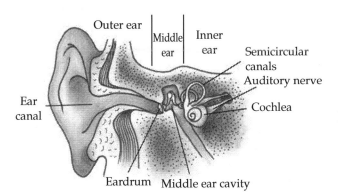

Figure 2.30 The structure of the ear. Adapted from hearingcentral.com, Credit: David Li.

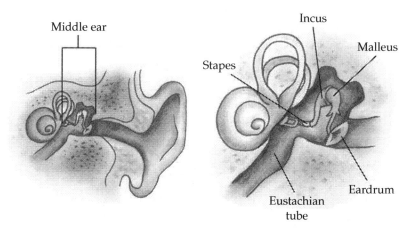

Figure 2.31   Middle ear. Adapted from hearingcentral.com, Credit: David Li.

malleus, is directly affixed to the tympanic membrane, and the last of these, the tiny stapes (about 3 mm long and 3 mg in weight), directly interacts with a much smaller thin membrane called the oval window. The oval window is the entrance to the fluid-filled inner ear and is about one-twentieth of the size of the tympanic membrane. Since the oval window is a much smaller structure, the vibrations of the eardrum are intensified as they are transmitted to it. Further, the series of ossicle levers ending in the small oval window also acts to significantly amplify (by about 1.3 times) the vibrations at the tympanic membrane. Overall, the middle ear increases the pressure from the eardrum of the outer ear to the entrance to the inner ear by more than 20 times. This increase in intensity is critical in this next transition to the inner ear. This is because the inner ear is filled with fluid, which would otherwise cause a great loss of sound energy. When the outer or middle ear fails to conduct sound energy properly due to some disorder, disease, or illness, we say that **conductive hearing loss** has occurred.

The **inner ear**'s structure is so complex that it is sometimes called the **labyrinth**. It is situated inside the very hard and protective temporal bone. Our organ of balance or **vestibular system** is found here – the semicircular canals – but we will be focusing on another structure in the inner ear – the **cochlea**, shown in Figure 2.32.

The cochlea is appropriately named after a snail's shell because its structure is hollow and spiral. With its two-and-one-half turns uncoiled, it would measure about 35 mm. This long cochlea is compactly organized into a coiled-up structure in mammals, contributing to their ability to hear a wide range of sound frequencies. The cochlea's cavities are fluid-filled, and waves in that fluid are created as the oval window moves due to the mechanical movements of the stapes. The function of the inner ear

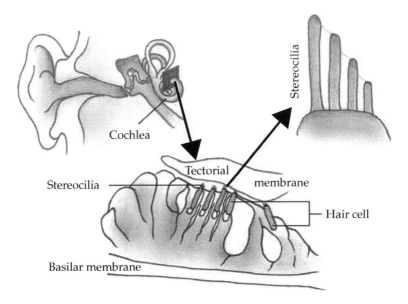

Figure 2.32 Cochlea. Adapted from hearingcentral.com, Credit: David Li.

is to provide some analysis of the composition of the sound wave that has now been translated into fluid waves, and to convert the physical movements into a neural signal for the brain. We will be developing only a rudimentary understanding of the highly complex inner ear structures, with the goal of showing how this transduction from mechanical to neural occurs.

As a consequence of the ossicles transmitting movement of the tympanic membrane into tiny sensitive movements of the oval window, the fluid in the cochlea is set into waves of motion. Running roughly down the middle of the long, curled-up cochlea is the **basilar membrane**, which separates fluid-filled cavities. This membrane is deflected by the waves moving through the fluid, and the basilar membrane is differentially responsive – resonates – to different sound frequencies along its length. This different response of portions of the basilar membrane is due to its physical properties, in particular its width. The part near the stapes – called the **base** – is narrow and stiff and responds to high frequencies, and the portions that are more interior in the spiral – near the **apex** – are wide and less stiff and respond to lower frequencies. We call this pattern of response of the basilar membrane a **tonotopic** organization. A schematic of this tonotopic organization of the basilar membrane is shown in Figure 2.33.

The tonotopic response of the inner ear means that it functions in a way that parallels a spectrogram; the inner ear analyzes the frequency components of sounds. So there are good reasons why a speech scientist would find a spectrogram to be an informative display – it represents

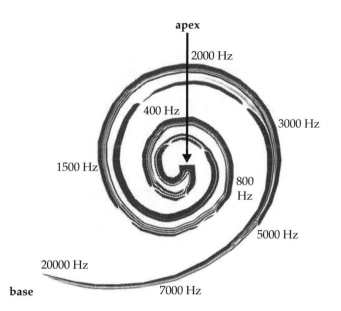

Figure 2.33 Schematic of the tonotopic structure of the basilar membrane.

information of a sort that we know is used by humans in hearing (and, as we will see, also consequently used in cognitive perception).

Overall, healthy young humans can hear from roughly 20 Hz to 20,000 Hz. A large portion of the basilar membrane responds to sounds below 1000 Hz and only a small portion to sounds above 12,000 Hz, an area that is not information-rich for human speech. This means that humans are most sensitive to sounds in the frequency range produced by their own species' communicative speech actions.

> The metabolic needs of the sensory hair cells are fed in a specialized indirect way that allows the blood vessels to be few and removed from the area. This is advantageous because the inner ear is so sensitive that it would be able to hear the blood flow if it were close by.

The next step to understand in the hearing process is how the wave-driven deflections of the basilar membrane are translated into chemical and, finally, electrical responses at the cellular level. The sensory cells of hearing are called **hair cells**. This is not because they are made of hair! It is because when a hair cell is seen through a microscope each cell has projections called **stereocilia** (about 100) coming from one end. At their other end, they have synapses connected to neurons that conduct electrical signals between the cells and the brain. It is a mechanical act of bending the projecting stereocilia that causes the chemical changes in the hair cells and a consequent neural signal. The hair cells are arrayed along the basilar membrane in the **organ of Corti** – our hearing sense organ that sits on the basilar membrane (Figure 2.34).

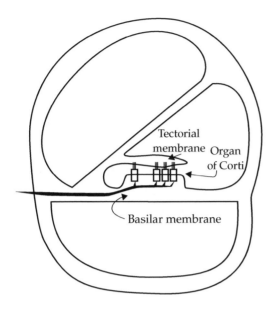

Figure 2.34 A schematic cross-section through the (unrolled) cochlea showing the Organ of Corti with hair cells whose stereocilia project against the tectorial membrane.

The stereocilia projecting from the hair cells extend upward into a collagen **tectorial membrane** of the organ of Corti. The deflection of the basilar membrane as the fluid in the inner ear is agitated pushes the stereocilia of the hair cells up into the tectorial membrane, causing them to bend. This bending changes the electrical potential in the cell, resulting in nerve impulses being sent directly to the brain via cranial nerve VIII.

There are actually two main types of hair cells, and while we will not discuss their different enervation and function at length, we will want to recognize that the **outer hair cells** function to adjust the sensitivity of the **inner hair cells**. We saw that the basilar membrane has different resonance behavior along its length. It's also the case that the inner hair cells themselves can respond differentially to sound frequencies, introducing another analysis capability in the cochlea. This allows the sensory cells of the inner ear to tell the brain that it is encountering sound energy at particular frequencies and intensities. This is important in recovering linguistic information from the speech acoustic signal.

In the brain, there is also a pattern of organization for auditory information (as there is for vision, as well) that allows it to reconstruct events in the world. One type of organization of neurons in the auditory cortex is in columns that correspond to a particular frequency. Another type of organization is tonotopic, like the cochlea. Frequency response ranges from higher toward the front of the relevant auditory brain region to lower at the back. The brain is also organized for physical auditory localization, such that different locations in the brain correspond to different locations of a sound in the world with respect to the body.

Recall that we used the term conductive hearing loss to refer to deafness or hearing loss due to problems with the mechanical conductive abilities of the middle ear. In contrast, when the cochlea (inner ear) or auditory nerve are impaired, we use the term **sensorineural hearing loss** to describe the resulting hearing deficit. The development and health of the inner ear is very delicate. It can be damaged by loud noises (see the fact box on "Noise-Induced Hearing Loss" and Chapter 11) and injury, and by disease (bacterial, viral, immunological, neurological), tumors, and drugs during fetal development, and in childhood and adulthood. We will discuss this further in Chapter 11. The National Institute on Deafness and Other Communication Disorders (NIDCD) – *www.nidcd.nih.gov/health/hearing/* – is an excellent source of information for health and hearing.

Noise-Induced Hearing Loss

- The sensory organ of the inner ear is tiny compared to the human body's other sensor organs, such as our visual abilities – with millions of photoreceptors – and the body's chemical and tactile receptors. The cochlea has less than 30,000 sensory cells. This means that losing even a relatively small number of cells in the cochlea can lead to significant hearing loss. And, since the cells are responsible for particular frequency responses, other hair cells cannot flexibly take over the function of damaged or dead hair cells in other parts of the cochlea.
- The number of hair cells you have is fixed early in fetal development and mammals are not able to regenerate damaged or dead cells.
- Repeated long-term exposure to loud sound pressure levels can cause hair cells to be destroyed, resulting in hearing loss. This type of hearing loss is called **noise-induced hearing loss**. It can be caused by exposure to mechanical, industrial, or engine noise, artillery, power tools, or listening to loud music (at concerts, clubs, or with speakers or headphones), or other loud sounds, even loud toys. The louder the sound the more quickly hearing loss can result with even less time of exposure. (And there is some evidence that loss is more rapid when carbon monoxide levels are high, such as on buses, subways, in traffic, or in certain industrial settings.) Of course, when people's hearing is diminished, they will often turn adjustable volumes up even louder, thereby exacerbating the cycle of hearing loss.
- Noise-induced hearing loss is epidemic in modern societies and is found in younger as well as older portions of the population. According to the NIDCD, 10 million Americans have suffered irreversible noise-induced hearing loss, and 30 million more are exposed to dangerous noise levels each day.

- Though scientists are working on hair cell regeneration, there is currently no cure or remedy for noise-induced hearing loss, and, if your hair cells die, the portions of hearing they are responsible for are gone forever. The moral of this story – and, yes, it does have one – is to be proactive in protecting your hearing. Supervise children, adjust volume levels downward when you can, and, if you can't, wear foam earplugs or other ear protection.

Terms to Know

Key terms for Section 3 are:

Basilar membrane
  Base
  Apex
Cochlea
Conductive hearing loss
Hair cells
Inner ear
Localization
Middle ear
The National Institute
  on Deafness and Other
  Communication Disorders
  (NIDCD)

Organ of Corti
Ossicles: malleus, incus, and stape
Outer ear
  Pinna
Sensorineural hearing loss
Stereocilia
Tectorial membrane
Tonotopic
Tympanic membrane
Vestibular system

Further Reading

Section 1

Goldstein, Louis and Phil Rubin (2007). Speech – Dances of the Vocal Tract. *Odyssey Magazine*, 16 (1), pp. 14–15. Also available at *www.haskins.yale.edu/Reprints/HL1452.pdf*

Ladefoged, Peter (2005). *A Course in Phonetics*, 5th edn. Boston: Wadsworth Publishing.

Section 2

Johnson, Keith (2003). *Auditory and Acoustic Phonetics*. Oxford: Wiley-Blackwell.

Ladefoged, Peter (2001) *Vowels and Consonants*. Oxford: Wiley-Blackwell.

Section 3

Johnson, Keith (2005). *Auditory and Acoustic Phonetics*. Oxford: Wiley-Blackwell.

Chapter 3

Phonetic Diversity in the World's Languages and Diversity Among Dialects of English

Section 1: Sounds of the World's Languages

Languages of the World

Knowing how many human languages exist is no easy question. Some languages are spoken by only very tiny groups of people in remote places. Most languages of the world are spoken by fewer than 10,000 speakers and more than a quarter are spoken by under 1,000 people. Most of the languages of the world are not written or regularly written languages. They occur only in their universal human form – as *spoken* languages. A reasonable estimate of the number of languages in the world is about 6,000 but estimates range as low as 5,000 and as high as 7,000. This is not a number that can be stated with surety.

It is even rather difficult to provide a scientific definition of what a "language" is. The Yiddish linguist Max Weinreich popularized (though apparently did not coin) the aphorism that "a language is a dialect with an army and a navy." This is, of course, meant to suggest that sociopolitical factors often play a large role in the lay definition of what is and is not a distinct language. A linguistic definition, which is by no means perfect, is that two linguistic communication systems can be considered to be one language (or dialects of one language) when they are **mutually intelligible** (this means that a speaker of System X can understand a speaker of System Y and vice versa), and can be considered to be two languages when they are not mutually intelligible. Of course, this is not a perfect definition since there are degrees of intelligibility, intelligibility isn't always bidirectionally equal, and experiences with a previously unintelligible "dialect" can make it much more intelligible. Nevertheless, this is an adequate linguistic definition for our purposes. It is worth noting that this definition doesn't always jibe with lay definitions of a language. Many different languages are often referred to by lay people as "dialects" of Chinese. For instance, Mandarin and Cantonese are distinct languages (though they share the same orthography). Furthermore, Danish, Swedish, and Norwegian are often mutually intelligible but they are generally referred to as distinct languages.

Although we can guess that there are 6,000 or so distinct languages in the world today, future textbooks written in the next century are likely to quote a much lower number – perhaps 3,000 or 1,000 or even fewer. This is because many of the languages of the world are in their final generation of speakers. These are called **endangered languages** or **dying languages**. Such languages occur around the world (including in Europe and the USA) but can be found particularly in Papua New Guinea, among the Native languages of the Americas, and in tribal or nonnational languages of Asia and Africa. A language becomes an endangered or dying language when the next generation of young people learn other languages, usually languages spoken by larger, more socioeconomically powerful groups of people, rather than continuing to speak the language of their parents and grandparents. About half of the world's population speaks one of 10 languages: Mandarin Chinese, English, Spanish, Bengali, Hindi, Portuguese, Russian, Arabic, Japanese, and German.

Linguists have a scientific interest in understanding the properties of the languages of the world. A renowned phonetician, Peter Ladefoged (1925–2006), spent much of his career studying and documenting the sounds of the world's languages, often with his colleague Ian Maddieson. They went into some of the most remote locations on the globe to make recordings of dying languages. Their work is documented at *phonetics.ucla.edu* Ⓦ. The reason Ladefoged invested a lifetime's scholarship in studying the sounds of the world's languages is that science's understanding of what is a *possible* human language depends on our knowledge of existing human languages and their properties. In those 10 most spoken languages, there are about 100 different consonants, but Ladefoged claims that in the known languages of the world there are nearly three times that number. Just as plant geneticists will suffer from a loss of biodiversity in their understanding of possible plant genes, cognitive scientists will suffer in their understanding of the cognitive structure of human language when the diversity of human languages available for study is severely limited.

That said, however, it is vital to remember that it is each community's and individual's decision as to whether their route to a happy, healthy, and productive future lies in continuing to speak a minority language or in adopting a majority language. Learning and speaking a majority language may offer much in the way of employment opportunities, resources, socioeconomic and cultural status, and education. Some parents who speak a dying language feel that their child's future would be brighter if they spoke a different language. Others prioritize the preservation of language and cultural identity. And even among those communities with an interest in preserving their indigenous language, there are differences in views regarding how welcome scientists are in helping with the endeavor of recording, documenting, archiving, and disseminating the language.

Contrast and Parameters of Contrast in the World's Languages

Linguists have an interest in understanding all aspects of diversity in human language. Some linguists study how parts of sentences can be organized. For example, some languages like English order their sentences subject–verb–object while others like Basque, Hopi, Nepali, Turkish, Japanese, and Korean order their sentences subject–object–verb. This is an aspect of the linguistic subfield of syntax. Other linguists might be interested in the mechanisms of how words are formed from smaller word pieces. Are suffixes used? Prefixes? What other ways exist to form words in different languages? We will examine this in Chapter 8 on morphology. Other linguists spend time examining the patterns of sounds in words and how to characterize those different patterns across human language. We will touch on this in Chapter 7 on phonology.

Yoda presents the linguistically unlikely example of an object–subject–verb language (certainly helping to enforce his exotic persona): "Help you I can." "Consume you it will." Occasionally, though, Yoda produces a verb–subject order as well: "Strong am I with the force." "Always in motion is the future."

In this chapter, we will pursue a characterization of phonetic variation among the world's languages. Rather than trying to create a giant list of all the consonants and vowels in the world's languages – a daunting task – we will lay out the primary dimensions or **parameters of contrast** that human languages are known to employ. Recall that the term **contrast** refers to the potential to change or *encode* word meaning. So we are interested in understanding the ways in which the human vocal, auditory, and cognitive systems are known to encode meaning in language.

How Humans Move Air to Make Speech Sounds

All languages make speech sounds with air coming up from the lungs and moving outward through the vocal tract. These sounds often but not always use this movement of air up from the lungs to vibrate the vocal folds. Some languages, however, also include consonants made with other

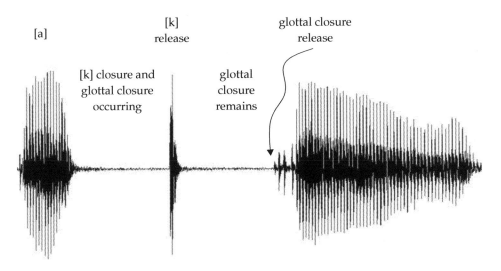

Figure 3.1   Waveform of [ak'a]

ways of moving air in the vocal tract. The mechanism of moving air in the vocal tract for speech is called the **airstream mechanism**.

Moving air by exhaling from the lungs is called a **pulmonic airstream mechanism**. All vowels and most consonants are made this way. However, there are three other airstream mechanisms. One other also moves air outward from the vocal tract; this is the **glottalic egressive airstream mechanism** and it is used to make **ejective** consonants. Ejectives are created by making a closure (or very narrow constriction) in the vocal tract *and* a glottal stop that seals the vocal folds together at the bottom end of the vocal tract. The column of air trapped between the oral and glottal closures is then squeezed or **compressed** by rapidly moving the whole larynx upward in the throat. Compressing the air causes a high pressure to be generated in the mouth. When the oral closure is opened or **released**, the resulting consonant has a loud popping sound to it. Figure 3.1 shows a waveform of the sequence [ak'a]; notice the loud release pop for the ejective as the compressed air is pressure-equalized with the outside air pressure.

Voicing for a following vowel will begin after a small delay as the glottal closure is released back to its normal voicing position. Ejective consonants are frequently found in Native American languages such as Navajo and Quechua, and also occur in languages spoken in southern and eastern Africa and in the Caucasus mountains.

Two other airstream mechanisms are used by human language and both of these

Throughout this chapter we will try to draw your attention to specific language examples that you can listen to at the UCLA Phonetics Lab Data page (currently at: *www.phonetics. ucla.edu/index.html*).

force air *into* the mouth rather than outward, so they are called **ingressive** airstream mechanisms. Let's first consider a **glotalic ingressive airstream mechanism**. Like the ejectives just described, these **implosive** sounds also have a closure in the mouth and a constriction at the vocal folds. In this case, however, the glottal constriction isn't generally a complete closure. In implosives, air still generally flows through the vocal folds vibrating them. However, the key quality of an implosive consonant is the *downward* movement of the larynx, thereby lowering the pressure of the column of air trapped in the vocal tract between the oral and glottal constrictions. Because the pressure is lowered, air may come into the mouth (though it doesn't always as the pressure may not be sufficiently negative). Recall that the opposite is true for ejectives in which raised pressure results in rapid outward airflow. Another property typical of implosives due to the expansion of the vocal tract produced by larynx lowering is an extra-voiced quality in which voicing during the stop closure is persistent and with high, even growing, amplitude during the closure. Figure 3.2 is a waveform of

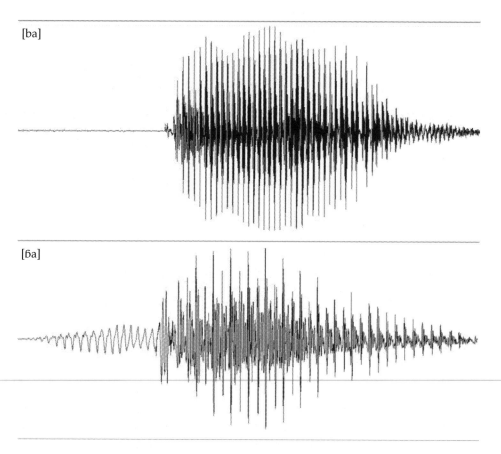

Figure 3.2   Waveforms of [ba] and [ɓa].

a pulmonic egressive [b] (such as in English) and an implosive [ɓ]. Notice the strong voicing vibrations during the implosive closure. Implosives occur, for example, in a number of languages spoken in Southern Africa and Asia, and even in languages found in India and South America.

The final ingressive airstream mechanism is the **velaric ingressive airstream mechanism** used to make **click** consonants. Click consonants are part of the regular consonant system of some languages native to Southern Africa and can also be found in a few East African languages. As you might now be able to guess from the term **ingressive**, these sounds have air flowing into the mouth. As with ejectives and implosives, clicks include an anterior closure in the mouth. However, in contrast to the ejectives and implosives, which have a glottal constriction, clicks have a posterior closure formed with the back of the tongue against the soft palate. These two closures create a pocket of air in the mouth. By drawing the tongue body rapidly downward, the air pressure in the pocket becomes quite negative (i.e., lower than the pressure outside the mouth). When the front closure is then released, air rushes into the mouth as the ambient and mouth air pressure are rapidly equalized. The great negative pressure and consequent rapid inward airflow results in an extremely loud consonant sound; clicks are the loudest sounds found in human language. Figure 3.3 shows a sequence of pictures of how an alveolar click is articulated (clicks at a variety of other anterior places of articulation are also possible). ⓦ Try this yourself (making sure that when you release your tongue tip it doesn't flop down and hit the floor of your mouth, but rather moves slightly downward and backward).

Places in the Mouth Where Human Languages Make Consonants

English includes many but not all places of articulation for consonants (see Chapter 2). For example, English does not have a very robust set of consonants created in the rear of the mouth and in the pharynx. Languages can encode contrast both in terms of the place along the vocal tract at which a constriction is made and also, for the flexible front of the tongue, in terms of the specific part of the tongue forming the constriction.

Since we have already discussed place of articulation for English consonants, let's describe some of the places along the vocal tract that other languages use to make consonants. Many languages of India and Australia, for example, curl the tongue tip up, and sometimes even flip it over, to make a constriction high up in the vault of the palate. Such consonants made with the tongue tip in the palate are called **retroflex**. In Figure 3.4, you can see an MRI image of a retroflex consonant being made by a speaker of Tamil, a language of southern India.

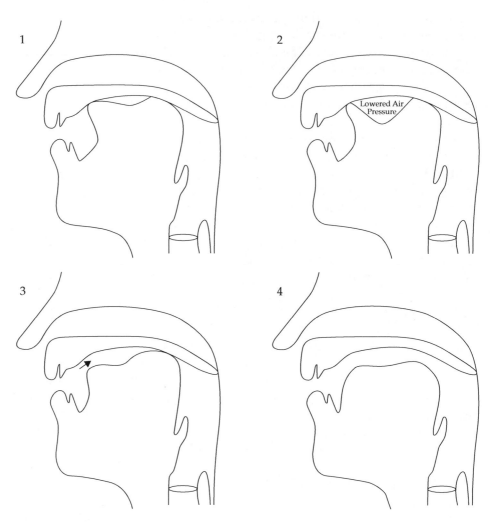

Figure 3.3   Steps in producing an alveolar click

1   Make the two oral closures: one with the tongue-tip to the alveolar ridge, the other with the tongue back at the velum.
2   Air rarefaction: The body of the tongue is pulled down, while the oral closures are maintained; resulting in a decrease in the pressure of the air cavity created by the two oral closures.
3   The front oral closure is released; air rushes in in an attempt to equalize pressure, producing the characteristic "popping" sound.
4   The back oral closure is released.

This same portion of the vocal tract, namely the vault of the palate, can be used by the body of the tongue as well as the tip of the tongue. Consonants made with the tongue body in the palatal vault and with the tongue tip down around the lower front teeth are called simply **palatal** consonants. You can approximate these sounds by paying attention to the

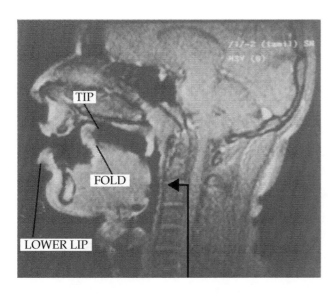

Figure 3.4 Image of a Tamil retroflex (created with Magnetic Resonance Imaging [MRI]) Used by permission of Shrikanth Narayanan

initial sound in *hue* or a strongly voiced *you* or the nasal in *poignant*. Palatal consonants are found for example in a number of languages of Europe: German (for example *ich*) and Spanish (for example *español*). Some Slavic languages, for example Russian, have a series of consonants that add a secondary palatal constriction to consonants whose primary place of articulation is elsewhere. For example, at the beginning of the word [tʲoplij] (meaning "warmth") the tongue is making an alveolar closure with its tip but the body of the tongue behind the tip is also simultaneously high and arched in the palate.

Moving into the soft palate area, English has **velar** stops and nasals; other languages add fricatives at this place of articulation – for example, German *Bach*. At the very rear of the soft palate is the uvula, and consonants made at this place along the vocal tract are called **uvular**. Uvular consonants are somewhat rare but are found in some Native American languages and in some languages of the Middle East and Caucasus mountains. You may have heard in certain dialects of French or German the uvular r-sound (French – *rouge*, German – *rot* "red") made with the rear of the tongue or in Spanish or many other languages the trilled r-sound made with the front of the tongue, for example, Spanish *perro* ("dog"), which contrasts the nontrill tapped r-sound in, for example, Spanish *pero* ("but"). These sounds are made when the tongue tip or the uvula vibrate due to airflow against the surface of the alveolar ridge (for the tip) or raised tongue rear (for the uvula). Such articulations are called **trills**. This vibration is caused entirely by aerodynamics and the posture of the tongue tip or uvula.

Finally, we reach the pharynx area of the vocal tract where **pharyngeal** and **epiglottal** consonants are articulated. In these sounds the tongue *root* (its mobile vertical portion in the pharynx) is moved backward toward the

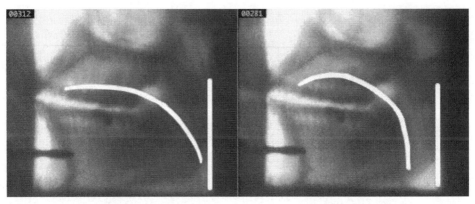

Pharyngealized initial consonant
(dˤaamˤ] "injure"

Non-pharyngealized
[daam] "last"

Figure 3.5   X-ray films of an Arabic speaker producing the contrast between a pharyngealized [d] (left) and a nonpharygealized [d] (right). The white tracings follow the curve of the tongue and the edge of the pharyngeal wall. Adapted from an X-ray film produced by Haskins Laboratories

rear wall of the pharynx or throat. These sounds are generally approximants or fricatives, not stops; though stops can have an additional pharyngeal constriction or narrowing added to their primary constriction. Figure 3.5 shows the articulation of a [d] in Arabic with and without an additional pharyngeal constriction.

If these sounds are particularly low in the throat, they tend to involve the epiglottis, so would be dubbed **epiglottal** sounds. These very back approximants and fricatives are found, for example, in some Semitic, African, and Native American languages.

Vowels of the World's Languages

Our discussion of English has already worked through a wide array of vowels, as English has a large number of vowels compared to most languages of the world. Some languages have only three vowels, and many languages have five vowels. However, there are vocalic dimensions of contrast in the world's languages that are not found in English. There are a number of languages that use the involvement of the lips or **rounding** more robustly than English does. You may remember that most dialects of English (though less so in the Western United States) involve the lips in articulating the high and mid *back* vowels. Other languages, particularly Turkish and a number of languages in Northern Europe, also contrast front vowels with regard to rounding. These languages – for example, Turkish, Danish, German, Swedish, Dutch, French, Hungarian – have both unrounded and rounded front and back vowels. You may have heard this front rounded vowel in the name for the German city *München* (which we usually change in English to Munich).

In English, you may have noticed that all vowels are made with air flowing only through the mouth. Only the three nasal consonants of English use air flowing through the nose due to the velum (soft palate) being in its low or open position.

A few of the languages with only three vowels are Quechua, Marshallese, and Amis, an Austronesian language spoken on the east coast of Taiwan. Examples of the many languages with five vowels are Spanish and Japanese.

English does not contrast any sounds that differ only in whether air flows just through the mouth or through both the mouth and nose. Other languages do just this. A number of languages have vowels that contrast in whether they are oral (air flowing only through the mouth) or **nasal vowels** (air flowing through both the mouth *and* nose due to the velum being in the low position). These languages are found all around the world from Europe (e.g., French) to India (e.g., Hindi) to Africa (e.g., Ijo) to Asia (e.g., Taiwanese) to the Americas (e.g., Chinantec).

Long Versus Short Contrasting Speech Sounds

Temporal length is another dimension of linguistic contrast not employed by English. Some languages show the distinction between a vowel or consonant that is shorter in duration and one that is longer, often more than twice as long, in duration. Sometimes the term **geminate** is used to refer to these long speech sounds. We will simply refer to the length contrast as one between **short** and **long**. It's important to note that sound duration is not something that varies continuously for the purpose of linguistic contrast. No language encodes meaning by a word or sound being short, a little longer, a little bit longer, even longer, really long, superlong. Language rely on the discreteness of phonological differences to encode meaning, and this extends to length as well. Languages may contrast sounds that are otherwise alike but belong to one of two length categories.

Length contrasts are found in diverse language families but are not hugely common in the world's languages. Some languages that use this parameter of contrast include Japanese, Italian, Thai, Vietnamese, Arabic, Lithuanian, and Finnish – all wildly different languages. Some of these languages employ a length contrast for just vowels or just consonants and some for both vowels and consonants, such as Japanese or Finnish. Figure 3.6 shows waveforms for long and short sounds in minimally contrasting word pairs in Japanese. You can see that the long sounds are quite long indeed in comparison to the parallel short sounds.

[okasan]   "Mr/Mrs Oka"

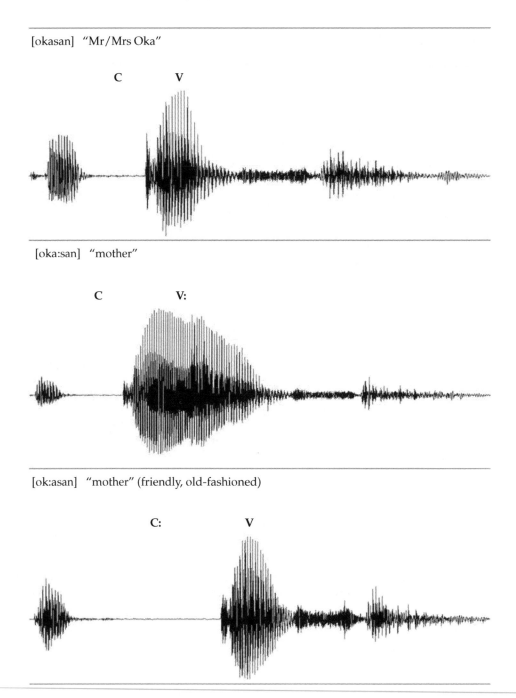

Figure 3.6   Waveforms showing Japanese length contrast. (The colon-type symbol indicates the long version of the symbol it is written after.) Ⓦ

Phonation Type – Using the Pattern of Vocal Fold Vibration for Linguistic Contrast

All languages use a normal pattern of vocal fold vibration called **modal voicing** that allows a moderate amount of air to flow through the glottis in their set of speech sounds. English uses only modal voicing in its phonological system. Modal voicing has regularly spaced glottal pulses without substantial noise in the normal frequency range of the speaker. It is possible to press the vocal folds together more firmly to make the glottis smaller and create lesser airflow or to hold the vocal folds more widely and create greater airflow. These laryngeal maneuvers result in voicing vibration patterns different from modal voice. When airflow is lessened for certain sounds in a language's inventory of sounds, this is called **creaky voice** or sometimes **laryngealization** or **pressed voice**. Glottal pulses may be irregular spaced and/or low frequency. This occurs occasionally in English at the ends of phrases. (To get a sense of creaky voice, try imitating a scary Halloween door slowly opening or a growl.) **Breathy voice** (sometimes called **murmur**) occurs when airflow is greater for certain sounds in a language's inventory of sounds; it may have a noisy component due to the higher airflow. (English speakers can think of the quintessential "bedroom voice" to get a sense of breathy voice quality.) Any individual's personal voice characteristics might include having a somewhat breathy or somewhat creaky voice, and certain disorders of the larynx can result in such sound quality as well. But when a language uses these alterations in vibratory patters to encode linguistic contrast, the distinction between modal, creaky, and breathy voice is referred to as **phonation type.**

Phonation type contrasts do not occur extremely widely in the world's languages but can be seen in languages of the Americas such as Mazatec, languages of Africa such as Hausa, languages of Asia such as Bruu, and many languages of India such as Hindi, Gujarati, and Nepali. Phonation type contrasts are more frequently found for vowels but can also occur for consonants, particularly nasals, as well. In Figure 3.7 you can see the waveforms for a modal, a breathy, and a creaky voiced vowel.

Tone – The Contrastive Use of Pitch in the World's Languages

You will recall that the pitch of the voice is determined by the rate of vocal fold vibration during vowels and nasals. Pitch can vary continuously to convey things like emotion or intonation. However, **tone** refers to the contrastive use of *portions* of a given speaker's pitch range to differentiate the meaning of one word from another. Tone never refers to any exact frequency

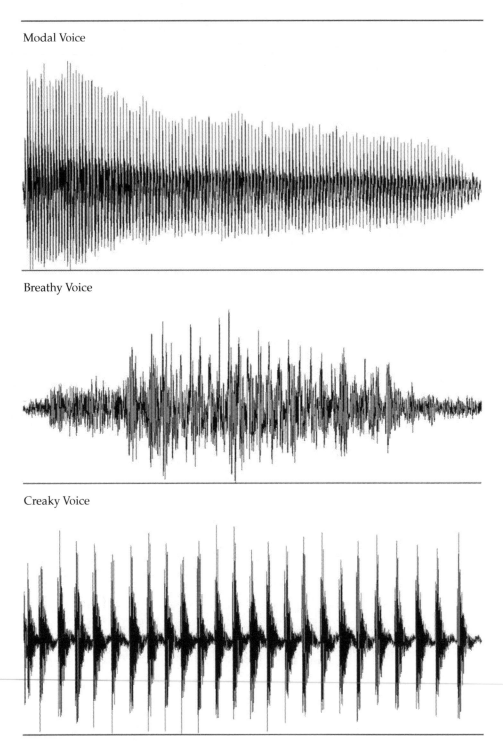

Modal Voice

Breathy Voice

Creaky Voice

Figure 3.7   Phonation types: Modal, breathy, and creaky voice

of vocal fold vibration because speakers of course differ in their pitch ranges. In fact, this is the reason we use the term tone instead of pitch to refer to this dimension of linguistic contrast.

Phonological systems can "carve up" the speaker's pitch range into no more than five regions to be used in a system of lexical contrast. Some systems contrast just the high region of a speaker with that speaker's low pitch region to determine word meaning. Others use differences among high, mid, and low, for example. In addition to contrasting the **level** tone of a syllable, a language may also allow **contour** tones that move between these designated tone regions.

Tone can affect the lexical meaning of a word, or even more commonly can be

Sometimes the tones in a language are referred to by names (such as superhigh, high, mid, and low) or sometimes they are referred to by numbers designating the pitch level(s) with 5 denoting the highest level and 1 the lowest, and sometimes scholars working on a particular language will just assign the tones used by that language arbitrary numbers (like Tone 3). This can be confusing, but is for now an unavoidable fact in the linguistics field.

used for grammatical or morphological meaning, such as past versus present tense or plural versus singular. It's sometimes startling for English speakers to realize that the *majority* of the world's languages are tone languages, that is, languages that use pitch regions to encode meaning. This includes the world's most widely spoken language Mandarin Chinese, spoken by about a billion people. Table 3.1 gives an example of a four-word minimal contrast in tone in Mandarin.

A number of ways of denoting linguistic pitch are used by linguists. In Table 3.1 the graphical symbols indicate the pitch range by the vertical bar on the right (top being highest pitch), and the pitch movement within that range is indicated by the connecting angled lines on the left. The adjacent numbers indicate the changes in pitch by reference to the pitch range from a low pitch of 1 to a high pitch of 5. Languages that use tone contrastively are most frequently found in Asia and Africa but are also found in some languages of the Americas and elsewhere.

Table 3.1 Tone example from Mandarin for the syllable [ma] as four different words contrasting in tone. From http://www.phonetics.ucla.edu/vowels/chapter2/chinese/recording2.1.html

Chinese character	Description of tone contour			English
媽	High level	˥	55	mother
麻	High rising	˧	35	hemp
馬	Low falling	˨	214	horse
罵	High falling	˥	51	scold

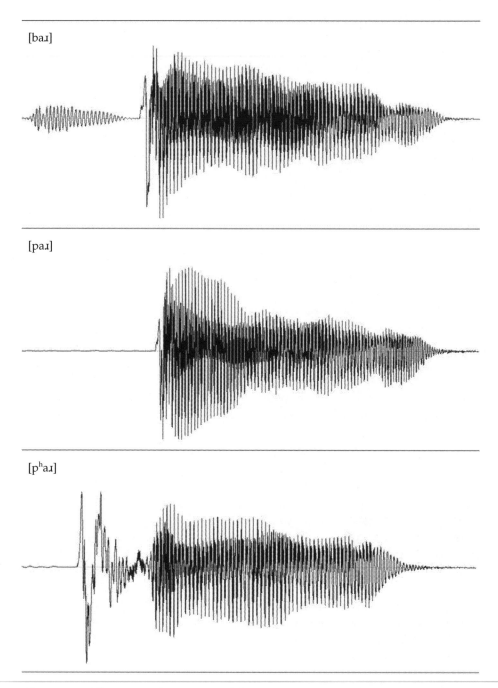

Figure 3.8   Three-way Armenian VOT contrast: a stop with an initial fully voiced closure (upper), a voiceless unaspirated initial stop (middle) and a voiceless aspirated initial stop (lower) Ⓦ

VOT – An Example of How Coordination Can Serve Contrast

We've seen in our IPA chart that speech sounds in the world's languages are classified as voiced or voiceless. We've also discussed that voiceless stops in English are generally aspirated, which means that they have a positive VOT during which air is moving through a still-open glottis before voicing for a following vowel has begun. To return to the cross-linguistic parameters of contrast, languages can adopt a small number of discrete categories of coordination between articulatory movements to serve the needs of linguistic contrast. Voice onset time is determined by the coordination of oral and laryngeal articulation. The positive VOT of English voiceless aspirated stops is one type of this coordination. A language could also choose to coordinate the oral closure release and the voicing maneuver synchronously, and there are languages that do so. Such a situation yields voiceless unaspirated stops having a near-zero VOT. Finally, the vocal folds could remain in a posture appropriate for voicing during the stop closure interval. This would yield a voiced stop having a negative VOT (meaning voicing is occurring before the stop closure release has occurred).

While most languages contrast two VOT categories, though they differ on the organization of which two, some languages contrast three coordinations of these articulatory maneuvers – that is, some languages have a three-way VOT contrast among voiced stops, voiceless unaspirated stops, and voiceless aspirated stops. This occurs in Armenian, Thai, Taiwanese, and other diverse languages. (Some languages like Korean, Icelandic, and Hindi even have more complex organizations of oral gestures and various types of laryngeal gestures.) Figure 3.8 shows an example of three waveforms for such a contrast in Armenian.

Phonotactics – It's Not Just the Inventory; It's How It's Put Together in Words

It would be simple to imagine that two languages with the same set of sounds or dimensions of contrast would have the same means at their disposal for encoding word meaning. But in fact we must also consider how those discrete elements of the phonological inventory are allowed to combine with one another in a word. This system of constraints on sound sequencing or combination is called **phonotactics** and is an important component of phonological or sound system diversity in the world's languages.

A language might constrain what sounds in its inventory are allowed to occur at the beginning or ending of a word or syllable. We know that syllables in English may not start with [ŋ]. Phonotactics may constrain what sequences of sounds are allowed to occur in a word or syllable. English does not, for example, allow words to end with the sequence [vr]. So when a word enters English from another language, perhaps a proper name like Favre (the great quarterback), we must pronounce it (if we are to sound as though we are speaking English) in some other way that is phonotactically allowed in English. In the case of quarterback Brett Favre, we pronounce his last name [farv] instead of [favr] or [favrə], which violate acceptable sound sequencing patterns or phonotactics in English, though they might be fine in French, for example.

Can you think of other phonotactic constraints in English? German has a word *pferd* ("horse"); would such a word be allowed in English? Why or why not? English has words like "clean" beginning with [kl] and "please" beginning with [pl] but does it have words beginning with [tl]? English has long strings of consonants possible in a word – like "sixths" [sɪksθs], but even English speakers would find eye-opening the consonant sequences allowed in Georgian, for example: in [bgera], meaning "sound" or [dgeba], meaning "he or she stands up." Polish also allows long strings of consonants within a word.

Summary of Dimensions of Contrast in Spoken Language

In summary, we have reviewed the parameters which human speech employs to encode word meaning. These are:

- Place of articulation
- Manner of articulation
- Voicing
- Airstream mechanism
- Vowel rounding and nasalization
- Length
- Phonation type
- Tone
- Coordination: VOT
- Phonotactics

You can listen to many of the sound contrasts described in the first section of this chapter at *phonetics.ucla.edu*.

Section 2: English in the United States and Around the World

Dialects

Dialects are distinct forms of a language. In fact, at the finest level of detail, every speaker speaks a form of his or her language distinct from all other speakers. Linguists even have a term for this personal linguistic system at its finest level of detail – an **idiolect**. But at a level a step back from this, the form of language each of us speaks has much in common with the speech of others we interact or have interacted with. These forms of language that are distinct for a particular group are called **dialects**. We all belong to groups and we all, in that sense, speak dialects of our native language. The group that speaks any particular dialect might be defined geographically or regionally, or it might be defined socioeconomically in terms of class, or it might be defined culturally. There are many possible qualities that a group of people who speak a similar form of a language may share. Do your friends (and you, with them) speak the same way as your parents or their parents before them? Probably not. Dialects can be shared by age-groups. Region, socioeconomics, culture, and age are just a few factors, and it's easy to see how even these four may combine in many ways. The dialect someone is speaking is never *purely* a consequence of a single aspect of that person's background. Can you think of the various groups that might shape the dialect you speak? Do you speak more than one dialect?

It is important to remember in our training as linguists that the term **dialect** carries no value judgment and simply refers to *a distinct form of language*. It would be completely outside the realm of science to consider any dialect of any language as "substandard," "lazy," or "corrupt" versions of that language. Nonstandard or marginalized dialects are not wrong or bad in any linguistic sense, but just like any "standard" or socially accepted version of a given language, every dialect is **systematic** in its structure and follows coherent patterns in its use. Every dialect (and idiolect) provides the cognitive scientist with a unique opportunity to study the workings and organization of the human mind and cognitive system. Which dialect(s) are considered standard is an accident of history, economics, and politics.

Englishes in the United States

Though dialects considered "standard" are not scientifically more valid than other dialects, it will be useful to have some common ground for the purposes of describing differences among dialects of English in the

United States and elsewhere. To some degree, postulating for teaching purposes such a common standard English is an artificial construct, since all individuals speak their own idiolect, which shares dialectal features with various groups. Nevertheless, we will indulge in this little bit of fantasy because it will help us understand patterns of variation. We will use the term **Standard American English (SAE)** to refer to a dialect of English found in dictionaries, much printed material, and national newscasts, and taught to English students. It is an *idealized* form of English that approximates the noncasual English of upper-middle-class, educated, US English speakers.

Throughout this section we will draw on examples found in the University of Arizona's Varieties of English website (maintained by their Language Samples Project) at *www.ic. arizona.edu/~lsp/index.html* where you can listen to some of these dialects. Ⓦ

Let's consider an example of the systematic behavior in particular regional dialects of American English. In **Eastern New England** or **ENE** (Boston, for example), there are speakers of a dialect that does not include an [r] sound in words in which SAE does have such a sound. However, this omission does not just appear willy-nilly in random locations in words. In words in which SAE has [ar] (or syllabic [r], i.e., no vowel in the syllable, only [r]), the ENE dialect has no [r] and, for a syllabic [r] a longer, different vowel than the SAE vowel: for example, "bar" pronounced [ba]. And in words in which SAE has [or], [ir], or [er], the ENE dialect produces a diphthong with [ə] instead ([oə], [iə], or [eə]): for example, "beer" pronounced [biə]. So for speakers of this Boston dialect, [r] does not "appear" or "disappear" randomly. Rather, the dialect is *systematic* in its pattern. The pattern of [r] distribution for these speakers depends on the preceding vowel (and on various other factors we have not discussed here).

Dialects do not only differ systematically in their sound systems. (In fact, such pronunciation differences alone are sometimes called simply an **accent**.) Dialects of a language can, and generally, do differ from one another in their syntactic (sentence-level grammar) and lexical (vocabulary) systems as well.

Let's consider a dialect of English that employs a different tense system than SAE – **African American English** or **AAE** (sometimes called AAVE [African American Vernacular English] or Black English or Ebonics or Inner-City English). Of course, not all African Americans speak AAE, and those who do generally do not do so all the time. AAE has a **habitual** tense that is also found in other languages of the world such as Irish and Scottish Gaelic, for example. SAE would use an adverb like "usually" to indicate this. This tense uses the unconjugated form of the verb "to be" to indicate a habitual or regular action. (The verb is also of course used in its conjugated forms for other meanings.)

Danny here.   meaning "Danny is here."
Danny running.   meaning "Danny is running."
That the way he is.   meaning "That's the way he is [right now]."
Danny <u>be</u> here.   meaning "Danny is usually here."
Danny <u>be</u> running. meaning "Danny usually runs/is usually running."
That's the way he <u>be</u>. meaning "That's the way he usually is."
[Based on linguist Lisa Green's work]

This habitual tense used in AAE isn't an arbitrary aberration from SAE but rather is an example of a perfectly grammatical (in the linguistic sense) tense system found in some of the world's languages. Consider the following sentences from Spanish exemplifying this:

Ella está triste.   meaning "She is sad right now."
(from verb *estar* "to be")
Ella es triste.   meaning "She is usually sad."
(from verb *ser* "to be")

Southern States English (SSE) also has grammatical features that differ from SAE. Many of you will recognize the word *y'all* as being a Southern English regional term, but have you thought about its explicit grammatical function? If you have studied other languages, you may realize that languages often have a different form of the second person "you" in the singular and plural. SSE uses *y'all* for the second person ("you") plural. Other forms of American English do this as well: *youse, you guys, you-uns*. Can you figure out what parts of the United States these forms are from? Do any of your dialects of English have a you-plural form distinct from the you-singular form? Southern States English also a verb type meaning "to intend to do something" which is a possible part of the verbal system in human languages. In SSE this form is *fixin to*. So "I'm fixin to go to store" means that "I intend to go to the store in the next little while." As a last example of a grammatical dialect variation, consider the use of double auxiliaries (or modals) in the perfectly grammatical SSE sentence like "I might could bake a pie later today." This means roughly that "I might be able to bake a pie later today though I'm not sure."

Finally let's consider an example of lexical variation in American English. Can you think of vocabulary that you use that is not found in SAE? Or in the English of your parents? Some terms that vary widely from region to region include those for grocery carts or carriages; highways, freeways, turnpikes, interstates; soda, pop, coke, tonic; subs, grinders, hoagies, heros. Can you pick out your regional dialect terms here? Or do you perhaps have other forms for these items?

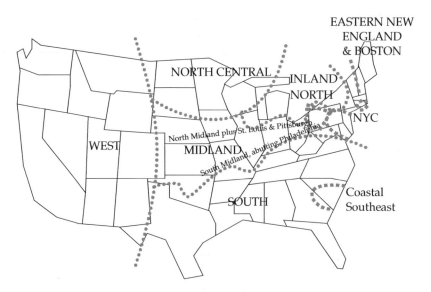

Figure 3.9   Broad dialect regions of the United States based on data from the *Atlas of North American English* (Labov et al., 2005; www.ling.upenn.edu/phono_atlas/home.html). Sophisticated dialect studies are more uncommon regarding the western United States, so less is known about dialect differences in this region.

We've seen that dialects of a language can differ in terms of their pronunciation, grammar (syntax and morphsyntax), and their lexicon. A number of linguists, but most notably William Labov, have devoted research to characterizing the geography of regional variation in American English. Based on Labov's work, Figure 3.9 presents an extremely rough map showing some geographical regions of American English; it is by no means thorough, however – for example, distinctions in the Western US are not well represented – but it gives some sense of regional variation.

Types of variation in vowel systems in the United States

One of the best-researched areas of variation among US regional dialects is variation in the vowel system. We certainly have no expectations of covering all the varieties of vowel systems found in US English dialects, but we would like to introduce some terms for talking about *types* of variation among systems.

The first type of variation you may want to recognize is **merger**, which describes the situation in which two categories in one system are realized as one category in another system. In the case of English vowel dialects, SSE is recognized to have certain mergers relative to SAE. For these

Table 3.2   Mergers in regional dialects of American English

Vowel categories of SAE that are merged	Examples of homophonous words	Possible regional locations
[ɛ] and [ɪ] before nasals	pen–pin	South and parts of Midwest
[a] and [ɔ]	cot–caught	Parts of: South, West, and Midwest
[i] and [ɪ] before [l] before [r] before [ŋ]	peal–pill dearer–mirror seeing–sing	Parts of: N. Carolina & Texas SoCal.
[u] and [ʊ] before [l]	pool–pull; fool–full	Certain places in: Pennsylvania, Indiana, California, Texas
[e] and [ɛ] esp. before [g]	fail–fell pag(an)–peg	e.g. before [l] in West Texas, Central and Western North Carolina, Western gulf states
[ɛ] and [æ] before [r]	merry–marry–Mary ferry–fairy	South, West, and elsewhere

speakers, [ɛ] and [ɪ] may not contrast before nasal consonants – that is, they are **merged** before nasals. So pairs like *pen* and *pin* and *Wendy* and *windy* are homophonous (i.e., they sound identical). Another merger found in various parts of the United States including the South and the West is a merger of [a] and [ɔ]. In some places, this merger may be limited to contexts before nasals like *Don* and *Dawn*; while in other locations, it occurs more widely across the lexicon, such as the homophony in this book's first author's Western English dialect between *cot* and *caught*. Table 3.2 shows some of the mergers that have been observed in regional dialects of American English (relative to SAE).

One can imagine that the opposite of mergers would be the **addition** of categories or contrasts. This is also a possible type of variation in regional US vowels systems in comparison to the vowel categories found in SAE. So in New York City and Boston, one is likely to find three different vowels in the words *merry*, *marry*, and *Mary*, where many other dialects have two vowels (or sometimes one). In Philadelphia, three different vowels might be found in the words *pen*, *pan*, and *pat* where some other dialect don't differentiate (or at least not to such a degree) the vowels in *pan* and *pat*.

It is also possible that the vowel categories and organization may not be the primary differences from SAE in a particular case but rather that **qualitative variation** in how exactly a particular vowel category is pronounced might be noteworthy. For example in SSE (Southern States English), the SAE vowel [ai] is pronounced as a monopthong [a]. In Bostonian English, a very low front vowel occurs in place of SAE [ar], such as in "park the car." In Southern California, as another example of qualitative variation, the back mid and high vowels, such as in words like *good* and *dude* are typically not rounded as they are in SAE, resulting in one of the canonical qualities of SoCal "surfer English."

Types of variation in consonant systems in the United States

Qualitative variation can also occur between dialects in how their consonants are produced. For example, Southern Californians typically have an interdental [θ] and [ð] rather than the dental place of articulation found in SAE. For our local Southern Californians, one can see the tip of the tongue protrude under the upper front teeth. You can check in the mirror which place of articulation you use (make sure to speak as "casually" as possible). Many dialects of English produce word final [ŋ] as [n] instead, for example in the South and in Inner City English. So words ending in "ing" [iŋ] or [ɪŋ] (e.g., "liking," "leaving," "winning") are pronounced with a final [ɪn].

Other types of consonant variation include **omission** (sometimes called **deletion**) and **metathesis**. We've already seen an example of omission in Eastern New England English's omission of [r] in certain circumstances. African American English or Inner City English will also omit consonants following a systematic pattern. This dialect will omit word-final consonants – especially alveolar ones and especially after other consonants – for example, *tes(t)* and *han(d)*. However, many versions of this dialect will only omit the second consonant of two when both share the same voicing property; that is, the omission occurs only when both are voiced or both are voiceless consonants. So the [t] is pronounced in *sent* (not *sen(t)*), but the [d] in *han(d)* is not. This is an example of the complex and regular patterns that can be observed across *all* dialect systems of a language, regardless if they are considered standard or nonstandard.

Likewise, **metathesis** – a reversal in the temporal order of two segments – is found both as a phonological pattern across the world's languages and as a characteristic of interdialect variation. So in a local Southern California Inner Cities English, the word "ask" is pronounced [aks]. Furthermore, because of this dialect's additional **omission** pattern, "ask" (SAE [ask]) and "asked" (SAE [askt]) are homophonous in this dialect – both are pronounced [aks]. We will see in Chapter 7 that omission or deletion and metathesis are phonological phenomena found across the world's language.

Englishes Around the World

Earlier in this chapter, we noted that Chinese is spoken by the largest number of people in the world. However, English is spoken in the most countries worldwide and is the official or influential minority language (e.g., in India) of more countries than any other language. It is the official or co-official language of approximately 45 countries and is spoken in about 115 countries. If the primary and secondary speakers are both considered, only Chinese is spoken by more people. Because of English's widespread geographical prevalence and the fact that it is the primary language of science, business, and the Internet, many consider English to be the most influential language in the world.

In addition to the United States, some of the countries where English is the main or official language or is widely spoken are the United Kingdom, India, Nigeria, Jamaica, Canada, Australia, South Africa, Liberia, Hong Kong, Kenya, New Zealand, Pakistan, Singapore, Israel, Zambia, Bermuda, Ireland, the Philippines, and Zimbabwe. Just as dialects of English in the United States exhibit grammatical, lexical, and pronunciation variation, so do dialects of English around the world.

My friend Edward from Britain might say barmy (crazy), bin (trashcan), and jumper (sweater). My friend Kie from Montreal might say KD (macaroni and cheese, from Kraft Dinner), keener (eager beaver), and garburator (garbage disposal). And my friend Susie from Australia might say duster (chalkboard eraser), globe (lightbulb), and ute (pickup truck). My friend Shri from India could say dickey (trunk of a car), godown (warehouse), prepone (to advance, as against postpone), and pass-out (to graduate). Sometimes varieties of English from other countries can be difficult to understand until one gets used to them. However, the same can be said for unfamiliar varieties of English spoken in one's own country!

The same sorts of mergers, additional contrasts, and qualitative variation occur in the vowel systems of Englishes around the world as we have seen for continental US dialects of English. Some examples of vowel differences are shown in Table 3.3.

Similarly, there are differences in the consonant inventory and behavior across the world's Englishes. English spoken in India, for example, tends to have [w] where American English would have [v].

Because American entertainment media is very widespread around the world, American forms of English may have an influence on worldwide Englishes. This can be seen both as phonetic influences on pronunciation and in word borrowings from American English into the English of other countries. Figure 3.10 shows how younger British people are more likely to use the vowel [æ] in words like *chance* than the [ɑ] favored by older

Table 3.3   Examples of vowel differences in American, Australian, and British English

Word	American English	Australian English	British English
heed	[hid]	[həid]	[hid]
hud	[həd]	[hɐd]	[hʌd]
hod	[had]	[hɒd]	[hɒd]
hoed	[houd]	[hɐud]	[həud]
hard	[hɑrd]	[had]	[hɑd]
herd	[hr̩d]	[hɜd]	[hɜd]
here	[hir]	[hɪə]	[hɪə]

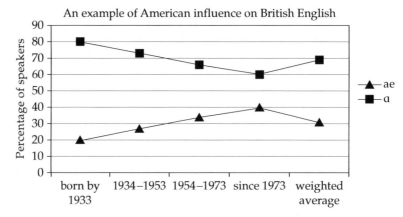

Figure 3.10   Change over recent years in use of [æ] and [ɑ] in British English, based on data from John Wells.

British speakers. This is presumed to be due to the influence of American English being more pervasive for the younger speakers.

Summary of English Dialects

In this section of Chapter 3, we talk about dialects of English. Similarly, those of you who are native speakers of other languages will be familiar with dialects that exist in those languages. Do they seem most likely to be thought of in geographic terms? Socioeconomic terms? Class or caste terms? In addition to dialectal variation in language, other language varieties also exist the world over. When speakers of different languages find themselves in a situation requiring communication – like trade – over a protracted period of time, a new language form develops called a **pidgin**. This restricted second language may take vocabulary largely from one language and, over time, form a rudimentary system of grammar. The speakers of the pidgin are still native speakers of their own language (or languages) but the pidgin is a language variety that serves an important function when these speakers without a common language come together. Interestingly, children living in such communities may start to learn a pidgin as a first language. If this happens, over generations it may become the primary language of a community. When a pidgin becomes a first language, it has now evolved into a **creole**. A creole is widely used in a community and has the full function, vocabulary, and rich grammatical structures of any other language. By way of example, Louisiana Creole, spoken in locations in southern Louisiana and elsewhere, arose from the extended contact over generations between French colonists and African slaves, many of whom arrived from the area between the Senegal and Gambia rivers. The vocabulary is in substantial measure derived from French (though there are even Spanish and Choctaw influences), but the grammar is different from French.

In summary, we have seen that everyone speaks a dialect and that each of these dialects is a systematic, fully endowed language. Every dialect – standard and nonstandard – is valuable and informative about the nature of the human capacity for language. Dialects are distinct forms of a language associated with groups that may be defined by region, socioeconomics, culture, age, or a number of other factors in combination. Dialects show grammatical and lexical variation and phonetic variation in both their vowel systems (e.g., mergers, qualitative variation) and consonant systems (e.g., omissions, metathesis). English is a widespread and influential language around the world and the dialects of English spoken around the world are diverse, just as the dialects of English spoken in the United States are diverse.

Further Reading and Resources

Ladefoged, Peter (2005). *A Course in Phonetics*, 5th edn. Boston: Wadsworth Publishing.

Rickford, John R. (1997). Suite for Ebony and Phonics. *Discover*, 18(12), pp. 82–87. Also available at *www.stanford.edu/~rickford/papers/SuiteForEbonyAndPhonics.html*

University of Arizona's Varieties of English website, maintained by their Language Samples Project, at *www.ic.arizona.edu/~lsp/index.html*

Language Log: *http://languagelog.ldc.upenn.edu/nll/*

Telsur Project: *www.ling.upenn.edu/phono_atlas/home.html*

UCLA Phonetics Lab Data: Index of languages, Index of sounds, at *phonetics.ucla.edu*

Chapter 4

The Scientific Method and Experimental Design

Introduction

In many of the chapters that follow you will read about experiments that have been carried out to test and develop theories about human speech and language processing. This chapter is designed to provide you with a framework for understanding those experiments, as well as to give you a basic background in the process of scientific discovery and progress. We will start broadly by discussing the **scientific method** whereby theories are generated and refined through experimental testing. We will then go into more detail about the components of an experiment, with particular emphasis on elements that are important for **psycholinguistics** experiments. We conclude with a related discussion of how experimental results are analyzed, and the role of **statistical analyses** in interpreting results.

Theories and the Scientific Method

What is a scientific theory?

In general terms, a theory is an explanatory description about how something works, or why something is the way it is. There is basically no limit on the form theories can take, what they can be about, or whether they are at all plausible. One could have a theory that when the pens go missing from one's desk it's because elves steal them in the middle of the night and stash them in a hollow tree somewhere. Or that smoking is good for you because the smoke kills off bacteria in your lungs. In contrast to this relatively unconstrained everyday notion of a theory, a core characteristic of modern *scientific* theories is that they are *falsifiable*. That means that there is, in principle, some piece of evidence that, if found, would render the theory false. An important part of the idea of falsifiability is that no scientific theory can conclusively be declared *true* in an absolute sense because there is always the possibility that tomorrow the theory will be falsified. Of course, this does not mean that as scientists (or as individuals) we must go through our days shrouded in doubt and uncertainty. There comes a point when a theory has defied all attempts to falsify it, and when it has persisted long enough, it is held to be true (or true enough). We can design and build successful airplanes, bridges, televisions, medicines, and so on, based on these tested theories. But there always is the possibility, however remote or improbable, that a well-established scientific theory will eventually be proven wrong. Our airplanes would still fly, our bridges still stand, and our antibiotics would still be effective, but perhaps not entirely for the reasons we thought. Our original theory would then have to be revised.

The scientific method: how theories are developed and tested

The role of scientific theories is to explain some aspect of the natural world. Their explanatory power generally comes from describing relationships between various components of the natural world and how those components influence each other. Aspects of the natural world that are valid subjects of scientific inquiry include human behavior, and even subjective feelings and emotions. The components of the theory may themselves be based on prior discoveries. For example, the source-filter theory in Chapter 2 explains certain acoustic characteristics of speech by linking prior theoretical knowledge about the physics of sound with observations about how speech is produced by the human vocal tract. Some components of a theory may not be observable entities in the world or prior theoretical knowledge but may instead be new assumptions about what the very components of the world are, for example, the properties of subatomic particles.

In the early stages of conceptualizing a scientific question, what scientists initially want to explain often come from everyday observations, experiences, and queries that anyone might have: What governs the rising and setting of the sun? How do children acquire language? What do we do in our mouths when we talk? Are sign languages like spoken languages? As knowledge within a scientific areas advances, the theories often become more focused. For example, it might be necessary to form independent (although not unrelated) theories that separately address how children learn the meanings of words and how they learn the sentence structure of their language. In addition, as knowledge about an area of inquiry advances, the related theories often involve prior scientific knowledge that only experts would have, and thus might address questions that would not normally occur to nonexperts. For example, developing the source-filter theory became relevant only after the acoustic characteristics of speech had begun to be studied. But in general, the seed of a scientific theory is curiosity and our desire to understand what we observe of the world around us.

Going from a question about how some aspect of the world works to a theory – a set of ideas or propositions that offer an explanation – involves combining experience, intuition, and knowledge, and is a highly creative process. It can be one of the most enjoyable and intellectually stimulating parts of scientific discovery, and is also somewhat mysterious (but rest assured, scientists are studying it!).

Once a theory has been formed it must be tested. Recall that a scientific theory proposes how particular components of the world are related and how they influence each other. As such, they make **predictions** – for example, of the sort: if X occurs, Y will be observed to follow. The predictions are tested with experiments. If the predictions are borne out, the theory is supported (although not *proven*), but if the predictions are not borne out, the theory is falsified. Given our discussion of falsifiability, one might conclude that if an experiment fails to obtain a predicted result, then the theory is false. In an ideal sense this is true; however, in practice the accuracy of any one particular experiment can be questioned: Was it well designed to test the prediction? Was it sufficiently well executed? Are there alternative explanations for the failure to find the predicted result? These are issues that can affect whether a theory is refuted based on a single experiment. We will discuss some of these issues again later in the chapter. For the moment, let's assume that it was a perfect experiment and we accept that our predictions were not borne out. In that case, we might have to throw out the entire theory and start from scratch, or we might be able to revise the theory in such a way that it makes different predictions. We would then start the process of testing the theory over again.

This processes of *observation→theory→ prediction→experiment→revision→theory* . . . is called the **scientific method**. It is the fundamental process by which progress is made in scientific knowledge. It is an

The term **theory** is generally reserved for comprehensive explanatory systems that come out of a history of testing and revision and that are built on a large body of evidence. When scientists are just starting to explore a research area, sometimes the explanatory ideas are smaller in scope and more tentative. The term **hypothesis** is often used in those situations (and it is also sometimes used interchangeably with theory). For example, one might have a hypothesis that ambient noise affects the speed of recognizing words without having a broader theory about word recognition. In this chapter we use the term theory to cover all ranges of scientific explanation.

incremental process of testing and refining theories so that they are best able to explain the relevant data. Although the process seems almost like a computer algorithm, at every step there are biases and judgment calls. In many cases, for example, scientific debates center around what the relevant data are that must be accounted for. There are also debates about what counts as the best kind of theory in a given situation. In general, simpler theories are preferred over more complicated ones, if both theories can explain things equally well (this is referred to as **parsimony**). But what if a more complex theory explains just a little more data, or makes slightly better predictions than a simpler theory? Scientists will differ as to which theory they prefer, and the differences are related to different interpretations about what facts or evidence need to be explained. In fact some scientists reject parsimony as an absolute tie-breaker between equally predictive theories.

Experiments in Psycholinguistics

This section introduces you to some technical terms and concepts relating to many kinds of scientific experiments, but with a particular focus on concepts relevant for psycholinguistics experiments.

Independent and dependent variables

In most experiments in psycholinguistics, including the experiments that figure in many upcoming chapters, a theoretical prediction is tested by manipulating some aspect of the environment and measuring the effect on some other aspect of the environment (where "environment" is construed broadly to include myriad aspects of what an individual might encounter). The experiment tests whether the predicted effect of the manipulation is obtained. In general, what the experiment purposefully manipulates is called an **independent variable**, and the effect that is measured is called the **dependent variable** (or **dependent measure**). For example, in Chapter 6 you will read about experiments that measure how quickly listeners can repeat out loud the words they hear when listening to speech through headphones. Suppose a version of the experiment manipulates whether the speech consists of meaningless sequences of words or words in a meaningful utterance. The theory being tested might predict that words in meaningless contexts will take longer to name than words in sensible contexts. In this case, what is measured is the speed of the response, called **reaction time (RT)**; this is the dependent variable. The term highlights the fact that, according to the theory, what is being measured depends on what the experiment manipulates. The variable under the experimenter's control – whether or not the words are presented in meaningful contexts – is the independent variable. Experiments generally make predictions about how changes in an independent variable affect the dependent variable.

The previous example described an experiment with one independent variable and one dependent variable. It is often the case that experiments will have more than one of either of these. For example, in the previous experiment the theory being tested might also predict that when speech is accompanied by static noise RTs will be slower; researchers might then want to test the effect of playing static noise with speech and introduce the additional independent variable of noise to the experiment described above. Or, if one were interested in the **accuracy** of listeners' responses, one could score whether or not the listener gave the right answer, introducing another dependent variable. (The dependent variable would not be accuracy *per se*, but rather whether a correct response was given. Accuracy would then be calculated based on the proportion of times on which a subject gave a correct response.) While it may seem unnecessarily complex to have more than one dependent or independent variable in an experiment, designs with multiple variables can be informative. For instance, perhaps *overall* words are indeed repeated more slowly when accompanied by static noise – they are more difficult to recognize. But if the meaningfulness of the context (the other independent variable) were also varied systematically in the static and no-static conditions, one could ask whether static noise was less of a hindrance in meaningful vs. meaningless contexts. In technical terms, such a finding would be an example of an **interaction** between two independent variables: the effect of one independent variable on the dependent variable is **modulated**, or influenced by the other independent variable. Two theories could differ on whether or not independent variables interact with each other in relation to a dependent variable, so being able to test for interactions within a single experiment can be valuable.

One can also test whether two dependent variables interact. For instance, in psycholinguistics and cognitive psychology in general there is often a **speed–accuracy tradeoff**, meaning that faster responses are more likely to be incorrect. These kind of patterns can be readily observed if, in a single experiment, both kinds of measurements are taken.

You will see in later chapters that reaction time and accuracy are very common

Although we've been describing experiments as testing predictions, experiments can also be **exploratory**. It may be that a theory isn't spelled out enough to make a specific prediction about a particular phenomenon: how manipulating a particular independent variable should affect a dependent variable. Yet the observations in an exploratory study could help further refine the theory.

dependent variables in psycholinguistics experiments, although they are not always collected together within a single experiment.

Conditions and groups

In the previous discussion we used the term **condition** to describe whether or not static was present in a particular part of the experiment ("the static and no-static conditions"). The term is a technical term for describing experimental designs and generally is associated with different values or **levels** of an independent variable. There may be just two conditions per variable, such as whether static noise is or is not present, or there could be more. For example, there could be no-static, moderately-loud-static, and very-loud-static conditions. In psycholinguistics experiments, conditions often differ on the type of **stimuli** the subject receives in **trials** of the condition. Stimuli are simply the experimental material the subject responds to, for example, a speech signal, and a trial is a single presentation of a stimulus and measurement of a response.

The term **group** is similar to condition but is generally reserved for situations in which any given individual is only tested in one condition. For example, if the experimental design is such that some subjects only hear words along with static noise and other subjects only hear words without noise, then one would refer to the noise group and the no-noise group. On the other hand, if each subject hears stimuli with and without noise then one would refer to the noise condition and no-noise condition.

The theoretical question and the logic of the experiment often dictate whether the design should include independent groups, or if all subjects should participate in each condition. It is generally preferable not to divide subjects into groups (for reasons we will discuss in detail later), but sometimes it is necessary. For example, if one is interested in testing whether practice in hearing speech with noise improves the speed of recognizing noisy speech, then the experiment would have an independent variable that manipulates practice (practice vs. no practice), and clearly one individual could not participate in both conditions.

When an independent variable defines groups, then measuring the effect of the independent variable on the dependent variable is said to involve a **between-subjects** comparison. In contrast, if the same individuals participate in all conditions of an independent variable then measuring the effect on the dependent variable is said to involve a **within-subjects** comparison. We will discuss the practical significance of this distinction in our discussion of noise and statistical analyses.

Control conditions and experimental conditions

Control condition and **experimental condition** are special terms that describe a little more precisely the conditions of an experiment. In general, a control condition allows one to measure the dependent variable when the independent variable in question is not explicitly manipulated. In a sense, it's a way of obtaining a baseline measure for a behavior. In contrast, the experimental condition (or conditions) is one in which the experimenter has done something to change the normal or typical environment. For example, in an experiment where the only independent variable is the presence or absence of noise, it would be reasonable to call the no-noise condition the control condition and the noise condition the experimental condition.

However, the concept of control condition is not always so clear or even relevant in psycholinguistic experiments, as in many cases the stimuli are manipulated such that all conditions deviate from "typical" or "neutral" enough to be viewed as experimental conditions. What's really the critical concept in the control/experimental distinction is that the two (or more) conditions that are compared (with respect to their effects on the dependent variable) should differ *only* on the dimension of the independent variable. In other words, the only thing that should differ between the noise and no-noise condition is whether there is noise accompanying the speech signal – everything else should be the same. This allows one to conclude that any effect of the independent variable on the dependent variable is due to that one manipulated dimension and nothing else. In the abstract, that's a clear concept; in practice it can be a challenge. Next, we discuss situations in which experiments are not well controlled.

Confounding variables

Both independent and dependent variables are manipulated or measured by the experimenter and are part of the experimental design. But there are many things in experiments that influence measurements and results that are not controlled. Sometimes these uncontrolled influences are random, which means that they affect the dependent variable in similar ways for all conditions of an independent variable. Random uncontrolled influences are called **noise** because their overall effect is to make effects of an independent variable on a dependent variable more difficult to detect. (This is different than the static noise we've been talking about!) In contrast, when the uncontrolled influences affect the dependent variable *more in one condition than in another*, the uncontrolled influence is called a **confounding variable**.

To illustrate the concept with our example experiment, suppose that the actual words used in the static condition were different from those in the no-static condition. Now suppose that, by chance, a large portion of the words in the static condition also happened to be rare words (like *bog*) and a large portion of words in the no-noise condition were common (like *car*). Word frequency did not enter into the design of the experiment, yet it is *confounded* with the static variable, so it is called a **confounding variable**. The importance of being aware of confounding variables is that one can't be sure if an effect on the dependent variable (predicted or otherwise) is due to the independent variable (which was part of the planned design) or the confounding variable (which was not part of the design). For instance, if our experiment shows that listeners respond more quickly in the no-static condition compared to the static condition, one can't conclude that the effect is in fact due to the presence or absence of static. It could equally well be due to how common or rare words are. The presence of a confound doesn't rule out the possibility that the independent variable had an effect, but it provides a plausible alternative account.

In the example experiment we've been working with, we discussed a property of the materials (the words used) that could be confounded with an independent variable of static versus no-static. Can you think of other uncontrolled variables that could be confounding variables in an experiment similar to this one? For each variable that you think of, what steps could be taken to ensure that it isn't confounded with the static versus no-static variable? For example, the proportion of common and rare words could be made equal across conditions.

When undetected, confounding variables can lead to incorrect conclusions about whether a theoretical prediction was borne out or not by an experiment. In this sense they are a nuisance and can hinder scientific progress. But part of scientific discovery and progress involves identifying variables that affect the phenomena of interest that might not have been considered at first. These variables might first be discovered as unintentional confounds in an experiment. In many cases these discoveries come from other scientists evaluating and commenting on each others' work – finding confounds (and alternative explanations) that the scientist who designed the experiment might not have considered. If previously unconsidered variables are discovered to be important, then they can be incorporated into the theory and the theory becomes more complete.

Uncontrolled Variables, Experimental Design, and Statistical Analyses

We have introduced above the concept of *noise* in an experiment. The concept includes all the sources of uncontrolled influences on the dependent variable that are not confounded with an independent variable (otherwise they would be confounding variables, not just noise). In any experiment there are limitless influences of this random type. For instance, the time of day that an experiment is administered could affect subjects' responses – subjects might be more alert in the morning and less so in the afternoon, affecting response time and accuracy. Subjects may respond differently, for example, on hot days versus cool days. Many sources of noise are understood broadly as *individual differences* between subjects – some subjects are overall faster than others. Noise can also be introduced by the experimental setup itself. The accuracy of the equipment that records and times subjects' responses could introduce slight variability in the measurements so that some responses might be measured as being slightly faster than they are and other as slightly slower. As you can imagine, the list of potential uncontrolled variables in an experiment is endless. Above, we've discussed the situation in which an uncontrolled variable is confounded with an independent variable, but what about noise? How can noise affect an experiment and what can be done to lessen the effects of noise?

There are two general avenues for addressing the question of noise or uncontrolled variables. One is to design experiments in ways that reduce the effects of noise, the other is to apply statistical analyses to interpret the results. Usually both paths are taken.

Designing experiments to reduce the effects of noise

In order to understand the effects of noise on an experiment, let's first imagine a hypothetical "perfect" situation in which there is *no* noise or uncontrolled variables. We have two conditions in our experiment and the conditions differ only along the dimension of interest. We predict that the different conditions of the independent variable should lead to different results in the dependent variable, so we measure the outcome in each condition. In the case where there is no noise from any source, we can simply measure one trial in each condition and see if our measurements differ in the predicted way. If so, our prediction is confirmed; if not, we conclude that our prediction was wrong.

Of course, in reality such a situation never exists. Instead, each time a measurement is taken, many sources influence the outcome, as we saw earlier. Suppose our measurement is a reaction time, and in our perfect no-noise world the outcomes for the two conditions (A and B) are 300 milliseconds (ms) and 400 ms, respectively – a clear difference. Now suppose we're in the real world and there's some random noise that influences our measurement such that Condition A is measured at 50 ms longer than it "really" is and Condition B is measured to be 50 ms shorter than it "really" is. Now we have RTs of 300 + 50 = 350 ms in condition A and 400 − 50 = 350 ms in condition B. That is, the underlying process generated different RTs (just as in our idealized no-noise world), but the effect of noise was to *obscure* this difference.

One way to address this problem is to take **multiple measurements**. In the previous example we had just one trial per condition, so we had just one measurement or **data point** per condition. Instead, what if we take multiple measurements per condition (perhaps with different stimuli, or multiple measures of the same stimulus)? If the uncontrolled influences are random, then the next time we measure, the effect of noise on the measurement will be different, but the underlying process will be the same as ever. For instance, the next time we measure the outcome in condition A, the random effect of noise might shorten instead of lengthen the measured RT, or might lengthen it less. In general, the more data points we have, the more likely the overall effect of the noise will "wash out" when all the data points observed in a condition are considered together. Ⓦ

So one way to decrease the influence of noise is to design experiments in which multiple data points are collected in each condition. A scientist might have an individual subject participate in a great many trials. This can be problematic in many kinds of cognitive experiments; not only can subjects get tired, which can alter their responses, but subjects sometimes will change the way they behave because they start to notice patterns as the experiment progresses or become aware of what's being tested. Subjects will develop **response strategies** that then lead to atypical performance on the experimental task. In order to avoid these outcomes but still collect sufficient data points to decrease the influence of noise, psycholinguistics experiments typically test multiple subjects.

Of course, as you now know, introducing multiple subjects introduces the possibility of yet more uncontrolled variables! But again, as long as the effects are random across conditions, they just contribute to the random additions and subtractions (noise) that affect the measurement. In this context, it's a good time to recall the distinction between within-subjects comparisons – when each subject participates in each condition, and between-subjects comparisons – when subjects are grouped into different conditions – from an earlier box. We said that when possible, within-subjects comparisons are preferred. To see why, consider two subjects who differ in their overall reaction time to stimuli: subject S responds more slowly

Including multiple subjects is a good way to obtain more data points. But including multiple subjects has other advantages as well. In general, theories in psycholinguistics are theories about humans as a species. As such, it is desirable to test many different individuals to get a representative sample of the entire population. If many subjects behave in similar ways there will be more justification for attributing the behavior to the species as a whole. Of course, it may also turn out that people differ in how they process language. Such differences need to be accounted for in a good theory, and they would only surface if multiple individuals are tested.

overall than subject F. This means that S always adds a little more to RTs relative to F. If we treat this variability as a contribution to the noise, we see that if S is measured in condition A *and* B, the fact that S is a little slower than F won't affect the relative difference in the overall measurement of A and B. Similarly, F's faster responses will have the same effect on the overall outcome of condition A as it will on condition B. In other words, the individual variation they bring will affect condition A and B equally. On the other hand, if condition A and B are in fact experimental *groups* (that is, they don't include the same subjects), and subject S is in group A and subject F is in group B, then the effects of the individual differences they bring are not equal across condition/group. Of course, if there are multiple subjects per group and subjects are randomly assigned to groups, then a given group should have approximately equal numbers of faster and slower subjects and the effects of these individual differences will then be diminished. What's important to realize, however, is that the effects of individual differences are always going to be more balanced in within-subjects designs than in between-subjects designs. When possible, then, within-subjects designs are preferred because they reduce the effects of individual variability.

Using statistics to analyze experimental results

We have just discussed the value of multiple data points and multiple subjects as a way of addressing the influence of noise and uncontrolled variables. But whereas in the perfect no-noise world we needed only one data point per condition, in the real world we now have many. How do we interpret them? How do we compare them? The answers to the two questions involve statistics. The first involves **descriptive statistics**; the second involves **inferential statistics**.

Central tendencies and dispersion

An implicit assumption in most psycholinguistics experiments is that the fundamental processes being measured are similar across trials of any one individual and across all the individuals in an experiment. Of course, there are individual difference and a myriad of influences that affect the actual measurement taken on a given trial, but the idea is that there is considerable constancy across trials and individuals as well (at least within an experimental condition), and that this constancy should be discernable in the measurements. This assumption is made more concrete in the notions of central tendency and dispersion. **Central tendency** covers a number of ways at arriving at a quantitative (i.e., numerical) representation that captures the similarity among a set of data points. One way to think about central tendency is that it represent the true value of a process once the noise has been removed. (This a bit of an idealization, since there are a variety of ways of calculating central tendencies that yield different results, and because it is generally not possible to really remove all the effects of noise, but the idealization is at the heart of the concept.) You are probably familiar with an extremely common calculation of central tendency called the **mean** (also sometimes loosely referred to as an average). To compute it, one adds up all the data points and divides the sum by the number of data points. (If you imagine that each data point is a lead weight, and you place each weight along a number line in the position that corresponds to the measured value for the data point, then the mean is at the balance point.) The mean is interpreted as an approximation of what the measurement would have been for each data point without noise and without individual variation that was not part of the underlying measured process.

The degree to which such an interpretation is justified depends on several factors but especially on the **dispersion**. Like central tendency, dispersion is a general term. It covers a set of ways of quantifying the degree of *variability* of the data – how much difference there is across data points. To see why dispersion is important to evaluating central tendencies, it's essential to realize that any collection of data points has a central tendency. For instance, 10 data points consisting of six 50s, two 49s and two 51s have a mean of 50, but so do 10 data points consisting of five 1s and five 99s. The dispersion of the first set is much smaller, which means that data points in the first set are overall much closer to the mean than data points in the second set – they are more tightly "clustered." This corresponds to our intuition that the mean is a much better representative value of all the data points in the first set than it is of all the data points in the second set. A typical measure of dispersion used along with the mean is called the **standard deviation**. Basically, it represents the average distance of the data points in the sample to the mean of that sample. The smaller the standard deviation, the closer the data points are to the mean.

Figure 4.1 graphs two sets of data with different central tendencies and different dispersions. The x-axis represents measurement values, the y-axis represents the number of data points at a given value. The data on the left have a lower mean and a higher dispersion than the data on the right. In this example each data set has a prototypical shape of a **normal distribution** (or bell curve), in which most of the values are close to the mean. This kind of **distribution** of data points is typical of many process in nature, and it has special mathematical properties.

Comparing conditions
In our discussion of noise we said that collecting multiple data points is beneficial because over many data points the effects of noise tend to cancel each other out. Sometimes noise might result in higher values, sometimes lower. This means that even if an independent variable in fact has

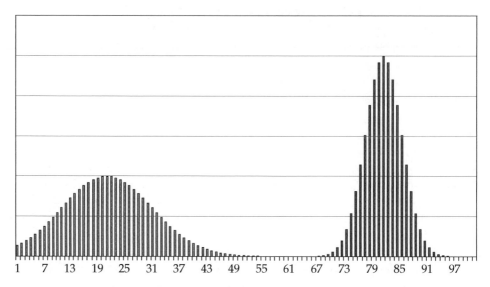

Figure 4.1   Two sets of data with different central tendencies and different dispersions.

no real effect on a dependent variable, random noise can still result in the means being different. Likewise, the means in two conditions could *really* be different, but noise might pull the observed means closer together. How can we tell if a difference between two means is "real"?

The problem essentially is determining whether two distributions of data points are reliably different. Sometimes we can see clearly by eye that two distributions are different. For example, Figure 4.2a shows hypothetical data from two conditions of an experiment in which the central tendencies are far apart relative to the dispersion. There is basically no overlap in the data points so it is obvious that the difference in means of the two distributions reflects a true difference in the underlying process being measured. Figure 4.2b shows two distributions that have closer means, but they also have less dispersion (the data are less noisy), so here as well it is easy to see by eye that the underling processes were different. In contrast, in Figure 4.2c the means of the two conditions are the same as in Figure 4.2b, but the dispersion in greater. As a result it is difficult to tell just by looking whether the differences are due to noise, or to a real underlying difference.

Fortunately, there are mathematical techniques for assessing this. A variety of statistical procedures consider properties related to central tendencies and dispersion to calculate the **probability** that the difference in the two means is due to random variability versus a real difference in the underlying process. General practice in many scientific fields is that if the probability that the difference in means is due to chance is less than .05 – less than a 5 percent possibility – then the difference is said to be **statistically significant**, and the difference is considered a real one and not

(a)

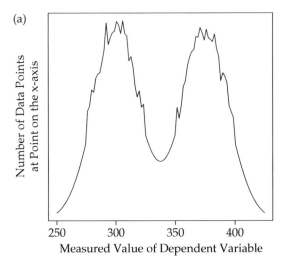

(b)

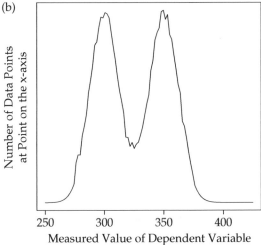

(c)

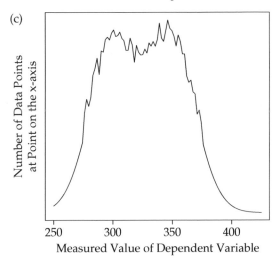

Figure 4.2 The three images depict distinct distribution of results (measurements) from two conditions of a hypothetical experiment. In (a), there are two clearly discernible values near which more of the results cluster – around 300 and 375. The distribution of data points – the number of measurements at the range of measured values – shows some dispersion in the data (many data points differ from 300 or 375) but the two central tendencies are far enough apart to be discernible as distinct patterns. If the left distribution – the leftmost "hump" – consisted of measurements largely from one condition and the right distribution from the other, you could tell without statistics that the conditions yielded different results. In (b), although the means are closer together than in (a) (roughly 300 and 350), the dispersion is less and so the two distributions are clearly discernible by eye. In contrast, (c) has two distributions of data with the same means as (b) but greater dispersion. It's hard to tell by eye whether the data constitute one or two distinct distributions. In such cases, statistical analyses could provide a more precise assessment of the data.

Most scientists will tell you that it's difficult to interpret a **null result** – an outcome when manipulating the independent variable has no statistically significant effect on the dependent variable. The reason is that statistical significance depends on the degree of noise and dispersion in the data. As you can see from Figure 4.2, the closer the means (i.e., the smaller the effect of the manipulation), the "cleaner" the data need to be for a difference to be detected. Statistical techniques are more precise than eyeballing the data when the differences aren't obvious, but they are not magic; there is simply no way to detect differences that may be real if the noise is too great.

This is one reason why when introducing the scientific method we said that any one experiment that fails to produce a predicted outcome may not be sufficient to falsify the theory.

due to noise. Of course, if we were testing for the safety of a part on the space shuttle, we might want to be more than 95 percent sure that our predictions were accurate!

Summary

This chapter introduced the idea of a scientific theory and the scientific method and provided an overview of the concepts and terminology of experimental design. A key concept was that scientific theories are *falsifiable*: in principle, there is some piece of evidence that would show that the theory is wrong. However, one experiment is sometimes not sufficient to falsify a theory because in practice there are many factors that can influence the outcome. Uncontrolled factors in an experiment might be confounded with an independent variable, or they might be a source of noise. Experimental designs can help reduce the effects of noise, and statistical analyses can help detect patterns in noise.

Key terms and concepts from this chapter include:

- scientific method
- falsifiability
- independent and dependent variable
- confounding variable
- noise
- between- and within-subjects designs
- central tendency
- dispersion
- statistical significance

Further Reading and Resources

Popper, Karl R. (1999). *The Logic Of Scientific Discovery*. London: Routledge.

How to Lie and Cheat with Statistics: *http://faculty.washington.edu/chudler/stat3.html*

Twenty science attitudes: *http://www.ksu.edu/biology/pob/modern_attitudes.html*

Chapter 5
Speech Perception

Section 1: The Lack of Invariance and the Use of Cues in Speech Perception

Introduction

In Chapter 1 we introduced the notion of the speech chain. In Chapter 2 we explored several links along the chain, from how a speaker converts mental representations of speech sounds into a physical speech signal using the vocal tract, to the properties of the signal that encode speech sounds, and finally to the ear – the biological device that registers the sound wave as sensory information sent to the brain. In this chapter we explore the next link in the chain – speech perception – or how listeners automatically **decode** the acoustic speech signal and reconstruct the sequences of phonological units, and the words, intended by the speaker.

An important idea that we develop in this chapter is that speech perception is the result of the brain detecting and evaluating the patterning of **cues** in the speech signal. Cues in speech perception are information about the intended phonological units. For example, voice onset time (VOT) is one available cue to the voicing of a speech segment. Speech perception can be understood as a process whereby the brain **computes** a representation of speech by interpreting the information or cues in the speech signal. Perception, then, is a result of a *process*.

At first glance it's not obvious why cues should be important in speech perception: why do we need *hints* about the identity of a speech sound? Why can't we just identify the speech sound by directly matching it to stored templates? We start this chapter by discussing the importance of cues as patterned information, by showing that a given speech sound can be

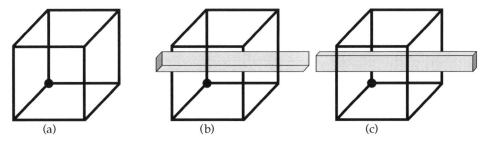

Figure 5.1 Image (a) is ambiguous as to whether the dot is in the back-left corner of a cube or the front left corner. Images (b) and (c) provide additional cues that favor one interpretation over another, resulting in complementary interpretations.

realized as many different acoustic patterns, and the same acoustic pattern can be perceived as different speech sounds in different circumstances.

More broadly, however, it's important to realize that the notion of cues is central to all domains of perception, in humans and other species. Figure 5.1 demonstrates this in the visual domain. Figure 5.1a depicts the classic Necker cube: a two-dimensional image that the visual system perceives as an ambiguous three-dimensional object – is the dot on a near corner or a far corner in 5.1a?

Our perception of the orientation of the cube shifts because the depth cues are ambiguous. However, Figures 5.1b and 5.1c add a cue in the form of a rod that penetrates the cube. Now the orientation is unambiguous and is determined by the lines of the cube that the solid rod occludes, or covers up, and the lines that occlude part of the rod. This additional cue – occlusion – changes the way the other cues to depth are interpreted, and changes how lines of the cube are interpreted. In other words, the same visual information – for example, the lines forming the "corner" where the dot is – produces two different perceptions depending on the other available cues.

The Lack of Invariance in the Perception of Segments and Words

Chapter 2 presented general facts about the acoustics of speech and how speech sounds are **encoded** in the acoustic signal. For example, we saw that formants are involved in distinguishing vowels, and voice onset time (VOT) helps to distinguish consonants. We also learned about visualizing sound waves as waveforms, spectrograms, and power spectra, and how patterns in each type of format correspond to speech sounds. From this, one might wonder whether perceiving speech involves simply "reading" the sound wave – sequentially examining patterns in each section of the sound wave and identifying the corresponding speech sound – much as we visually identify letters and words on the printed page. This kind of process would be possible if speech sounds could always be uniquely identified, for example, if an [a] always corresponded to the first two formants being at specific frequencies, or if voiced consonants always had 0 ms VOTs and voiceless always had 60 ms VOTs. If this were the state of affairs, we might describe speech sounds as being in **one-to-one correspondence** with patterns in the acoustic signal.

In reality, perceiving speech is not so straightforward. There are many factors that introduce variability in the way the acoustic signal corresponds to the intended (and perceived) phonological units. Rather than one-to-one, the correspondences between the indented or perceived speech sound and the acoustic signal is many-to-many. The technical term for this state of affairs is **the Lack of Invariance**, which means that there is no one-to-one correspondence between the intended/perceived phonological unit and the acoustic signal. The mapping from the acoustic signal to phonological units is many-to-many. Just as the Necker cube can be interpreted in multiple ways, portions of waveforms that correspond to a speech sound can be interpreted as different speech sounds (a one-to-many mapping), and different acoustic patterns can represent the same speech sound (many-to-one). Another way of putting this is that there is variability in the way a given speech sound is realized in the speech signal and, just as with the Necker cube, a given pattern in the speech signal can be ambiguous. Yet in perceiving speech, we generally have no problem recovering the intended phonological units, and we don't have the impression that we are hearing lots of ambiguous patterns. Our experience is of **phonetic constancy** – stable perception despite variability in the signal. How do our brains compute constant, accurate perceptions in face of all the ambiguity and variability? To understand this, it will help to examine more closely some forms of variability and in particular the *sources* of variability. We then can start to understand how the brain can perceive invariant speech sounds despite the acoustic variability.

There are three predominant sources of variability in the way a particular speech sound is realized acoustically: **within-speaker variability**, **between-speaker variability**, and variability introduced by articulations that overlap in time during speech production – **coarticulation**. We first discuss the two kinds of speaker variability, and then coarticulation.

Speaker variability

Each spectrogram in Chapter 2 represents the speech of a unique speaker at a unique moment in time. The formant values are tied to the particular resonating frequencies of the major cavities in the vocal tract in a specific configuration. But the sizes of the resonating cavities varies between individuals, and thus the absolute formant values for a given articulatory posture will differ from speaker to speaker. Therefore, although the first two formants reflect vowel identity, we cannot identify a vowel, say, [a], merely by "looking up" its formant frequencies in a mental table, since the actual values will differ across individuals. This is a source of between-speaker variability that results in mappings between speech sounds and the acoustic signal that are many-to-one (many different signals give rise to the perception of one sound).

Between-speaker differences also give rise to one-to-many mappings – where a particular acoustic pattern gives rise to different perceptions of phonological units in different situations. The physical differences in vocal tracts mentioned above, in addition to differences in pronunciation between individuals, means that a given acoustic pattern (say, the first and second formants that are critical for vowel identity) might be perceived as an /ɔ/ when spoken by one speaker, an /a/ when spoken by another. Figure 5.2 shows the F1 and F2 values for individual vowels produced by

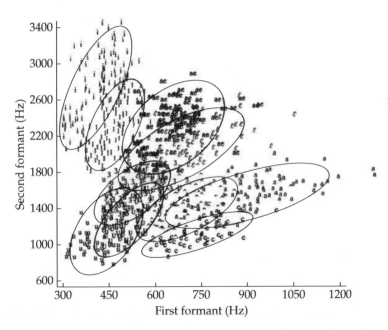

Figure 5.2 Vowels produced by men, women and children, plotted by their first and second formant values. Ellipses show approximate boundaries for vowel categories. Areas contained in more than one ellipse correspond to one-to-many mappings between the acoustic signal and the perceived vowel. Reprinted with permission from Hillenbrand, J., Getty, L., Clark, M., & Wheeler, K. (1995). Acoustic characteristics of American English vowels. *The Journal of the Acoustical Society of America, 97*(5), 3099-3111. Copyright 1995, American Institute of Physics.

men, women, and children. The ellipses show the approximate boundaries in the F1 x F2 vowel space for each vowel. As you can see, there are many points in the space that fall within the boundaries for two or more different vowel categories. In other words, for different speakers the same acoustic pattern will be perceived differently by listeners.

Other sources of between-subject variability are the fundamental frequency (F0) of the voice (perceived as pitch) and speaking rate. The average F0 and its range of fluctuation differ from speaker to speaker, as does the average speaking rate. Both properties can affect speech perception, as we'll see below. These properties vary within speakers as well. For example, one's emotional state, one's alertness, and the conversational circumstances can all affect the rate at which one speaks, as well as the average pitch of the voice and its moment-to-moment variability. These are additional sources of between- and within-speaker variability that make a many-to-one mapping from acoustics to perception.

Lack of invariance due to coarticulation

We saw above how between-speaker variability contributes to the lack of invariance in the realization of vowels. The realization of consonants is also extremely variable, but in contrast to vowels the variability is due predominantly to local effects of the phonetic context in which the consonant is produced – in other words, the sounds the speaker is producing before and after the sound in question. In order to understand these effects, it's first necessary to understand the properties of the speech signal that contribute to our perception of consonants.

Formant transitions and the perception of consonants

As we have seen above, vowels are distinguishable to a large degree by the first two formants, F1 and F2, which for most vowels (with the exception of diphthongs) show up as relatively flat, horizontal lines on the spectrogram when spoken in isolation (that is, not preceded or followed by any other speech sound); this is referred to as a steady-state vowel. Recall that vowels are characterized by a relatively unrestricted airflow, whereas consonants involve a complete or partial restriction in the vocal tract. Therefore, articulating a consonant *in the context of a vowel* (**coarticulation**) requires changing the configuration of the vocal tract. This change involves changing the size of the resonating chambers. As an example, if you experiment with articulating the syllable [dæd] you'll notice that your jaw starts out somewhat raised for the initial /d/, then lowers to form the [æ], then rises again to form the final /d/. The lowering and raising of the jaw, and the movement of the tongue, result in changes to the resonating frequencies of the vocal tract and to the consequent formants. Since /dæd/ is voiced throughout, thereby putting acoustic energy into the formant

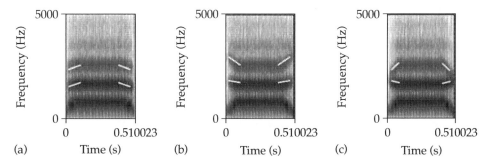

Figure 5.3 Computer synthesized examples of the syllables (a) [bæb], (b) [dæd], and (c) [gæg]. The steady state vowels are identical in each syllable; only the formant transitions differ. Note: The spectrograms do not include the stop closures or release bursts, only the formants and formant transitions.

frequencies, the changing vocal tract configurations result in changing formant frequency values called **formant transitions**. Formant transitions are rapid changes over time in formant frequency values as the vocal tract moves from one configuration (e.g., from producing a consonant) to another (e.g., producing a vowel). Figure 5.3 shows spectrograms for the syllables [bæb], [dæd], and [gæg], with the formant transitions highlighted.

You can see from Figure 5.3 that the middle of each syllable looks the same, and is characterized by the horizontal formants associated with the steady-state vowel (and those formant values are the same across the syllables because it's the same vowel).

If you were to splice out and play only that middle portion, you would perceive a vowel. Now notice that preceding and following that stable, flat portion, the formants slope slightly. These sloping formants are the formant transitions. Because the formant transitions reflect the vocal tract shaping of the consonant constriction release (at the left edge) and formation (at the right edge), the formant transitions logically must give rise to the consonant perceptions. However, consider that in each syllable, the first and final consonants are the same, yet the formant transitions are different. For example, in [gæg], the F3 transition rises for the initial [g], but falls for the final [g], and the other transitions also display this "mirror image" property. In other words, the formant transition patterns preceding a vowel are *opposite* what they are following the vowel, yet the perception is identical! This is another example of the many-to-one mappings from acoustics patterns to perception, this time due to coarticulation.

The reason that the shape of the formant transitions depends on the position of the consonant with respect to the vowel becomes clear when one recalls where the formants and formant transitions come from. We've been stressing the importance of the vocal tract and its movements for creating formants and formant transitions, respectively. Returning to our earlier

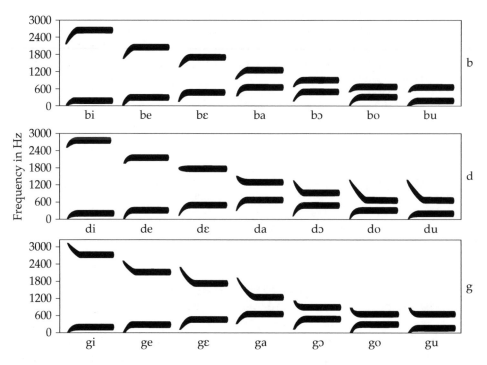

Figure 5.4   Idealized images of formant transitions and steady state vowels for a series of vowels following three different voiced stops. For a given consonant, the contour of the formant transitions changes depending on the following vowel. Reprinted with permission from Delattre, Liberman, & Cooper, *Journal of the Acoustical Society of America*, Vol. 27, Page 769–773, 1955. Copyright 1955, American Institute of Physics.

example of [dæd], since the movement of the articulators to transition from the steady-state vowel to the final [d] – the raising of the tongue tip to the alveolar ridge – is (roughly) the reverse of the movements to transition from the initial [d] to the vowel – the lowering of the tongue tip, it makes sense that the formant transitions (which reflect the movement of the articulators) should be the reverse as well. So, by considering the movements responsible for generating formant transitions, we can explain why the initial and final consonant transitions are mirror images. But that still leaves a many-to-one problem that the speech perception mechanisms have to cope with and that we would like to understand: how do radically different acoustic patterns give rise to the same perception?

The many-to-one challenge gets even more impressive: even when a consonant occurs in the same position relative to a vowel, formant transitions differ depending on the identity of the *vowel*. Figure 5.4 shows idealized depictions of F1 & F2 for a series of syllables, specifically, the consonant [d] followed by a range of vowels. (These were actually hand-painted spectra used for experiments in speech carried out at Haskins Laboratories; they were fed into a machine that produced speech from drawn spectrograms. Ⓦ) Notice that the slope angle and length of the formant transitions are different, depending on the following vowel. Yet the acoustically different formant transitions all produce the same perception of [d] in listeners. This is once again a situation where different acoustic patterns produce a single perceptual experience. Below we introduce a theory about the kinds of computations listeners might be carrying out to produce identical perceptions for varying acoustic patterns. In particular, we will consider what might in fact be invariant despite all of these many-to-one correspondences.

Invariance in Speech Perception

You have now seen a number of examples of the lack of invariance in speech. Specifically, you have seen how speakers and the overlap of neighboring speech sounds introduce variability in the acoustic realization of speech segments. Yet despite this variability, we perceive the intended segments extremely accurately. This puzzle has stimulated considerable research into finding **invariant cues** in the speech signal. One idea that has been proposed is that invariance can be found in the acoustics-to-gesture/ articulation mapping. This idea is based on the observation that there are lawful, predictable relationships between the acoustic patterns in speech and the articulatory gestures that produced them. So while there is variability in the acoustic realization of the mental representations of the phonological units that speakers intend to produce, much of the variability follows naturally from the mechanics of speech production, and could be, in fact, *informative* about the gestures that produced the acoustic signal. (For example, the acoustic effects of coarticulation can be informative about the gestures that were the source of the coarticulated sounds.) If the knowledge of these gesture-to-acoustics relations is part of listeners' unconscious linguistic knowledge, then perceiving speech could involve recovering the gestures that produced an acoustic pattern. Going from gestures to a representation of phonological units in the mind of the perceiver could make use of the same mental-to-gestural relationships the perceiver uses when speaking. Alternately, mental representations of phonological units might simply be the representations of the gestures themselves. In either case, the general idea is that considering the gestures that could have given rise to a particular acoustic signal could provide a *context* for interpreting potentially ambiguous elements.

In an influential theory of speech perception called **the motor theory of speech perception**, the representations of gestures in the listener's mind plays a central role. The "motor" part of the name refers to the idea that the perception process involves representations of the motor command structures for the gestures that produced the acoustic signal. (We will discuss this theory again later.) Other theories that differ in many details from the motor theory also propose that gestural representations play a role in perception as one of several sources of information that could provide a context for interpreting an ambiguous acoustic signal.

Cues in consonant perception

Recall our discussion about the acoustic differences of consonants produced before or after a vowel. We linked the pattern of the formant transitions to facts about the articulatory movements involved in producing a consonant in each position. In the examples in Figure 5.3, the vowel was the same in the three examples, so the target of the articulatory movements was the same, and just the starting point (or ending point) for the syllables differed according to the consonant. However, in Figure 5.4, the consonant is the same in each panel but the vowel varies. This means that the target of the articulatory movement is different. It stands to reason, then, that the formant transitions would differ, since they are determined by the change in configuration of the vocal tract. In Figure 5.4 the starting targets are the same, but the ending targets are different; the formant transitions are therefore different as well. What is stable, however, in all these examples, is the link between the formant patterns and the articulatory gestures that created them. In Figure 5.4, the differences in the formants of the vowels are lawfully related to the formant transitions that result from the coarticulation of the preceding consonant. Speech perception, then, might involve working backwards: computing a representation of the gestures that would have produced the formant patterns in question, and perceiving a speech sound based on the computed source gestures.

We note that some scientists believe, as do proponents of the motor theory, that speech perception involves gestures, but differ as to how gestures are recovered in the minds of listeners. One theory holds that the acoustic signal does, indeed, have invariant cues that directly activate the gestural sources in the mind of the listener – we just haven't discovered them yet.

Cues in vowel perception

Recall from Chapter 2 that a vowel's identity is in large measure reflected by its F1 and F2 values. In general, the more closed the vocal tract is, the lower F1 will be; the longer the vocal tract is (including, for example, lengthening due to lip rounding), the lower the formants will be. The relation between the frontness–backness vowel dimension and F2 is somewhat more

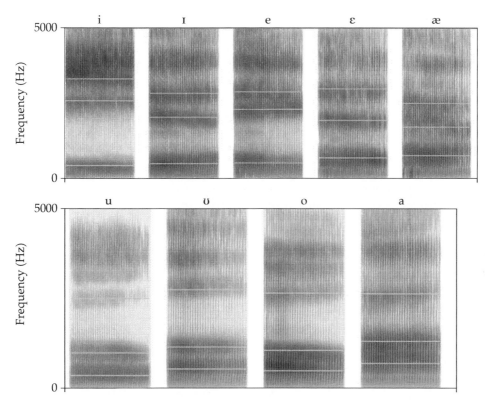

Figure 5.5 Spectrograms of English-like vowels with F1 and F2 highlighted. The top image shows front vowels, the bottom image shows back vowels. Adapted by permission from Louis Goldstein.

complicated, but for our introductory purposes, it suffices to say that F2 falls in frequency as the English vowels move from frontmost to backmost. These facts suggest that identifying vowels requires considering a *relationship* between F1 and F2. Since individuals differ in the absolute values of formants for any vowel, the F1 and F2 relationship must look to *relative* values between formants. By relative values we mean a relationship of one formant value with respect to another formant value.

Figure 5.5 shows spectrograms, with the formant frequencies highlighted for a set of English-like vowels. Try to identify the changes in F1 and F2 as a function of height and backness.

A **ratio** is one common way of representing relative values. For example, the numbers 2 and 4 are different absolute values from the numbers 3 and 6, but they are similar in that the second number of the pair is twice the first: they have a 1:2 ratio. At one point, it was thought that the ratios of F1 and F2 were invariant across individuals for a given vowel. So, an [æ] for Mark might have an F1 at 700 and an F2 at 1500, but for Sally,

F1 might be 900 and F2 about 1930. The absolute values are different, but the ratios are almost identical, and the perceived vowel would be the same. The relationship between formants provides a potential source of stability because while the absolute formant values are determined by the size of the resonators, which varies across individuals, the ratios involve relative sizes. Between individuals, the relative sizes are more constant (if the oral cavity is larger, the vocal tract length is likely to be as well), so computing the ratios of formants is one possible way of extracting reliable properties of particular vowels. Later, some researchers proposed that F0 and F3 might be important in how these relative relationships are interpreted. While the fundamental frequency (F0) is not determined by resonator sizes, it is nonetheless biologically influenced (and correlated with biological size) and thus is also available as a cue to guide interpretation of the other formants. So while theories differ as to the contribution of F0 and F3 in guiding the interpretation of the F1 and F2 relationship, many theories have in common the idea that computing the relationships between formants provides a greater source of stability across speakers in the formant patterns that correspond to vowels.

Recalling our earlier discussion, the type of invariance involved in F1/F2 ratios is related to the lawful effects of differences in vocal tract size and shape on the acoustic patterns for vowels. However, although considering F1/F2 ratios instead of absolute frequencies may reduce variability, and although F0 and F3 can guide the interpretation of F1 and F2, these properties do not appear to be sufficient to entirely solve the lack of invariance problem for vowels. For one thing, the degree to which these characteristics can entirely account for acoustic differences brought about by vocal tract difference between speakers is not entirely clear. But even if they could account for the differences, there are important speaker variations that are independent of vocal tract differences. For example, recall from Chapter 3 all the varieties of English in the United States, and in particular regional differences in vowel pronunciation. A pair of identical twins could be brought up in different parts of the country and have differing vowel spaces. The overall size and shape of their vocal tracts would be (nearly) identical, but nevertheless the formant values for their vowels would be different simply because they pronounce things differently. In other words, some of the variability depicted in Figure 5.2 would remain, even if we could remove all the variability due to vocal tracts. Although as listeners we can usually detect even subtle regional differences in pronunciation, these differences don't generally impede our comprehension. Therefore there must be some other sources of information aside from vocal tract gestures that we use in perceiving speech. Some scientists think that part of speech processing involves simultaneously evaluating several possible interpretations of the acoustic signal and selecting the one that is most coherent (e.g., that results in a meaningful word). On this view, there are processes involved in speech perception that consider the context of the acoustic signal, where context can include the context of surrounding phonological units (i.e., coarticulation) as well as factors like the listener's familiarity with the speaker or the expectations about what might be said. These sources of information play a role in generating and evaluating possible interpretations of the signal.

The role of vision in speech: The McGurk effect

One fascinating piece of evidence in support of the idea that listeners' perception of speech involves considering a broad range of information comes from the **McGurk effect**. Broadly, the McGurk effect, named after one of the scientists who discovered it, describes a situation in which the visual information a listener gets from watching the mouth of a speaker alters the listener's perception of what the speaker is saying. Experiments exploring this phenomenon involve listeners watching a talker's mouth on a video monitor. The talker utters several syllables, one after the other, and the listener reports hearing syllables, for example, "ba, va, tha, da." Next, the identical audio portion is repeated, but now with no video. This time, listeners will report hearing one repeated syllable, "ba, ba, ba, ba" yet the sounds were *exactly the same* as the sounds they were presented with before, when the video portion was present and they heard nonidentical syllables. Ⓦ In fact, in this experiment the pairing of the audio and visual portions of the syllables was contrived – the audio was the same acoustic syllable, "ba," repeated several times; however, the video was of the talker pronouncing different syllables, *ba, va, tha,* and *ga*. So the visual information presented by the talker's lips and tongue indicated different syllables than the audio, in almost every case. The fascinating effect was that the visual information was integrated with the audio information, resulting in a perception of speech that took into account both information sources. In other words, *visual* information of a sound's source fundamentally affects the way we process *auditory* information – vision affects the perception of speech. In this case, the acoustic and visual information were "in agreement" that the vowel was an [a]; the acoustic signal also provided information that the consonant was a voiced stop, [b]. However, in three of the syllables the visual information conflicted with the acoustic information for the initial consonant, indicating a place of articulation that was incompatible with [b], that is, that did not show the lips closing. In the case of [va] and [θa], perception was guided by the place of articulation information from the visual information, not the acoustic signal, and that information, rather than the acoustic signal, determined what consonant was perceived. However, the acoustic signal contributed the information that the consonant was voiced (which has no visual cue), so that all the consonants that were perceived were voiced. The perceived [da] is especially interesting because it is neither exactly what was produced visually (which was [ga]) or acoustically. The place of articulation for [ga] is hard to see just by looking at the front of the mouth, yet the articulation clearly wasn't that of a [b] (what the acoustic information was indicating). The perception was a kind of blend of the two sources of information. Of course, it's not the case that if the acoustic signal was [ba], and the visual information came from *cat*, the listener would perceive something more like *cat* than *ba*. There has to be enough overlap of cues so that the visual and auditory information are processed as contributing to the same sound. When that happens, the visual cues have a tremendous impact on speech processing.

In normal situations, of course, we never come across individuals like the talkers in the experiment just discussed whose mouths' actions don't match the sounds that emerge. But these kinds of contrived or impossible situations can be very informative as experiments about the way we perceive speech in normal situations (much like visual illusions are informative about the computations involved in vision). The McGurk effect might seem like strong evidence in support of the motor theory, or other theories in which gestural information plays an important role. After all, visual information from movements of the mouth is incredibly informative about the articulations that generated a speech sound (you can see many of them). However, some scientists have argued that through learning from experience with talkers, mature listeners have formed an association between the visual information and the intended phonological units simply because they occur together so frequently, not because the visual information is about gestures *per se*. If this is the case, then the associations must be formed very early because five-month-old infants have been shown to be influenced by visual information in similar ways to adults.

Although there is some disagreement about the underlying mechanisms involved in the McGurk effect, the phenomenon reinforces the notion that speech perception depends on *cues* – not only in the speech signal itself, but in other modalities, coming from other senses. As listeners, we use all the bits and pieces of information that are available to us in order to figure out what the intended message was. Sometimes, as in the integration of visual information, the cues are not even in the acoustic signal, even though they profoundly change the way we experience and perceive speech. In addition, the McGurk effect offers another example of one-to-many relationships in speech perception: one acoustic signal produces different perceptions, depending on other available cues.

Finally, this phenomenon introduces a theoretical idea that will be important in our further discussion of speech perception: **top-down processing** and **top-down information**. We will discuss these concepts more in Chapter 6, but broadly, **bottom-up processing** in language refers to cognitive operations that build more abstract representations of language from less abstract ones. A perceptual process that generates representations of the building blocks of words strictly from information in the acoustic signal would be a bottom-up process since it uses only concrete sensory information to determine the identification of phonological units. But a perceptual process that incorporates higher-level knowledge in constructing representations – for example, knowledge of how speech sounds are produced – would involve top-down (as well as bottom-up processes). On the view that the McGurk effect involves using visual information and knowledge of the articulatory gestures tied to speech sounds, it is an example of top-down processing in speech perception.

Summary of Section 1

This section introduced a fundamental property of speech: the lack of invariance between the acoustic signal and the speech sounds that listeners perceive. A guiding question in speech perception research is how listeners experience phonetic constancy in the face of significant variability. One approach has been to search for invariance in the vocal tract gestures and the lawful relationships between gestures and the acoustic patterns they give rise to. More broadly, we described how speech perception involves identifying and interpreting cues to – or patterned information about – speech sounds. The information is not a guaranteed indicator of one speech sound or another, but rather is interpreted in the context of other cues in recovering or decoding phonological units. The key topics are summarized below.

- Within-speaker variability
- Between-speaker variability
- Variability from coarticulation
- Formant ratios as a cue in vowel perception
- Formant transitions as a cue in consonant perception
- Visual cues in speech perception: The McGurk effect
- The motor theory of speech perception

Section 2: Ways in Which Speech Perception Might be Special

Categorical Perception

We have been discussing how gestures in speech production influence each other, so that the acoustic information associated with a given speech sound can change from context to context, depending on the surrounding sounds. This is due, in part, to the fact that speakers produce the sequence of individual speech sounds in a fluid, continuous, and overlapping manner. This aspect of speech production also introduces variability in the production and coordination of the gestures a speaker intends to produce. Speech gestures are produced incredibly quickly, and some of the important contrasts are quite small. For example, a syllable-initial voiced stop, say [b] in [ba], has a typical voice onset time (VOT) of near 0 milliseconds, whereas the voiceless counterpart, [p] in [pa], has a typical VOT of around 60 milliseconds. However, speakers are not able to reliably produce sounds at these precise VOT values. Rather, one instance of a [p] might have a VOT of 60 milliseconds, and another may have a VOT of 40 milliseconds. Likewise, one [b] may be produced with a VOT of 0 milliseconds, the next one with a 10 millisecond VOT. In other words, there is variability along the dimension of VOT due to the variability in the way sounds are articulated from instance to instance. This fact about production has interesting consequences for perception: when we hear a stop consonant with a VOT somewhere between 0 milliseconds – say, an ideal [ba] – and 60 milliseconds – say, an ideal [pa] – do we perceive the consonant as falling somewhere between [b] and [p]? Interestingly, we do not; we hear either a [b] or a [p], but not some blend of both. This phenomenon is called **categorical perception**, referring to the fact that we normally perceive speech sounds categorically as one sound or another, but not as a blend of sounds or as an intermediate or indeterminate sound. Categorical perception implies that perceivers pay attention to the variability that matters – the variability in VOT that distinguishes [pa] from [ba] – and ignore variability that is not linguistically relevant, such as the variability in VOT between two different [pa]s. Figure 5.6 provides a schematic depiction of categorical perception of VOT. We will fill in more details below. Categorical perception operates on a variety of articulatory/acoustic dimensions, including for example, place of articulation.

Coarticulation and other factors affect the precise location of the consonant constriction, which, in turn, results in variability in the formant transitions for each instance of a given consonant-vowel (CV) sequence, in particular in the initial frequency of the transition. As in the case of VOT, certain differences in the initial frequency of a formant transition result in the perception of different consonants when the two values are on opposite sides of a category boundary. But the same difference in initial frequencies does not give rise to any perceived difference in speech sounds when the two frequencies are on the same side of the category boundary. Figure 5.7 shows a depiction of the first three formants for an idealized [da] and [ga], as well as the F3 transitions along a kind of continuum from [da] to [ga] that might be used in a typical categorical perception experiment. As with VOT and voicing, consonants with formant transitions somewhere

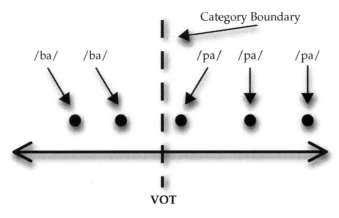

Figure 5.6 Depiction of categorical perception of the consonant in a CV syllable. The horizontal axis represents the dimension of voice onset time (VOT).

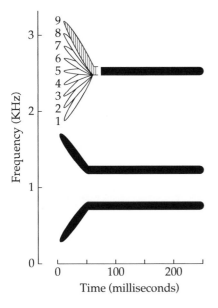

Figure 5.7 Idealized F1, F2, and F3 showing superimposed steps in the F3 transition. The F3 transition labeled (1) corresponds to a typical [ga], and (9) corresponds to a typical [da]. The intermediate steps correspond to stimuli that vary on the F3 transition continuum between [ga] and [da]. Adapted from Liberman, A. M., & Mattingly, I. G. (1989), A specialization for speech perception, *Science*, 243, 489–494. Reprinted with permission from AAAS.

between the two extremes are not perceived as a mix of consonants but rather as one or the other. So, as with VOT, perceivers apparently attend to the differences in formant transitions that signal different consonants and ignore differences that are linguistically irrelevant. A general description of categorical perception is that perceivers have *good between-category discrimination* – the ability to perceive differences between two items from different categories – and *poor within-category discrimination* – difficulty perceiving differences between two items from the same category.

Experiments assessing categorical perception

There are several widely used methods of assessing categorical perception. In one method, which we'll call *forced-choice identification*, subjects hear a CV syllable (usually created as synthetic speech on a computer) and have to report which of two possible syllables they heard (e.g., [ba] or [pa]). The syllables are synthesized to vary along a phonetic dimension, such as VOT, sampling many points along the **continuum** throughout the experiment. For example, a subject would hear a series of <bilabial-stop>+[a] syllables, where the VOT might be 20 milliseconds in the first trial, 0 in the second, 50 in the third, then 30, then 25, and so on, sampling many points along the VOT dimension. The subject simply has to report, after hearing each syllable, whether the syllable was [pa] or [ba]. Figure 5.8 shows a schematic graph of what the results would look like if the perception of voicing along the VOT dimension were **continuous** rather than categorical. The *y*-axis represents the proportion of [pa] responses, and the *x*-axis represents the range of VOT values. The hypothetical graph shows that as VOTs increase in equal increments from the voiced to the voiceless end of the continuum, the perception of "[pa]-ness," or voicelessness, also increases incrementally; each increase in VOT results in an increase in the perception of [pa]-ness of the consonant – the greater the VOT, the greater the number of responses of a voiceless consonant.

However, Figure 5.9 plots typical results from this type of experiment and depicts categorical judgments rather than the continuous perception shown in Figure 5.8. The important differences between categorical perception curves, like Figure 5.9, and continuous perception curves is that many incremental changes in VOT along the *x*-axis do *not* result in different perceptions of [pa]-ness. For example, in Figure 5.9, from 0 to about

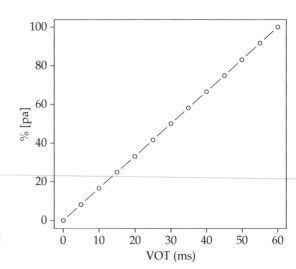

Figure 5.8 Hypothetical graph depicting continuous judgments of voicing ([ba] vs. [pa]) along the voice onset time (VOT).

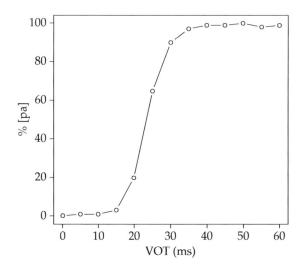

Figure 5.9 Hypothetical graph depicting categorical judgments of voicing ([ba] vs. [pa]) along the voice onset time (VOT) continuum.

25 milliseconds, listeners perceive only [ba], and from about 25 to 60 milliseconds, listeners perceive only [pa]. The area right around 25 milliseconds VOT results in mixed perceptions – some listeners reporting [ba], others [pa]. This means that a difference in VOT between two syllables of 20 milliseconds results in no perceptual difference if the values are 0 and 20 (both [ba]s), or 35 and 55 (both [pa]s), but the same 20 ms difference results in different consonant perceptions if the values are 20 ms and 40 ms.

These results exemplify good between-category discrimination because in order to consistently label two sounds as different, the listener must discriminate between them. It might also seem that the results demonstrate poor within-category discrimination because two different sounds on the same side of the boundary are always given the same label. However, even if listeners report two syllables with differing VOTs as being the same syllable, they might still be able to tell the difference between the two sounds – they both may sound like the syllable [ba], but one could be a better [ba] than the other. If that were so, then the categorical perception curves could be an artifact of *labeling* rather than of discrimination (or lack thereof). This would be similar to our perception and labeling of color: we might call two different colors *green* even though we can clearly perceive a difference in the hue. The labeling facts are very important for speech perception: they show that something different happens in the judgments of speech sounds depending on where along a cue's continuum an acoustic difference falls – there is a clear category boundary in this respect.

The point at which perception switches from one speech sound to another is called a **category boundary**. The VOT boundary for voicing differs slightly depending on the place of articulation. For bilabials, such as in Figure 5.6, it's +25 msec, for alveolar +34, and for velar +42.

What *do* we perceive continuously? An example of continuous perception is our perception of pitch as the frequency of a sound changes. When the frequency of a sound increases, we perceive an increase in pitch. We are accurate at assessing whether two frequencies are the same or different (because we perceive different frequencies as different pitches), and, given two sounds with sufficiently different frequencies, we are fairly accurate at judging whether a third sound is closer in frequency to one or the other.

Nevertheless, for understanding how speech perception works, it's important to determine whether listeners really do perceive differences between two sounds, even if they label them the same way. Another kind of experiment, the ABX discrimination task, tests just this question.

In the ABX task, listeners hear two sounds, A & B, that differ along an acoustic dimension, for example, VOT. The listeners then hear the X sound, which is identical to either A or B, and then have to say which alternative (A or B) matches X. If listeners are able to discriminate A and B as different sounds, then it should be clear which one matches X, and the responses should be very accurate. On the other hand, if A and B sound the same to listeners, then they have no basis for deciding which one matches X, and would essentially be guessing. The responses to guesses will be about 50 percent correct, since half the time, by chance, listeners will select the matching sound. Figure 5.10 shows a typical ABX discrimination graph for VOT plotted over the categorical perception curve from Figure 5.9.

The plotted points on the new ABX line (plus signs) fall between the two VOT values that make the A and B for that test item; in other words, the first point falls between 0 and 10 msec, meaning that A was 0 and B was 10 for that test item. The *y*-axis on the right represents the proportion of times listeners correctly matched X to A or B. As you can see, in the very same range of VOT values for which listeners label the syllables as the same, listeners cannot accurately discriminate two syllables that have different VOTs. We know this because the responses fall at the 50 percent correct discrimination level. However, the differences in VOT do lead to high matching accuracy when the A and B syllables fall on *opposite* sides of the category boundary (that is, when one is labeled [pa] and the other [ba]). We see this at the point where the discrimination is close to 100 percent accurate. So the ABX discrimination results are consistent with the forced-choice identification results, in that syllables that are labeled equivalently are also not discriminable.

Summary so far

Our ability to perceive categorically is one way in which we can cope with the lack of invariance in speech. For example, variability in speakers'

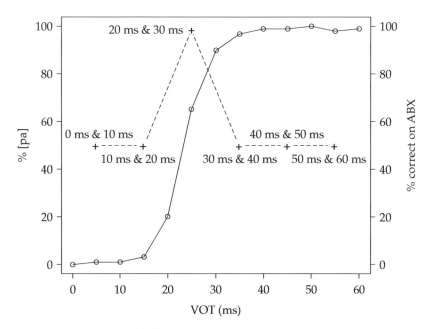

Figure 5.10 Idealized ABX discrimination curve plotted over a categorical perception curve. Values for A and B are indicated for each point on the ABX curve. A & B always differ by 10 ms. Points are plotted between the two values comprising A and B, and chance correct discrimination is 50% (axis on right side).

articulations of VOT in voiced consonants does not confuse us because we treat a range of VOTs as being voiced. Everything we've said about categorical perception of voicing with respect to VOT is true of other acoustic dimensions as well. For example, incremental shifts in formant transitions from, say, a [g] to a [d] do not result in increasingly mixed perceptions of [g]s and [d]s, but rather result in reports of hearing [g] followed by a categorical shift to [d]. ABX discrimination tasks on formant transitions yield similar results as for VOT. The fit between humans' speech perception and production mechanisms

The kind of perception engaged in this speech process has been termed by some researchers a different **mode** of perception from general auditory perception, and one that might be specially evolved for perceiving human speech. In this chapter we will be discussing other facts about categorical perception, some of which challenge this view.

is remarkable: while intending to produce the same phonological unit from instance to instance, speakers introduce acoustic variability due to the nature of fluent speech production, and that's just the kind of variability that listeners' perceptual system "ignores" in determining phonological categories. In contrast, the acoustic variability speakers produce between two intentionally different phonological units is just the variability that yields differing perceptions on the part of listeners.

Categorical perception in infants

Now that we have established what categorical perception is and what advantages it offers in speech perception, we turn to the question of what is the source of categorical perception. Is perceiving speech categorically something we are born with, or is it a skill that has to develop or even that we have to learn? The answer to this question is important because it touches on many aspects of language processing and language development. Most directly, it helps us understand more about a fundamental component of speech perception and how each individual comes to have it. But it also tells us, for example, whether infants and young children hear language as adults do. If there's a period during which they don't perceive speech categorically, or when they perceive different categories than adults, that means that they can't "correctly" hear the words that people around them are uttering. That could pose important limitations on early stages of language learning, as infants' perception of the very words of their language would change as their ability to perceive the adult categories changes.

The question really involves two related but independent questions. The first is about categorical perception in general: is it the way humans normally perceive speech from the first moments after birth? The second is more specific, pertaining to the actual categories infants and children have: once children do perceive speech categorically (whether at birth or later), do they perceive the same categories as adults, or do they have to learn the categories? Below we will look at some research that demonstrates that very young infants perceive speech categorically, and also discuss how categories change with development.

Experiments testing categorical perception in infants

The experiments for assessing categorical perception in adults described above were relatively straightforward: ask an adult whether a syllable is a [pa] or a [ba] (forced-choice identification), and play three sounds for an adult and ask whether the last sound matched the first one or the second one (ABX discrimination). But these kinds of experiments are not possible with infants, for obvious reasons. A number of clever methods have been developed to "ask" infants a range of questions about their perception of language, and you'll read about several of them in this book. A common property of all these methods is to leverage behaviors and proclivities that infants naturally display under various situations and use them to make inferences about their speech perception.

One natural behavior for very young infants is sucking. As you know, infants suck for sustenance, but infants also will suck on something in their mouth if they are excited, amused, entertained, or for comfort. This is called **nonnutritive sucking**, and it can be used as an indication of infants' interest in what's going on around them; the technical term for this is **arousal**. Another characteristic of infants (and perhaps of humans in general), is that they become bored with repetition. Something infants find interesting and exciting on the first encounter becomes less and less stimulating the more they experience it. This is called **habituation**. In the early 1970s a group of researchers developed an experiment that took advantage of these two infant characteristics to test for categorical perception. The experiment was essentially a discrimination experiment, not a labeling experiment. The experiment tests for the discrimination of two sounds by first habituating the infant to one sound (A), then playing the second sound (B) and testing whether the infant **dishabituates**; in other words, does the infant show an increased interest in sound B over the now-boring sound A. If infants dishabituate, it means they must have been able to discriminate A from B. As you may have guessed, the measure of interest in the sounds involves nonnutritive sucking: the more frequently infants suck the more interested they are in what they're hearing.

Now for the details of the experiment. First, to measure nonnutritive sucking, a pacifier is modified with an air-filled tube connected to special hardware and a computer (see Figure 5.11). When the infant sucks on the pacifier, it increases the pressure inside the pacifier, which in turn increases the pressure inside the tube. The special hardware counts this

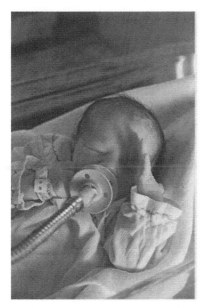

Figure 5.11 Newborn sucking on pacifier connected to an air-filled tube. The other end of the tube is attached to a device that measures changes of pressure in the tube caused by the infant sucking. Photo used by permission from Anne Christophe.

pressure increase as a suck and records how many sucks per minute the infant produces.

At the start of the experiment, before any sound is played, infants will naturally suck from time to time on the pacifier placed in their mouth. This establishes a **baseline sucking rate** for each infant, and also allows the researchers to calibrate the system to the range of intensities of the infants' sucking responses. Then the more intense sucks are "rewarded" by playing a syllable. Infants are interested by this, which causes them to suck at a faster rate, and more intensely; this, in turn, provides them with repetitions of the syllable, each time they produce an intense suck. For a while, this results in a considerable increase in sucking rate over the baseline. But then, since the sound never changes, the infants begin to get bored and the sucking rate decreases. Several continuous minutes of a decreasing sucking rate indicates that the infant has habituated to the syllable. Up to this point, all infants participating in the experiment have heard the same sound. But at the point of habituation, a given infant participates in one of three different versions, or **conditions** of the experiment. In the Same condition, an alternate version of the same sound in played. For example, if the first sound (A) was a [ba] with a VOT of +20 msec, the second sound (B) might be a 0 msec VOT [ba]. In the Different condition, the sound is switched to a different adult category. However, the *acoustic* difference between the A and B is *the same* as the acoustic difference in the Same condition. For example, the +20 msec [ba] is switched to a +40 msec [pa] after habituation. In *both* conditions, the difference in VOT between A and B is 20 msec, but in one case A and B are different adult categories and in the other case they are not. Finally, in the Control condition, the sound is not changed.

Again, discrimination of A and B is indicated by dishabituation and an increase in sucking rate after the syllable is switched. If infants' perception of VOT were continuous, then they should behave similarly in the Different and Same conditions, since the difference in VOT is 20 msec in both cases. What the researchers found, however, was that infants perceive VOT categorically: they dishabituated in the Different condition but not in the Same condition (nor, of course, in the Control condition). Moreover, the boundary that defines the voicing category for infants was found to be the same as for adults: about +25 msec for bilabial stops. Additional experiments went on to test categorical perception of VOT using different places of articulation, and also to test categorical perception of formant transitions and place of articulation. The results of all of these studies demonstrate that infants perceive speech categorically, as adults do. Furthermore, infants' category boundaries are just the ones that occur in the languages of the world.

So, returning to the questions we began with: it does appear that infants perceive speech categorically, at least as early as one month of age.

It also appears that they do not have to completely learn all the categories they need, as the phonological boundaries they start with are all used in at least some languages. However, that does not mean that no learning has to take place. As discussed in earlier chapters, languages differ in which category contrasts they make: what are distinct categories in one language (e.g., aspirated vs. unaspirated stops in Thai) are not contrastive in others (e.g., in English). Consequently adult speakers of different languages perceive the same piece of an acoustic signal differently, depending on what language they speak. Below, you'll find out about some fundamental discoveries about when infants "tune in" to the particular categories for their language.

The tuning of categories through experience: Phonological acquisition
The experiments on speech perception in early infancy, including the one you just read about, showed that infants perceive virtually all the contrasts that human languages make use of. Since adults do *not* perceive contrasts that their language does not use, this is a rare example of infants having greater capabilities than adults! But of greater scientific interest, it means that following experience with their particular language, infants learn to attend only to the contrasts that are important in their language and lose the ability to perceive potential contrasts that are not at work in their language. This process is called **phonological development**. We give an overview here of experiments that have examined the time course of phonological development in children.

The most general question these studies have asked is: how quickly does phonological development happen? While the details differ slightly for consonants and vowels, within the first year of life infants appear to learn how to selectively perceive only the contrasts in their language, and lose the ability to perceive other contrasts. For both types of speech sound, by the time they are only a year old infants appear to perceive only the categories that are contrastive in the language they've grown up with. What kind of experiments lead to these conclusions?

A typical experiment in phonological development uses the **conditioned headturn** procedure. Headturns are another natural behavior for babies. Similar to the nonnutritive sucking procedure, the conditioned headturn procedure tests for discrimination, but rather than using habituation and recovery from habituation as the indicator of discrimination, this procedure does something different. The other natural behavior the experiment makes use of is infants' inherent interest in stimulation. The experiment *conditions* or trains infants to realize that they can get a reward when they hear a change in the repetition of a background syllable. The conditioning is achieved by repeating the same syllable through a loudspeaker, then changing to a contrasting syllable – one that the infant is known to be able to discriminate. For an English-learning infant, this might mean starting, for example, with [ba] and switching to [da]. A short (and variable) time after the switch, an interesting, attention-getting event – typically involving stuffed toys becoming "magically" animated with blinking lights and sounds – is made to occur off to one side of the room. Infants naturally orient their gaze towards the activity and find it enjoyable to watch the display. Soon, the infants associate the switch in syllable to the imminent activation of the toys and will turn to the toys' direction *in anticipation* of their activation. Looking *in advance* of the toys activating is the conditioned response that indicates that the infant perceived the switch in sounds; only noticing that a switch has occurred would allow the infant to reliably predict the upcoming activation of the toys.

Next, this learned response is used to test for the infant's ability to discriminate two nonnative sounds. In one such experiment, Janet Werker and her colleagues tested English-learning infants' ability to discriminate the two ejective stops (see Chapter 3) in the minimal pairs [k'a] and [q'a], which differ in the place of articulation. These are contrastive sounds in the Salish language Nthlakapmx (spoken in British Columbia); however, both consonants sound more or less like [k] to adult English speakers, who cannot discriminate between them. Ⓦ If infants can discriminate the two minimal pairs, they should look in the direction of the toys right after the switch, but *before* the toys become active. Turning to the toys immediately after the sound switch but before the "reward" of the toys being animated, indicates that they heard the switch and therefore can discriminate the two sounds. The researchers tested infants at different ages and found that younger infants (up to about eight months) could discriminate the two sounds, but older infants could not (just as adults cannot).

Researchers have examined a range of contrasts in a variety of languages, with infant learners of a range of languages as subjects. The overall conclusion from these studies is that infants are born with the ability to perceive all the contrasts used by the languages of the world. But between 8–10 months, infants lose the ability to perceive most consonant contrasts that are not meaningful in their language. So, by the time they are a year old, infants can no longer perceive contrasts that they could perceive less than six months earlier if their language doesn't utilize those sounds. For vowels, the selective tuning happens even earlier, starting at around six months of age.

Categorical perception for speech in nonhumans

Many researchers viewed the existence of categorical perception as an indication that human speech perception involves a special mode of processing that is specifically linguistic. If this were so, one would not expect to find this kind of processing in other species. But what if it were discovered that other animals also perceive speech categorically?

In the 1970s, Patricia Kuhl and James Miller set out to test this question by testing for categorical perception of VOT in a nonhuman animal species. Testing animals in categorical perception experiments encounters similar problems as testing infants – how do you ask if they've heard a [ta] or a [da]? They had to train the animals to respond in distinct ways to different sounds, which meant that they had to test animals that could be (relatively) easily trained. They also wanted to test a species that had a similar enough auditory system to humans so that it would be reasonable to expect that the sounds would be encoded in roughly the same way when entering the brain. For these scientific requirements, they chose the chinchilla. Chinchillas can be trained in the laboratory, and they also have auditory systems similar to humans' (e.g., they have a similar cochlea). They're also cuter than rats (see Figure 5.12).

The experiment involved first training the chinchilla to respond differently to speech sounds at the ends of the VOT continuum. The animal was placed in a cage that had a water dispenser at one end. The dispenser was rigged so that it only allowed water to flow after a number of licks by the chinchilla, so that the animal would have be motivated to be on that side of the cage. At various times a syllable would be played, either a 0 ms VOT [da] or a +80 ms VOT [pa]. After one type of syllable, say [da], the animal would receive a mild shock from a pad located beneath the floor if it didn't run to the other side of the cage after the sound was played. After the other sound, [ta], the water dispenser would freely dispense water for a brief period. Chinchillas learned to accurately move to the safe

Figure 5.12 Chinchilla research subject.

side of the cage after hearing [da], and to stay at the water station after hearing [ta]. This training allowed the researchers essentially to "ask" the chinchillas whether they thought they heard a [da] or [ta], by observing their behavior after playing the syllable. So next the researchers played synthesized syllables that varied along the VOT continuum, just as in the human adult labeling experiments, and they observed whether the animals moved (indicating that they perceived a [da]) or stayed near the water (indicating that they heard a [ta]). They also tested human adults on the same sounds. What they found was a striking correspondence between the human labeling results and the chinchillas' behavior. Chinchillas would move to the "safe" side of the cage for one range of VOTs, and stay near the water for another range. Chinchillas, therefore, appeared to perceive speech categorically. Moreover, the VOT boundary that differentiated the two responses was around +33 msec – almost identical to humans.

The remarkable overlap between human's and chinchilla's perception of speech provides an alternative explanation of human speech perception. Since chinchillas were not likely to have evolved special processing mechanisms for human speech, it must be something about the nature of their normal auditory processing mechanisms that produces categorical perception. And since our auditory systems are similar to theirs, it strongly suggests that categorical perception in humans may be due to similar normal processing mechanisms. Human speech may have evolved to take advantage of certain boundaries created by processing mechanisms, rather than the other way around.

Categorical perception for nonspeech in nonhumans

We discussed how categorical perception provides a solution for dealing with some aspects of the lack of invariance in speech. Other species also use sound for social and survival functions – for example to identify a friend or a foe – even if they don't have speech. One might expect that these auditory signals are also subject to variability, and therefore might benefit from something like categorical perception.

This idea was tested on a species far removed from humans and chinchillas: the cricket. Crickets use sound for rudimentary social functions. For example, crickets emit sounds at 4–5 kilohertz (a kilohertz is 1,00 Hertz – 1,000 cycles per second – and is abbreviated kHz) to identify themselves to other crickets – this is a sound that attracts them. In contrast, bats, predators of crickets, produce higher frequency sounds (upwards of 25 kHz) for echolocation – this is a sound that crickets want to avoid! Crickets, then, have different responses to sounds at different locations across the *frequency continuum*: at the lower frequency end, they might want to approach the source of the sound, but at the higher frequency end, they would want to flee. How do crickets respond to sounds along the continuum? Does their likelihood of approaching or fleeing depend on the closeness of the sound to one end or the other of the frequency continuum, as would be expected if their perception of frequency was continuous? Or is there a category boundary at some frequency such that lower frequencies result in consistent approach behavior, and higher frequencies result in consistent fleeing, as would be the case in categorical perception?

Researchers tested crickets' perception in two kinds of tasks: a "labeling" task and a discrimination task. In the labeling task, crickets in flight were played cricket-like sounds that varied in frequency between 4 and 40 kHz. It was noted whether they altered their flight in a way that suggested that they interpreted the sound as attractive or threatening. Interestingly, crickets always showed one of these responses (they never just ignored the sound or flew in confused circles). And furthermore, sounds below about 13–16 kHz were categorically treated as attractive, and sounds above that were categorically treated as threats.

The discrimination task resembled the habituation–dishabituation experiment with human infants. Crickets habituate to repetitions of threat sounds, so that they show less and less of a fleeing response the more times they hear the sound – in other words, they habituate to the sound. Discrimination of two sounds can be determined by measuring whether crickets *dishabituate* – show an increased fleeing response – to a second sound after habituating to the first sound. Crickets showed discrimination of sounds only when they came from opposite sides of the same category boundary that was implicated in the labeling experiment. In other words, crickets have good between-category and poor within-category discrimination, a hallmark of categorical perception. Interestingly, sound in frequencies above about 5 kHz and below about 25 kHz serve no known survival function for crickets, yet they do not ignore these sounds, and they are not equivocal about them; those middle-frequency sounds are also categorized as friend or foe.

These experiments suggest that categorical perception may indeed be special, but not special for speech and not special to humans. Rather, it may be a strategy that has evolved in animals to efficiently and accurately process sounds that are important for survival.

Categorical perception in other domains

So far, all of our discussion about categorical perception, whether in humans or nonhumans, for speech or nonspeech, has focused on the auditory modality, in other words, sound. However, categorical perception would be useful in other domains as well. For example, visually identifying (same species) individuals is something that's very important socially to humans and other animals. Yet each time we look at someone, the visual signal is somewhat different. The differences could be due to relatively minor things, like a change in the person's hairstyle, or more (visually) significant things, like a change in the direction or intensity of the lighting or viewing the individual from a different angle. All these potential changes mean that the image on the retina from one viewing to the next of the same person will be different; in other words, there is a lack of invariance in visually identifying individuals. It would be advantageous, then, if something like categorical perception operated in visually perceiving individuals, so that we could effortlessly identify our friends and family, regardless of the orientation of their head, the lighting, and so on. In fact, experiments have shown that humans have just such a capacity.

James Beale and Frank Keil carried out a clever series of experiments showing categorical perception for famous faces. Recall in the speech domain, speech sounds were artificially synthesized to fall in consistent intervals across an acoustic–phonetic dimension, like VOT or F3 transition, where the endpoints of the continuum corresponded to two different consonants. Similarly, Beale and Keil defined a continuum of faces with the endpoints being images of two famous people, for example President John F. Kennedy and President Clinton. The continuum was created by synthesizing visual images using visual "morphing" software. The software started with one endpoint face and incrementally modified it, little by little, until it matched the other endpoint face. Some of the steps along the way were used as the intermediate faces, somewhere on the (artificial) visual continuum between JFK and Clinton. The researchers used three face-pair continua: JFK and Clinton, Pete Townsend and Sylvester Stallone, and Arnold Schwarzenegger and Clint Eastwood. Subjects in the experiment participated in both an ABX discrimination task and a forced-choice labeling task.

The results from both kinds of judgment tasks were strikingly similar to categorical perception results in speech perception. In the forced-choice labeling task, there was a clear boundary in subjects' judgments. That is, there was a point along the face continuum such that subjects labeled all faces on one side as JFK and all faces on the other side as Clinton. The labeling boundary correlated with results from the ABX task: two faces were easier to discriminate when they were drawn from different sides of the boundary, but were difficult to discriminate when they were drawn from the same side of the boundary, though the number of morph-steps in each situation was identical. These findings are analogous to the way speech sounds that differ in VOT, for example, are discriminated and labeled.

There is an interesting difference between categorical perception for faces compared to speech. We saw that, in speech perception, infants start out perceiving categorically virtually all contrasts a language might make, and then lose the ability to perceive contrasts their language doesn't use. In speech, experience and familiarity with the sounds was necessary to maintain categorical perception that was in place from the start. In contrast, the establishment of categorical perception for faces appears to require experience and familiarity to arise. When faces were of unfamiliar, or of less well-known individuals, perception was not categorical: there were no clear face category boundaries, and face-pairs were just as easy to discriminate no matter where on the continuum they fell. With faces, then, experience and familiarity seems to be required for categorical perception to come into play. This might be because the particular "face categories" (i.e., individuals) that will end up being important to recognize varies from person to person to a much greater degree than in speech, so face perception has to be more flexible.

Such differences in the operation of categorical perception for speech and faces are important for understanding the details of how these processes function, for example, at Marr's algorithmic level (see Chapter 1). But the similarities are telling as well: in a domain other than speech, in which we must have constant perceptions in the presence of variable signals, we perceive categorically – we have good between-category discrimination and poor within-category discrimination. Categorical perception may be a general way that our perceptual systems have evolved to cope with perceiving and representing our environment.

Shifting Category Boundaries

We have discussed several ways in which categorical perception is well suited for dealing with the variability that is inherent in the auditory speech signal. Here we discuss additional properties of categorical perception that demonstrate further ways in which our perceptual mechanisms operate to make perceiving speech more robust. In particular we discuss two very different ways in which the category boundaries we use to distinguish speech sounds – for example, the voicing boundary on the VOT dimension – can shift, depending on the context in which a target speech sound is produced. We look at one kind of shift that considers bottom-up information (see Section 1) relating to coarticulation, and another kind of shift that considers top-down information relating to a listener's vocabulary. As we will see, in both cases, the result is a shift in how we perceive speech that "makes sense" in light of the other pieces of information available to us.

Compensation for coarticulation: Bottom-up effects on category boundaries

One of the benefits of categorical perception is that a speech sound will be perceived as intended by the speaker, even if the speaker introduces some articulatory, and hence acoustic variation from production to production. Some sources of variability are basically random, but other can be predicted somewhat from the presence of coarticulation. For example, consider the syllables [da] and [ga], which differ only in the place of articulation in the consonant. In isolation – that is, not coarticulated with any preceding sound – the constriction for the [d] in [da] is produced at the alveolar ridge, in other words, forward in the mouth. In contrast, the constriction for [g] in [ga] is velar, in other words, relatively far back in the mouth. Now we'll consider what happens in the production of these consonants in fluent speech, when they are coarticulated with a preceding consonant. For this discussion, we'll consider VC_1C_2V sequences, where the second consonant (C_2) is the [g] or [d] we just discussed. The articulations of the two consonants partially overlap, and so dimensions like the place of articulation of C_1 can alter the way C_2 is produced. To take some specific examples, let's consider [da] and [ga] each preceded by [al] and each preceded by [ar]. Looking at the effects of C_1 on C_2, in the case of [alda] the coarticulation of [l] with [d] does not change the production of [d] that much because they have the same place of articulation. In contrast, the lingual constriction for [r] is farther back than for [d], so, when coarticulated, the [d] constriction will be pulled farther back, having an effect on the formant values. Things are reversed for [ga]. In the case of [g], coarticulation with [l] shifts the otherwise low third formant of [g] a bit higher, and coarticulation with [r] has a minimal effect.

To understand the coarticulation effects on the formant transitions, let's review the differences between [d] and [g] by looking at spectrograms of the syllables [da] and [ga]. Figure 5.13 shows F1, F2, and F3 for a synthesized version of each syllable. The primary difference is in the F3

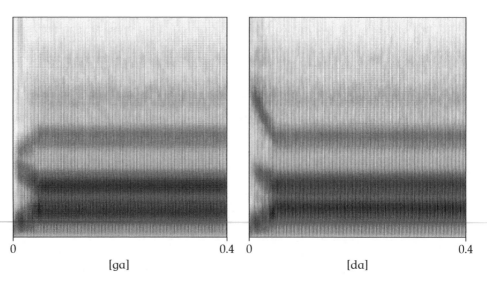

0   0.4 0   0.4

[ga]   [da]

Figure 5.13 Spectrograms of synthesized syllables [ga] and [da] showing F1, F2, and F3.

transition. Coarticulation of the type we just discussed would result in an F3 transition for [ga] that would start at a higher frequency (closer to that for [da]) when preceded by [l] versus [r], and the F3 transition for [da] would start slightly lower when preceded by [r] versus [l].

As we discussed earlier, the F3 dimension is another dimension on which we perceive speech categorically: there is an F3 start-frequency value that is a typical boundary for perceptually distinguishing between [da] and [ga]. The coarticulation effects on F3 of the type just discussed effectively bring [d] and [g] closer to that boundary. In particular, [d] following [r] is closer to the boundary (compared to no coarticulation), and likewise, [g] following [l] is closer to the boundary. When discussing categorical perception curves, we noted that right around the boundary there is some ambiguity in identifying the consonant, so one might expect that coarticulation might make the perception of C_2 less clear or less certain when F3 shifts closer to the boundary. Interestingly, however, it turns out that our speech perception mechanisms are sensitive to coarticulation effects. Our category boundary on the F3 transition dimension *shifts* depending on the context in which the consonant is occurring. If a coarticulated constriction influences an upcoming (or following) constriction, the perceptual system is able to take this into account. This means a particular acoustic signal that is perceived as a [ga] when it follows [al] might be perceived as a [da] when it follows an [ar], or when it is heard by itself. In other words, how the second consonant is categorized is influenced by the identity of the first consonant, resulting in another one-to-many relationship between the acoustic signal and perception. This perceptual adjustment is called **compensation for coarticulation**, because it shifts the category boundary in a way that compensates for the acoustic effects of coarticulation. Without this compensation, we might indeed misperceive consonants that were articulated close to a typical category boundary. By shifting the boundary according to context, we avoid these potential misperceptions.

Experimental evidence for compensation for coarticulation involves having subjects perform forced-choice identification on synthesized syllables where the F3 transition is made to be somewhere between that for [ga] and that for [da]. This is just like a typical categorical perception test. The difference is that the consonant to be identified is preceded by another syllable, say [ar] or [al]. Figure 5.14 shows three simulated categorical perception curves for an experiment like this. The solid line represents the percentage of [da] responses in a neutral context, the dashed line represents the percentage of [da] responses in the context of [al], and the dotted line represents the percentage of [da] responses in the context of [ar].

Compensation for coarticulation is another example of how cues to speech sounds are interpreted in context. The perception of a consonant that results from a particular pattern of formant transitions depends on what other

Figure 5.14
Identification curves
showing shifting of
[da]-[ga] category
boundary depending
on the preceding
phonetic context. For
example, item 5 (on the
x-axis) is ambiguous
between [da] and [ga]
when heard alone
(middle curve) but is
heard as [da] when
preceded by [ar] (left
curve) and as [ga]
when preceded by [al]
(right curve).

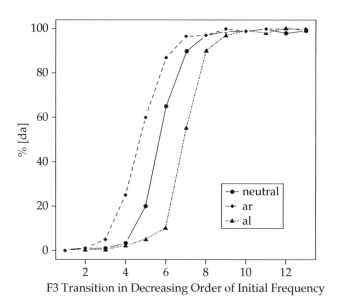

F3 Transition in Decreasing Order of Initial Frequency

speech sounds occur before it. This is also, then, another example of the relationship between speech *perception* and speech *production*: the way speech is perceived reflects facts about the way it is produced.

The Ganong Effect: Top down influence on category boundaries

The ultimate goal of perceiving speech is understanding the message or idea the speaker had in mind, as conveyed in a spoken utterance. An important part of the process is recognizing the individual words the speaker uttered, as well as their order in the utterance. We will discuss word recognition in more depth in Chapter 6, but for now it's simply important to realize that extracting words from the speech signal is the reason correctly identifying the consonants and vowels is important for listeners: they are the building blocks of words.

An important discovery in speech perception was that our **lexicon**, or knowledge of words, has a **top-down** influence on how we perceive speech. In particular, word knowledge can shift categorical boundaries just as compensation for coarticulation does. A researcher named William Ganong synthesized syllables containing consonants that were acoustically near a category boundary. For example, he synthesized a [de], such that the VOT for the [d] was close to the boundary, around +15 msec; listeners all agreed they heard [de]. Other subjects were played the same sound with the consonant [p] spliced (pasted) on to the end. You might expect, logically, that listeners would hear [dep], a nonword, as a result. However, listeners reported hearing the real word *tape* [tep] instead. It's as though the VOT boundary had shifted slightly in order to make a word rather than a nonword – in fact, that's exactly what happened.

This phenomenon was coined **the Ganong effect**, after the scientist who discovered it. It is further evidence for the role of top-down processing in speech perception because it shows that the abstract knowledge of words in the language affects lower-level processes of perception. In the example above, a sound that would normally be perceived as voiced is perceived as voiceless, guided by top-down word knowledge.

Duplex Perception

We have been discussing ways in which speech sounds are processed and categorized in special ways (although we have also seen examples showing that some special ways of processing like categorical perception are not unique to speech or even to humans). A classic series of experiments at Haskins Laboratories demonstrated that the brain processes speech in two different ways at the same time, both as speech and simply as sound. **Duplex perception** refers to the dual modes of perceiving speech sounds. These experiments work by starting with a normal speech sample, such as a CV syllable, and splitting the formant transitions into two parts, one that's played to the right ear and one that's played to the left ear. The sound either ear receives independently is not normal speech, and in some cases it is processed simply as sound. But at the same time, that nonspeech-like portion is integrated by the brain with the other portion, and in that context, it's perceived as speech. The listener hears thus both a word and a noise simultaneously. So the *same* signal is perceived as speech and nonspeech (normal sound) at the same time.

Let's look more closely at a specific example of this kind of duplex perception experiment. Figure 5.15 shows the spectrogram for [da] that has been digitally manipulated. There are actually two spectrograms, representing the sounds that are played separately to the left and right ears. On the left is simply the formant transition for the third formant, and on the right is the rest of the syllable (without the formant transition). We'll call the latter the **base**, as it contains the majority of the signal. The left and right portions are presented to its respective ear through headphones – a method that is called **dichotic presentation** – but let's first consider what each portion sounds like by itself.

The F3 formant transition is very nonspeech-like. Heard alone, it sounds like a very short "chirp" falling in pitch. It does not trigger any kind of speech recognition in listeners. Nevertheless, as we discussed earlier, in normal speech it critically contributes to our perception of the place of articulation of the consonant that starts the syllable. Indeed, listeners who hear the base without the F3 transition – something that couldn't

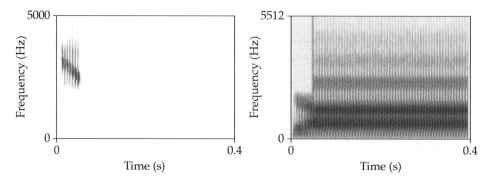

Figure 5.15   Two spectrograms representing the left and right channel in a duplex perception experiment. The F3 transition is excised from the original signal and presented in isolation to one ear while concurrently the syllable without the transition (the base) is presented to the other. Listeners hear an unambiguous syllable ([da]) and also a "chirp" corresponding to the F3 transition.

normally be produced by a human vocal tract – hear an ambiguous sound, sometimes sounding like a [da], sometimes like a [ga], or even a [ba]. In normal circumstances when the F3 transition is fully integrated with the base and the whole syllable is heard in both ears, the transition is a cue to the identity of the consonant and the "chirp" perception is not experienced at all. However, a fascinating thing happens when the transition and the base are artificially separated between the two ears. Listeners report hearing the "chirp" from the isolated F3 transition, but they *also* report clearly hearing a [da]. Recall that the base by itself is ambiguous and not necessarily heard as a [da]. This means that the F3 transition contributed to the interpretation of the base, even though the two pieces of the syllable signal were heard by different ears – at some level of processing the sounds were integrated and treated as a whole, giving rise to a clear consonant percept. *But at the same time*, the F3 transition was processed as raw sound, creating the perception of the "chirp." The transition was processed in two ways simultaneously, as speech and as simple sound. That is the phenomenon of duplex perception.

Duplex perception and categorical perception

Earlier in this chapter we mentioned that categorical perception is involved in perceiving place of articulation, as cued by formant transitions. We briefly mentioned a version of a categorical perception experiment in which the F3 transition was synthetically made to vary between a frequency onset for a [da] and a frequency onset for a [ga] (see Figure 5.7). What happens when that *varying* F3 transition is presented *dichotically* only to one ear and the base to the other? Do listeners still perceive the same category in duplex perception for these intermediate transitions as they do when both ears receive the full signal? Is the F3 "chirp" also perceived categorically?

In fact, the true "dual" character of duplex perception becomes even more apparent when just such an experiment is performed. When subjects are asked to report what syllable they hear, they report hearing [da] or [ga], and what they perceive depends on the starting frequency of the F3 transition. It's the same as if they heard the transition and base as one complete signal, rather than dichotically; the category boundary is unaffected. As in the case of the single F3 transition, the two separate pieces of the signal are integrated by the brain and treated as a normal speech sound, subject to the same categorical perception processes. However, as before, the F3 transition is also perceived as a "chirp"; but now, as the F3 transition varies along the continuum, different transitions are perceived as *different* "chirps," even if they fall on the *same* side of the [ga]–[da] boundary (e.g., listeners can discriminate them in an ABX task). In other words, when two different [ga] transitions are perceived as part of the speech signal, they both give rise to the same [ga] perception, but their simultaneous processing as simple sound yields a clearly perceived difference in that sound. The brain treats the F3 transition in two distinct ways, simultaneously.

Summary of Section 2

Section 2 of this chapter dealt with some ways in which listeners deal with variability in the speech signal. One way we cope with variability is to perceive a range of values on a phonetic dimension (e.g., VOT) as one category. Category boundaries are shifted in sensible ways depending on the context of other sounds (compensation for coarticulation) and the expectations that sound sequences should form words. Perceiving continuously varying dimensions categorically is a very general phenomenon, occurring in other domains, and across species. Key topics from this section are:

- Categorical perception of speech
- Categorical perception of faces
- Categorical perception in other species (for human speech and other sounds)
- Compensation for coarticulation
- The Ganong effect
- Duplex perception

Section 3: Discovering Words

So far, we've talked about some of the complexities in perceiving speech sounds, and about how listeners make use of a variety of cues to help in interpreting the information in the speech signal. As complex as that is, it's only a first step in comprehending speech. It's all well and good to perceive the sounds, but those sounds make up words – the fundamental meaning-bearing units of language. Perceiving speech sounds is in service of perceiving the words that they make up. We devote a whole chapter to discuss **word recognition**, and the issues involved in activating words in our **mental lexicon**. But in the remainder of this chapter we discuss simply how listeners detect words in fluent speech – how they figure out where one word ends and the next word begins. This is the problem of **word segmentation**.

Word Segmentation by Fluent Language Users

It may be difficult at first to appreciate that understanding how word segmentation occurs is really a scientific challenge since we, as fluent speakers, have no trouble identifying the words we hear and figuring out when a word begins and ends. We simply perceive distinct words. One could even go so far as to say that our auditory perception of words mirrors what our visual perception is like in reading. Words on the page are separated by white space, providing clear visual boundaries between words, and we have the perceptual sense of clear boundaries between aurally processed words as well. Are there acoustic boundaries like spaces on a page? The most natural, analogous kind of boundary would be small silences between words. But in fact, in fluent speech there are very few silences between words, and there are many instances in which small silences occur within words (such as during voiceless stops). Figure 5.16 shows the waveform and spectrogram of the sentence, "Where were you a year ago?", spoken by one of the authors of this book (can you figure out which one). As you can see, there is continuous energy throughout all the word boundaries, and there is a brief silence (or at least relatively low energy) before the release of the [g] in *ago*. Putting this in the language from Section 2: there is no one-to-one correspondence between silences in fluent speech and word boundaries – many short silences occur within words, and many word boundaries do not coincide with silence. Furthermore, there appears to be no cue directly accessible in the acoustic signal that reliably corresponds to word boundaries. In other words, word segmentation is subject to a lack of invariance, just like the identification of speech sounds.

For fluent speakers and comprehenders of a language, the lack of invariant cues to word boundaries in the speech signal is not terribly

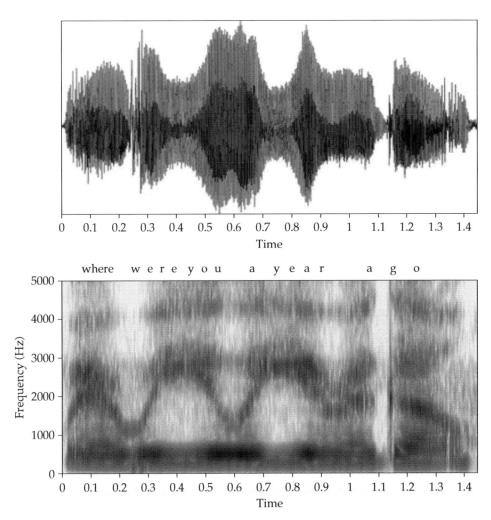

Figure 5.16 Waveform and spectrogram for the sentence *Where were you a year ago?* There is no one-to-one correspondence between points of minimal acoustic energy and word boundaries.

problematic. This is because we have a number of **segmentation strategies** at our disposal for making very good guesses about where words begin and end. As with the process of speech perception we discussed earlier, we generally employ these strategies automatically, unconsciously, and efficiently, which is in part why most people are unaware that segmentation is an accomplished skill. What are these strategies, and what kinds of representations and processes do they involve?

Perhaps the most obvious method for determining when a new word begins is recognizing that you just heard the end of a word, so the next sounds have to be the start of a new one. This would mean that we simply listen to the sounds coming in, and we recognize when the sequence of sounds matches a word that we know. Indeed, there is evidence that fluent language users use this strategy. As simple as it may sound, Chapter 6 will examine the processes by which comprehenders actually recognize known words, and some of the challenges and ambiguities in those processes. One aspect of those challenges that is relevant for the issue of segmentation is that there are frequent situations where possible real words occur within other words. An example is in the previous sentence: the word *within* contains (in both spelling and sounds) the word *with* and the word *in*. So if the only segmentation strategy listeners used was to segment (construe a word boundary) immediately after they recognized a word, they would make many errors. One segmentation error could have ripple effects and cause further confusion as the listener hears more of the utterance. For example, imagine if *within* occurred in the phrase "within supportable amounts." Missegmenting *with* results in the sequence *in supportable*, which is two words that could be interpreted as one: *insupportable*. As you can imagine, the errors could quickly grow, leading to increased confusion and lack of communication. Indeed, these kind of errors do occur, and you're probably aware of them happening to you occasionally. Nevertheless, they are not the norm, and they occur far less frequently than they could. Listeners are apparently using other sources of information as well to segment words. As we'll see in Chapter 6, some of this information involves the content of what is being said, and listeners' judgments about what likely segmentations might be based on that context, but there are other kinds of information that are more direct properties of the speech signal that listeners also appear to use.

One such cue involves the **stress patterns** of words. As we will see in Chapter 7, in any English word with more than one syllable, one of the syllables is more prominent than the others: it is generally louder, longer, and often has more variability in pitch than the other syllables in the word. This is the syllable with **primary stress**. Some longer words also have syllables with secondary stress, but for our discussion of word segmentation, we'll use "stressed syllable" to refer to the syllable with primary stress. In many languages, stressed syllables can be useful cues to word boundaries. For example, in English, nearly 90 percent of the words we typically encounter in everyday speech have stress on the first syllable. This means that when listeners hear a stressed syllable they would often be accurate in assuming that it begins a new word. But, as with the previous strategy, it is not error-free. Words like *excuse* have primary stress on the second syllable, so requiring stressed syllables at the beginnings of words would result in *cuse* without the *ex* – an undesirable result. These, too, are not errors we make all the time, but they are among the most common types of errors in segmenting words in fluent speech.

A third kind of information fluent adult listeners can use is information about the phonotactic constraints of their language. Recall from Chapter 3 that one way in which languages differ is in the sequences of sounds they allow in various positions in words and syllables, called phonotactic constraints. For example, the sequence [bk] would be very rare within words in English. Therefore, when listeners hear that sequence, they know there is a boundary between the [b] and the [k]. There is considerable evidence that comprehenders are sensitive to the phonotactic regularities in their native language and do indeed segment words based on phonotactic constraints. However, as accurate as sequences like [bk] might be as cues to word boundaries, in many cases the junction between words contains sequences that are perfectly legal within words. That is, many word boundaries could not be detected by considering only phonotactic constraints. As with the types of information previously discussed, phonotactic information is just one of many sources of information available to fluent language users to figure out where the words are in a continuous stream of speech.

Learning to Segment Words

There is evidence that fluent, adult language users consider all the information sources just discussed when segmenting words from fluent speech. The integration and use of these various sources of information is subtle and not entirely understood. It's interesting to consider that successful word segmentation is one of the aspects of computer speech processing that has been notoriously difficult to achieve. Given the ambiguity in the speech signal and the variety of cues that fluent language users use to segment words from speech, it's natural to ask how infants perform word segmentation. The question is particularly interesting because a commonality in all of the word segmentation strategies you just read about is that they call on aspects of people's knowledge of their native language. Obviously, recognizing words as they unfold in fluent speech requires having a vocabulary. But the way in which stress coincides with word boundaries, or even if stress is a reliable cues at all, varies from language to language. Whereas in English most words begin with a stressed syllable, in French, words with two syllables carry stress on the final syllable. Therefore, stress plays a different role in segmentation for listeners of French than it does for listeners of English, and the particular way of using stress must be learned during the language acquisition process. In a language like Russian, stress is not a reliable boundary cue at all. Finally, by definition, phonotactic constraints are specific to languages, such that sound sequences that are not permitted within words in one language may be permitted in another. So the particular phonotactic constraints that are relevant for word segmentation in a given language have to be learned. This is one reason why you might be comfortable reading a foreign language, but have a lot of difficulty understanding it when spoken. Simply segmenting the words

In this context, the term **bootstrapping** refers to a seed process or source of information that gets a developmental or learning processes going. The origin of the term comes from *bootstraps* – the straps of leather, or other material, attached to some styles of boots that aid in pulling the boots onto one's feet. In word segmentation, since many segmentation strategies require already knowing some words, infants need a bootstrap that provide them with sufficient information about word boundaries to start to learn some word forms in order to put those strategies to use.

can be a challenge if you are not using the correct strategies for the foreign language, and if your vocabulary is not very large.

In sum, none of the strategies outlined above could be used by infants before they know a sizeable number of words in their language: (1) they must have already segmented a sufficient number of words to be able to use words themselves as a basis for segmentation, (2) they have to have already segmented words in order to figure out what way (if any) stress patterns within words, and (3) they have to have already segmented words in order to start to figure out what the phonotactic regularities are in their language. So, without the benefit of the cues to word boundaries that proficient language users rely on, how do infants initially break into the words of their language? This is called a **bootstrapping** problem.

Infants' sensitivity to repeated patterns in continuous speech

While it is not known conclusively how infants initially segment fluent speech into words, a number of studies have pointed to a kind of information that is related to phonotactic constraints but that does not require already knowing words in order to use. The information has to do with how likely it is that sequences of sounds (or syllables) follow each other in spoken language. The assumption is that two sounds that co-occur in sequence within a word, like the syllables [prɪ]+[ti] in *pretty*, are more likely to occur together in a sample of spoken language than sequences that occur across word boundaries, like [ti]+[be] in *pretty baby*. There is no phonotactic constraint that prohibits [ti]+[be] within words, but the idea is that simply because the sequence [prɪ]+[ti] is within a word, they will be more likely to occur in sequence (one after another). This is because every time the word occurs, the sounds will occur in sequence, but the word that follows can begin with almost any syllable. Therefore, when infants hear a sequence of two sounds that they've frequently heard together, they can be pretty safe in assuming that there is not a boundary between them. On the other hand, if they hear two sounds that don't often occur together, they can make a good guess that one sound is the end of one word and the other sound is the beginning of another word.

Experiments have shown that infants as young as eight months of age use this kind of information to segment continuous sequences of syllables into smaller word-like units. One of the initial demonstrations of this by Jenny Saffran and her colleagues involved constructing a miniature "language" composed of a handful of words that could occur in any order (obviously not like any real language, but probably sufficient for testing word segmentation). The words were not words of English, but they could be, in that they included only sounds of English and did not violate phonotactic rules. The words were placed one after another and randomly repeated to create a final sequence that was around two minutes long, repeating each word 45 times. The sequence of words was produced by a speech synthesizer to enable precise control: there were no breaks between words, and the sequence was produced in a monotone pitch and without stress differences from syllable to syllable. This ensured that stress could not be used as a cue to word boundaries. Finally, a crucial feature of the words was that any particular syllable only occurred in one "word." This has the effect that, within a word, the transition from one syllable to the next is perfectly predictable. In contrast, at the end of a word, the transition from the last syllable to the first syllable of the following word is variable, since any word could follow. For example, the entire sequence might contain sections as follows (shown orthographically):

pabikutibudodaropi . . . tibudogolatupabiku . . . golatutibudopabiku . . .

Note that whenever *ti* occurs it is always followed by *bu*, which is then always followed by *do*; that is because *tibudo* is one of the words, and its syllables only occur within that word in the sequence. In contrast *do*, which occurs before a word boundary, is sometimes followed by *da*, sometimes by *go*, and sometimes by *pa*. Overall, the syllable-to-syllable transition for two syllables that cross a word boundary is less predictable than the syllable-to-syllable transition of syllables that fall within a word in the miniature language. Infants were exposed to two minutes of this continuous string of syllables. The expectation was that if infants use syllable-to-syllable predictability – called **transitional probabilities** – to segment words, they should segment out the experimentally intended words of the language. How was this tested?

The testing procedure used in these kinds of experiments is called the **headturn preference procedure** (HPP). Essentially, infants are offered a series of speech sounds to listen to, but they have to turn their head in the direction of a loudspeaker in order for the sound to be repeated. In this way, infants' preference for some sounds over other sounds can be determined by noting how long they are willing to turn their head to keep hearing the repetition of the sound. In this particular experiment, two types of sounds were played: syllable sequences that were words (such as *tibudo* in the previous example), and syllable sequences that were partial words (such as *budopa*, which has a word boundary after *do*). Part-words were syllable sequences that did occur in the two minute familiarization sequence but only across a word boundary. Infants showed a systematic preference difference between words and part-words, showing that they processed these sequences differently when listening to the familiarization sequence. Since the only systematic difference between words and part-words was the transitional probabilities of the syllables that made them up, such a listening preference indicates that infants were sensitive to and did pay attention to the transitional probabilities in the continuous stream of speech, and segmented the sequence based on those patterns.

Once infants can make inroads into identifying the words of their language, they can then start to notice what other cues coincide with word boundaries: do most words have stress on the first syllable? What are the phonotactic constraints? Experiments similar to the HPP experiment just discussed demonstrate that infants start to learn about these language-specific properties relatively early on, and well before they're speaking themselves. By nine months, infants use stress as a cue to word boundaries, and they are also sensitive to the phonotactic constraints of their language at this age. Fairly rapidly, then, after using repeating patterns to make the initial inroads to the words of their language, infants start to notice and use other partially reliable cues to segment words from fluent speech.

Summary of Section 3

This section discussed the lack of invariance with respect to word boundaries. Unlike printed text, there are no spaces between words in fluent speech, and more generally, no one-to-one cues to word boundaries. Nevertheless, there are semireliable sources of information that experienced language users capitalize on to segment words, such as recognizing known words, phonotactic information, and the position of stressed syllables. This section also discussed evidence concerning how young infants who don't yet know many words, or the phonotactic and stress patterns in their language, could nonetheless begin to segment words from fluent speech, thereby "bootstrapping" themselves into language recognition. Highly predictable syllable sequences are likely to be words, and could serve as an initial source of segmentation information. Once enough words are segmented using transitional probabilities, infants can start to notice what other cues in their language correlate with word boundaries.

Key terms from this section are:

- Segmentation strategies
- Bootstrapping
- Transitional probabilities
- Headturn preference procedure

Chapter Summary

This chapter introduced key concepts and questions in speech perception. The lack of invariance in the acoustic signal has led researchers to investigate the kinds of information that influence a listener's perception of ambiguous speech signals. We discussed how context can affect the perception of a sample of speech, both the context provided by other parts of the signal – for example, neighboring coarticulated sounds – from lexical knowledge, and even context from visual information. Many scientists hypothesize that articulatory gesture information is an important component of speech perception, since much acoustic variability is a lawful and predictable outcome of the process of producing speech via the human vocal tract. Nevertheless, there are many open questions as to how listeners perceive phonetic constancy in the face of acoustic variability.

Section 2 introduced some perceptual processes that help listeners cope with variability in the signal. Categorical perception is a critical ability that allows us to attend to the acoustic variability that is linguistically meaningful. It is not restricted to speech, or even to humans. Rather, it seems to be a broader biological strategy for allowing organisms to cope with inherent variability in a complex environment.

Section 3 introduced the lack of invariance problem in word segmentation, and the difficulties involved in recovering word beginnings and endings from the acoustic signal. We discussed the kinds of strategies fluent language users use to segment words, and theories about how young infants could initially segment words before they could make use of those strategies.

Development

In several areas, this chapter examined whether certain perceptual skills that adult language users have develop through maturation and experience, or are available from early on in infancy. The ability to perceive speech categorically is present at birth; in fact, infants are able to perceive category contrasts that their parents cannot. For instance, English-learning eight-month-olds can perceive the difference between Salish uvular and velar ejectives ([q'] and [k']) that to English-speaking adults both sound like [k]. However, between 10 and 12 months infants start to lose the ability to perceive nonnative contrasts, a process of phonological tuning.

In addition to categorical perception, infants' speech perception is similar to adults' in other ways as well. In particular, infants are influenced by the visual information from a talker's mouth and are prone to the McGurk effect, just like adults. The integration of visual and auditory information may be a fundamental, inborn characteristic of speech perception.

We also discussed some differences in the ways infants and adults process speech. Much of the evidence about how adults segment words from fluent speech suggests that they use knowledge that depends on properties specific to a particular language – its vocabulary, phonotactic constraints, stress patterns, and so on. Since these are pieces of knowledge that children have to *learn*, and since learning them requires having segmented a considerable number of words, they are of no use to infants at the beginning of language learning. We discussed how infants are able to make use of statistical regularities in continuous speech, and tend to segment the speech stream at points where the transitions from one syllable to the next are relatively variable. Applying such a procedure to natural speech could provide an entryway for infants to start identifying possible words of the language, and to start to learn about the other cues that could further help them to segment words from fluent speech.

Further Reading and Resources

Eimas, Peter D. (1985). The Perception of Speech in Early Infancy. *Scientific American*, 252, pp. 34–40.
Werker, Janet F. (1995) Exploring Developmental Changes in Cross-Language Speech Perception. In Lila R. Gleitman and Mark Liberman (eds.), *An Invitation to Cognitive Science*, 2nd edn., *Vol. 1: Language*, pp. 87–106. Cambridge, MA: MIT Press.
The Sounds of Language: *http://whyfiles.org/058language/baby_talk.html*

Chapter 6
Word Recognition

Introduction

In Chapter 5 we discussed word segmentation as one aspect of word recognition. We saw that one strategy experienced language users employ to segment continuous speech into discrete words is to posit a word boundary whenever the unfolding signal matches a word they recognize. In fact, many factors other than the speech signal itself affect the process of word recognition, and it is these topics we turn to now in this further chapter on word recognition. Word recognition is such a rich and complex area of research that many books and even careers have been devoted to understanding it. The purpose of this chapter is to acquaint you with foundational research on word recognition and the core phenomena that theories of word recognition were developed to address. You will read about several major theories of word recognition and the evidence used to support them. This will include discussions of the past and present technology that allows researchers to probe the representations and processes of word recognition in real time as listeners actively perceive speech. As you will see, while there is still much debate about the correct theory of word recognition, there is nonetheless much that can be agreed on regarding the phenomena that the theories must explain.

One thing that many current theories have in common is the idea that word recognition is an **interactive process** – a process that involves multiple levels of representation (e.g., phonological units, words, word meanings) in which representations at each level interact with each other and, according to some theories, where interaction may occur between competing representations within a single representational level. Many current theories also view word recognition as a **parallel process**, in which the representation of many words become active as a listener processes a particular auditory signal. Let's take a look at some psycholinguistic experiments that have helped lead scientists to these views.

Bottom-Up and Top-Down Effects on Words Recognition

If you were designing a device to recognize words in a speech signal, you might design a device that monitors the signal, detects phonological units, and, as each unit is processed, scans the mental lexicon (the mental representations of words you know) until the sequence of phonemes matches a known word, as depicted in Figure 6.1. Indeed, this is the first step in the strategy discussed in Chapter 5 for determining the location of word boundaries – when a word is recognized, a new word is about to begin. A process such as this that constructs representations entirely from the signal is called a **bottom-up** or **signal-driven** process, because the information used to construct representations is determined entirely by the speech signal. In this case, the signal determines the recognition of phonological units, which in turn are used to construct the word.

Recall from the previous chapter that this procedure is not entirely without complications, since it is common for plausible word forms to be words embedded within other words. So on hearing the word *cognition*, a listener using only the procedure outlined above would incorrectly activate his or her representation for *cog* after hearing just the beginning of the word. Setting that issue aside (and we will soon see other kinds of information listeners use to avoid some of these errors), there are other phenomena discussed in Chapter 5 that suggest that word recognition involves more

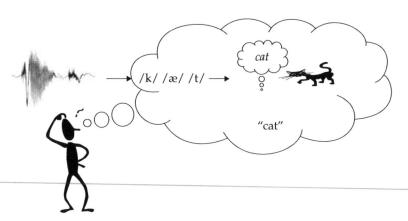

Figure 6.1   A hypothetical bottom-up word recognition system that extracts a sequence of phonological units from the speech signal and puts them together to form a word and to access the corresponding concepts.

than purely bottom-up processing. Recall that phonological units are not directly present in the speech signal but are constructed during the process of speech perception. In particular, as the Ganong effect shows, speech perception is affected by **lexical knowledge**, such that the phonological unit perceived in a section of speech can shift (for example, from a [d] to a [t]) if such a shift would yield a word versus a nonword (e.g., *type* vs. *dype*). So word recognition cannot be completely bottom-up, since the representations at the level of the phonological units depend on representations at the level of words. The Ganong effect was an example of **top-down processing**, in which representations at one level (e.g., words) influence representations at smaller compositional levels (e.g., the phonological units that make up the words).

A related issue is that the simplistic bottom-up model we started with assumes that phonological units are perfectly recoverable from the speech signal. However, in everyday situations, the speech signal is degraded by environmental noise (e.g., the open window of a moving car, the jackhammer across the street, the people next to you talking loudly), as well as being influenced by variability in the articulation by the person speaking. Moreover, we often listen to speech over a mode of transmission that degrades the signal, such as a cell phone, radio, or even a regular telephone. Although word recognition is harder and more prone to errors when several factors conspire against a "perfect" signal, the fact is that we recognize words remarkably accurately and effortlessly most of the time, despite all the sources of interference.

A striking example of our ability to recognize words in degraded signals has been demonstrated experimentally in a phenomenon known as **the phoneme restoration effect.** This effect is produced when a section of the speech signal corresponding to a speech sound, say the [s] in *legislature*, is removed and replaced by white noise (like static) or the sound of a cough, roughly of the same duration as the extracted section. This is a way of introducing, in a controlled manner, the kind of signal degradation that occurs in everyday situations. Listeners are aware of the static nose or cough, but interestingly, they are quite inconsistent and inaccurate

A metaphor that most theories of word recognition incorporate is **activation**. To understand the notion of activation, you can think of the word representations in your mind as light bulbs – when they're active, they're turned on, and that means you are considering that word as a possible candidate for the identity of the word you're hearing. In the phoneme restoration effect, it appears as though the activation of a word causes the activation of its component phonological units, even those that were not recoverable from the acoustic input. Later in this chapter you'll see an example of a theory of word recognition that takes the notion of activation quite literally, as a fundamental part of its representations and processes.

in judging where in the word it occurred. Moreover, listeners also report hearing the missing phonological unit. In the *legislature* example, listeners are certain that they've heard the missing [s] that was in fact removed from the sound signal – they have restored it in their perception. However, this kind of restoration does not happen in situations in which a restored sound would not make a word; for example if the [s] in the nonword *rensim* were manipulated in a similar fashion, it would not be restored. The phoneme restoration effect demonstrates that words can be recognized even when parts of the signal are missing, and demonstrates in another way that top-down information from word representations influences the recognition of the phonological units from which the words are composed.

The Ganong effect and phoneme restoration effect demonstrate the interactive nature of speech perception and word recognition. They also show that top-down processing is involved from the word level to the level of phonological units. But what about the activation of words themselves? Is there information other than bottom-up information that influences what words are recognized, as listeners attend to the unfolding acoustic signal? As we will see in the remainder of this chapter, auditory word recognition involves integrating a variety of different pieces of information from different sources: the meaning of the unfolding sentence, how common the word being recognized is in the language, and how phonologically similar other words are to it. In different ways, these are all top-down influences on word recognition. We now consider each one in more detail.

The effect of context on word recognition

Most of the time when you are listening to speech and recognizing words, you are recognizing words that are in meaningful utterances and that are part of a meaningful conversation or narrative. In many cases, because of what you know about the world and the topics being discussed, you can predict what the next word will be. For example, if someone is describing to you their hectic morning rush to get to work on time, they might say, "I jumped in the car, put it in gear, and stepped on the . . . ." You might not need to hear any of the next word to expect that it will be *gas*. If it's not, and you instead hear "[æks . . .]," that might be all you need for *accelerator* to pop into your head. Your ability to do this kind of prediction indicates that you are interpreting the sentence as you're hearing it and building up a conceptual representation of its meaning. Moreover, it suggests that you can use this high-level information to make predictions about what words you're likely to hear next; that is, it suggests that you engage in top-down processing when understanding spoken words in sentences.

The thought experiment just described taps into your experiences and intuitions to illustrate how top-down information is used in word recognition. But intuitions can be misleading about what's really going on in psychological processes; controlled experiments are required to ascertain scientifically whether the intuitions are valid. Furthermore, in our thought experiment, while listeners may indeed be able to predict words based on context, it could be that such an ability involves conscious, deliberate (albeit quick) reasoning, which is different from the immediate, automatic, online word recognition processes we would like to understand. Some of the seminal studies in top-down effects on word recognition were carried out by the psycholinguist William Marslen-Wilson and his colleagues in the early 1970s. In some of these studies, subjects were instructed to **shadow** or rapidly repeat words as they heard them through headphones. Their task was to repeat the words they heard as quickly and accurately as they could. Subjects spoke their responses into a microphone connected to a recording device. With very accurate measuring and timing devices, the researchers were able to determine subjects' **reaction times** when shadowing words – that is, how quickly after the **onset** (beginning) of a word a subject began to shadow it. The recordings also allowed them to measure the accuracy of subjects' performance.

In many shadowing experiments, the words to be shadowed (the target words) occurred in normal sentences that were part of a short, coherent narrative. One of the interesting findings from the earliest studies was that a portion of subjects started to shadow words at around 250 milliseconds after the target onsets – this extremely short interval was well before the entire word had been heard. The existence of these **close shadowers** provided evidence about the rapid speed of word recognition, as well as the fact that words were often recognized before all the bottom-up information had been processed. What was even more telling was how these close shadowers behaved in situations where the experimenters had introduced "pronunciation errors" in the target words. For example, instead of an expected word *company*, the target word might be changed to *comsiny*, for example in the passage "My wife works for a computer software *comsiny*." To do the shadowing task correctly, then, subjects had to repeat a nonword. Most of the time subjects were able to do this, but sometimes shadowers made "errors" that consisted of substituting a correctly pronounced real word for the target nonword, and they were just as likely to do so before or after they heard the syllable that made the word a nonword. For example, in the case of *comsiny*, close shadowers might say "compa . . ." after hearing just "com" (before the mispronunciation), or after hearing "comsi," in which the second syllable is heard before it is (incorrectly) shadowed. Even distant shadowers who waited to hear the whole word would sometimes "restore" the mispronounced portion to create a real word. Remarkably, these corrections would not be noticed by the shadowers, just as in the phoneme restoration effect. When shadowers repeated back the corrected version of the word, it was because that's

Who are these close shadowers? Marslen-Wilson reported that the close shadowers in his experiments were all women, and that about 25 percent of the women in his experiments were close shadowers. Other studies have suggested that general shadowing speed is caused by a **response strategy**, whereby some individuals (the close shadowers) will start to shadow before they really know what the word is, just based on the phonological information, and others (the distant shadowers) wait until they have confidently identified the word before they repeat it. Because differences in response strategies are not due to fundamentally different ways of processing speech, it is justified to extend what is learned from studying close shadowers to word recognition in the general population.

In this shadowing experiment, what are the independent and dependent variables? Remember, there can be more than one of each type (see Chapter 4).

what they actually *perceived*. Furthermore, if the modified target word was placed in an incoherent context, it was far less likely to be incorrectly shadowed and turned into a corrected real word. For example, if the word *astronaut* had been changed to the nonword *asfinaut* in the passage, "My car has just been fixed. The mechanic said the *asfinaut* needed to be cleaned," it was much less likely to be shadowed as *astronaut* than if it had been put in a coherent context like, "The space shuttle needs to be fixed. On the last space flight, the *asfinaut* reported many serious problems."

Taken together, these findings strongly suggested that word recognition processes take into account high-level information about the meaning of unfolding narratives and conversations, and that this high-level information has top-down effects on how phonological information is processed in word recognition. In other words, in the context of spacecraft, the nonword *asfinaut* was phonologically close enough to a sensible real word that listeners sometimes "incorrectly" recognized the real word in the speech stream. So, not only does top-down information from the word level affect how phonological units are recovered from the speech stream, top-down information from meaning and context affects word recognition as well.

So the scenario we sketched out in our thought experiment – "I jumped in the car, put it in gear, and stepped on the acce . . ." – has support from rigorous scientific experiments. The evidence from the shadowing studies suggests that listeners can indeed recognize the word *accelerator* when only a portion of the signal has been processed, and that the meaning of the sentence (or sentences) up to the point of the target word directly influences what words might be recognized from partial phonological information. Moreover, because the reaction times of shadowing responses are often so rapid (250 milliseconds), it is assumed that they tap into online, real-time word recognition processes, and not after-the-fact conscious reasoning about what one might have heard (which also clearly can happen but takes much more time).

The cohort model and the importance of the beginnings of words
In the first shadowing studies that used mispronunciations to test for context effects on word recognition, the placement of the mispronunciations was systematically varied. Mispronounced target words were always three syllables long and the mispronunciations were split between the first, second, and third syllables. However, when shadowers erred by correcting the mispronunciations, they rarely corrected mispronunciations in the first syllable. In other words, the very first sounds of a word appeared to be driven exclusively by the bottom-up signal and were relatively impervious to top-down context effects. The words that listeners ultimately recognized apparently had to match the bottom-up signal in the very first sounds.

This finding gave rise to a theory of word recognition called the **cohort model**. According to this theory, the first phonological unit of a word, as recovered from the speech signal activates *all* the words in the listener's mental lexicon that begin with that sound. Assuming that the first sound was accurately perceived, one of those (potentially many) words is the target word, and all the other active words are collectively the **cohort**. According to the theory, the cohort represents all the words the brain is considering at a given moment as candidates for the word being heard. The bottom-up signal then continues to play an important role by removing words from the cohort: as more of the signal is processed, words in the cohort that are no longer consistent with the bottom-up information are removed from the cohort and, consequently, from consideration. The cohort then becomes successively smaller as more of the speech

As depicted in Table 6.1, the phonological units are processed sequentially, one by one in the cohort model. Of course, as we saw in earlier chapters, the effects of coarticulation are such that a particular section of acoustic signal might contain information about more than one sound. For example, in Table 6.1, the formant transitions that are critical for perceiving the [t] contain information about the following [ε]. The theory makes a simplification by treating speech processing as purely sequential. This kind of simplification is common in scientific theories. Devising experiments that test key aspects of a theory is often easier given the simplifying assumptions. You will see other examples of simplification in models later in this chapter.

Think of how the predictions of the cohort model might change if coarticulation information was represented in the model. What effect might it have on the point at which words are removed from the cohort?

Table 6.1 Sample of initial cohort when a [t] is processed, and subsequent shrinking of the cohort

[t]	[tɛ]	[tɛl]	[tɛlə]	[tɛləf]
temperature	temperature	telegraph	telegraph	telephone
technical	technical	telephone	telephone	
telegraph	telegraph	television	television	
telephone	telephone			
television	television			
tap				
teepee				
tie				
. . .				

signal is processed. Eventually, only one word remains active, and that word is then the word that is recognized. See Table 6.1 for an example.

But how does context affect word recognition in this model? Two important characteristics of the cohort model are that bottom-up information determines the initial cohort – the initial set of active words – and that words can never be added to the cohort after that, only removed. So top-down information from context cannot add words; however, it can deactivate words that are inconsistent with top-down information. It can also maintain the activation of words that might start to diverge from the signal as it unfolds, so long as they are highly consistent with the context. In the *astronaut/asfinaut* example, *astronaut* would be in the cohort after the [æ] and [s] are processed. When the [f] is processed, bottom-up information alone would remove *astronaut* from the cohort; but because top-down influences from the context (a discussion about spacecraft) favor keeping *astronaut* activated, it might nevertheless remain in the cohort (whereas activation for a word like *Astroturf*, which at the point of the [f] would be just as divergent as *astronaut* in the speech signal, would not be maintained by the context). In this way, high-level context information can keep words active even as they start to differ from the bottom-up signal. Note that if the "mispronunciations" were in the first sounds, say, *kestronaut*, the cohort theory would not predict that shadowers would say *astronaut*, because it would not have been in the initial cohort.

Frequency and neighborhood effects: Words' effects on word recognition

You read above about top-down effects from the discourse context on the process of word recognition. There are other top-down effects that come from listeners' word knowledge, their mental lexicon. Specifically, most researchers believe that **word frequency** influences word recognition, and a number of theories hold that **phonological neighborhood** influences word recognition.

Word frequency is simply a measure of how frequently an average person would hear a particular word in everyday speech. Grammatical words like articles and prepositions are extremely frequent – think how many times in a day you must hear the word *the*. But within the grammatical classes of nouns and verbs, there is a considerable range of frequencies. Verbs like *come* and *go* are extremely common, whereas *gesticulate* and *embalm* are relatively less frequent. Likewise, nouns like *dog* and *mother* are frequent, but *barb* and *fragment* are less so.

The term **phonological neighborhood** refers to words a listener knows that are "close" to the target word (the word to be recognized). For our purposes, we will use a standard definition that two words are phonological neighbors if they differ by just one phonological unit: either a unit is changed, deleted, or added to make a phonological neighbor. For example, some phonological neighbors of [kɑr] (*car*) are [bɑr] (*bar*), [skɑr] (*scar*), [tʃɑr] (*char*), [ker] (*care*), and [kor] (*core*). (The *car–core* neighbors should make clear that the concept involves closeness in sound, not spelling.) **Neighborhood density** refers to how many phonological neighbors a target word has, relative to other words. A word like *cat* has a dense phonological neighborhood because there are many words that differ from it by just one phonological unit. On the other hand, *sphere* ([sfir]) has only a handful of phonological neighbors, so its neighborhood is relatively *sparse*.

Both word frequency and phonological neighborhood density have been shown to influence word recognition. Because these are not characteristics of the bottom-up signal, they can be considered top-down influences; however, these are features of the word-level representations themselves, not something truly higher up in the speech chain, such as context. We now consider effects of word frequency and phonological neighborhood density in greater detail.

Effects of word frequency

Considered more broadly, the top-down effects on context discussed earlier have the flavor of some of the speech perception effects we discussed in Chapter 5. Context appears to act as a kind of cue that guides listeners in their interpretation of the bottom-up signal. Incorporating context information during the process of word recognition adds robustness and efficiency to the process, allowing listeners to activate the correct word rapidly, before all of the signal has been heard. This capacity for early recognition doesn't result in many errors, since speakers generally utter words that make sense in the ongoing context. Word frequency could play a similar role: if a listener can only partially recover the phonological material in a word so that it is ambiguous between two words, and those two words would be coherent in the discourse, then chances are good that the speaker was uttering the more frequent one. (A consequence of having a high frequency in the language is being a very probable word: if word A occurs 20 times in 1 million words, and word B occurs 40 times in 1 million words, B is twice as frequent, and is also more probable or more likely to occur in an average sample of speech.) It would make sense, then, for word recognition to require less bottom-up information to recognize frequent words and to require more information to recognize less frequent words. If that were the case, then we would predict that word recognition might be *faster* for relatively frequent words compared to relatively infrequent words, as infrequent words would require more bottom-up information to be recognized.

A number of experiments have shown that this speed prediction is correct: high frequency words result in faster recognition than lower frequency words. Several different experimental techniques were used to test the effects of frequency; unlike the shadowing experiments described earlier, these methods involved listening to individual words in isolation, rather than in a passage of connected, meaningful speech. (This was done, in part, to make sure that any effects of frequency that were found were independent of context effects.) The techniques in the experiments overviewed here are called lexical decision and cross-modal priming.

A **lexical decision** experiment simply requires subjects to make a decision whether a word is a real word or a nonword by pressing a *yes* button or a *no* button. Generally, subjects are instructed to respond as quickly as possible to ensure that the response reflects immediate, "online" word recognition processes. In one experiment, Marslen-Wilson and colleagues selected word pairs that were phonologically identical until the very end, for example, *street* and *streak*. One word in the pair was substantially more frequent than the other; for example, *street* was reported to occur 130 times in every million words, and *streak* only 3 times. Since the words were identical until the very end, if frequency does not play a role in word recognition then the amount of time listeners take to recognize the word from its end (its **offset**) should be identical for each member of the pair. The time needed to make a lexical decision should therefore be the same for each word. On the other hand, if frequent words can be recognized more quickly, then recognition time and therefore lexical decision responses should be faster for the more frequent word in the pair. This is exactly what was found: participants responded to frequent words on average about 90 milliseconds faster than infrequent words. Although this difference (just under a 10th of a second) might seem small and might not be an important difference when it comes to understanding speech in normal situations, the fact that there is a reliable difference shows that frequency plays a role in the way words are accessed. This, in turn, means that a good theory of word recognition should be able to explain frequency effects.

The **cross-modal priming** technique offers further insights into the influence of word frequency. In a cross-modal priming task, subjects hear a word, called the **prime,** through headphones and then have to make a response to a written word presented on a computer screen, called the **probe** – that's the *cross-modal* part, meaning that two sense modalities – vision and hearing – are used. As it turns out, the response to the probe is often faster when the prime and probe are semantically related (like *dog* and *bone*) than when they're unrelated. This is understood by scientists to be the case because the probe (e.g., *bone*) is partially activated or **primed** by hearing the prime (e.g., *dog*) that is related in meaning; because of the pre-activation of the probe, subjects make faster responses to it than if it were not primed. In many cross-modal priming experiments the response is a lexical decision: is the visually presented word a real word or not?

Cross-modal priming was used to test for subtle and immediate effects of word frequency in the following way. As in the previous experiment, word pairs were chosen that differed in frequency but that were similar in the way they sounded. For example, *captain* (high frequency) and *captive* (low frequency) were paired. They differ in frequency, but match in the first four phonological units, differing in the last two sounds; the words in pairs like this served as the prime words in the experiment. Each prime word had a related probe word, but a probe was related to only one of the two prime words in a pair. For example, the probe *ship* is related to *captain* but not *captive*; the probe *guard* is related to *captive* but not *captain*. As a listener attended to the prime word, the visual probe word appeared at a point when the bottom-up signal could not differentiate between the two members of the prime pair; for example, just at or before "capt..." in either *captain* or *captive*. At this point, the cohort model would predict that both words would be active and competing for recognition, because both match the bottom-up signal so far. The concepts relating to each of these words would then be equally active, so neither probe word (i.e., *ship* or *guard*) should be primed any more than the other, and recognition of the visual probes should be equally accurate and fast. On the other hand, if frequency somehow affected activation, even at the point of hearing a portion of the bottom-up signal that was consistent with either word, the concept relating to the more frequent prime word might be preferentially activated. If this were so, the probe word that was related to the more frequent prime would be made active and result in faster lexical decision times. In fact, that is precisely what was found. Probe words like *ship*, which were related to the more frequent word in the prime pair (*captain*), were responded to faster than probe words like *guard* (which was related to the less frequent *captive*), even when the bottom-up signal was consistent with both prime words (up to "capt..."). This suggests that word frequency plays a role even when multiple competitor words are active in the cohort: the concepts relating to high frequency words in the

How do researchers know the frequencies of words? In the late 1960s two researchers at Brown University, Henry Kučera and W. Nelson Francis, tallied a sample of about one million words of American English from various written sources. This tally of word frequency was used extensively by researchers in psycholinguistics and **computational linguistics**. Today there are many online databases of spoken and written English, including speech to and by children.

cohort are more active or more available than concepts relating to the less frequent words.

To summarize, the first experiment – lexical decision – demonstrated that frequent words were recognized faster than infrequent words after the entire word was heard. The second experiment – cross-modal priming – showed that frequency plays a role even earlier, when there are still multiple words that correspond to the signal processed so far, any one of which could be the actual word that was spoken. Notice that the more basic lexical decision task in the first experiment could not be used to address the second issue because it would be very hard to push listeners to start making lexical decisions in the middle of processing a spoken word. But in the cross-modal priming procedure, the visual probe can be manipulated precisely to come on at any point during the unfolding of the prime word.

The discoveries about the role of word frequency in speeding up word recognition led to some modifications to the cohort model. In the revised theory, instead of words either being in or out of the cohort – instead of the light bulb representing a word being on or off – words in the cohort varied in how active they were, as though each light bulb has its own dimmer switch. According to the cohort theory, when activated, frequent words would initially become more active than infrequent words. And unlike in the earliest version of the theory, recognition could occur before the all-but-last word was removed from the cohort: if one word is sufficiently more active than then others, it will be the word that is recognized in the speech signal.

Effects of phonological neighborhood
The cohort model incorporates a notion of **competitors**; basically, competitors are all the words that are active in the cohort at a given time (one of which is presumably the target word). They are called competitors because they are all competing for selection as the recognized word. As long as a target's competitors remain sufficiently activated, the target word will not be recognized. Other word recognition models share this notion of competition between words during the recognition process, but models differ in how they define competitors. One such model, the **neighborhood-activation model**, considers competitors to be all the phonological neighbors of the

target word – that is, words that sound a lot like the target word are its competitors for recognition.

This hypothesis about competitors came about from a series of experiments by Paul Luce and colleagues that used mostly different methodologies than the ones you've read about so far. One method involved subjects listening to speech that had been degraded by the addition of **noise** (like static) to the speech signal. In one study, the speech consisted of isolated words (i.e., words presented alone, not in any context nor in connected speech). The subjects' task was simply to identify each word, and their accuracy was measured. The addition of noise made the identification more challenging, so it provided a way of testing what factors related to the words themselves could ease or increase the difficulty of recognizing the words. The words were carefully chosen by the experimenters for a number of characteristics. First, words were either high frequency words or low frequency words, as in the studies described above. In addition, the phonological neighbors of each word were either high frequency or low frequency words. Finally, words had either dense or sparse phonological neighborhoods, that is, many or few similar sounding words. Therefore, there were a total of eight different types of words (2×2×2), and the researchers could measure how the three independent variables (word frequency, neighborhood frequency, neighborhood density) affected accuracy of word recognition in noise. Consistent with the last Marslen-Wilson experiments described above, these experiments found that listeners were more accurate in recognizing high frequency words, but they also found that recognition was more accurate if the phonological neighbors were relatively low frequency. Furthermore, recognition was better if the phonological neighborhood was sparse rather than dense. Put differently, being a low-frequency word, having many phonological neighbors, and having highly frequent phonological neighbors each made recognizing words in noise more difficult.

These results were confirmed using yet different methods. One method used a lexical decision task, but unlike the experiment you've just read about, the words that provided the important experimental data were actually nonwords. These nonwords were designed to match real words up until the last phonological unit so that until the very end, the English words that were consistent with the speech signal would be active in the listener's mind. In order to correctly decide that the target was *not* a word, the activation of the real English words would have to decline sufficiently. In addition, the experimenters designed some words to have a dense phonological neighborhood and some words to have a sparse phonological neighborhood. For each group of those words, some had high frequency phonological neighbors, and some had low frequency phonological neighbors. This meant that every possible combination of neighborhood density and neighborhood frequency was reflected in the total set of words that subjects heard (dense+high frequency, dense+low frequency, sparse+high frequency, sparse+low frequency). The scientists measured the response times to accurate "nonword" responses from the word offset (when the information from the signal was inconsistent with any known word), and they evaluated whether neighborhood density and neighborhood frequency influenced the speed of the responses. They found that nonwords with sparse phonological neighborhoods led to faster nonword responses than nonwords with dense phonological neighborhoods, and separately, they found that nonwords with high frequency phonological neighbors resulted in slower nonword responses than nonwords with low frequency neighbors. Taken together, these findings added further support to the idea that words compete for recognition, but they further suggested that words *interact* as part of the competition process.

In summary, many studies have shown that the *frequency of a word*, the *number of competitors*, and the *frequency of the competitors* affect the speed with which we are able to recognize words.

Reevaluating the Importance of the Beginnings of Words

The TRACE model

An important part of cognitive science research uses computers to create and test **computational models** of cognitive processes. These models usually involve actual **implementations** on a computer, so that the computer carries out tasks in a way similar to human subjects in experiments. These models are sometimes based on theoretical models like the cohort model and implement the various components in the theory, with the goal of demonstrating that the computational model will "behave" like humans to some reasonable approximation. Such demonstrations provide a validation, or support, for the theory of how humans perform the task in question. In early stages of developing a theory, it might be sufficient to show that the model comes up with "the right answer" after doing some processing. For example, given some representation of an acoustic signal, a word recognition model should recognize the corresponding word. But as theories evolve and become more sophisticated, researchers demand more of their models. What counts as "the right answer" then includes making errors when humans make errors (and making the same kind of errors), and going through similar steps as humans to get to the final outcome, for example, the timing of when representations become active. The TRACE model of speech perception is one such model. This computational model was designed by James McClelland and Jeffrey Elman to model human speech perception and word recognition. The computer simulation was given a (roughly) phonetic input signal, and its output was the word that corresponded to the signal. Because of the way the model was designed, the researchers were able to examine from moment to moment the words that the model was "considering" at each point of processing the bottom-up signal (much in the way that some of the experimental techniques we've discussed allow researchers to probe the words that human listeners are considering from moment to moment). This allowed researchers to test what was going on "behind the scenes" in the model, and to compare that with human performance in word recognition tasks.

The TRACE model shares many characteristics with the cohort model, particularly that word recognition involves the interaction of multiple levels of representation and the idea of **parallel activation** of words. It also incorporates the idea that words compete for recognition. But unlike the cohort model, and similar to the neighborhood-activation model, it incorporates the idea that competition involves interaction *between words*, such that highly active words lower the activation of less active words – so the competition is much more interactive. It also allows for a word to become active even if its beginning is inconsistent with the beginning of the bottom-up signal, so long as there is sufficient match to the signal elsewhere in the word. As you will see, this fact predicts that words that rhyme with the target will be somewhat active, even if the initial sounds are inconsistent with the signal. So, for example, *tar* might be active during the processing of the word *car*. This idea is closer in spirit to the phonological neighborhood notion of competitor in the neighborhood-activation model (where candidate words can mismatch the speech signal in the beginning of the word) than in the cohort model.

It is because of the specific types of representations and processes employed in the TRACE model that it has the characteristics of parallel activation of words and interactivity within a level of representation – between words themselves – as well as between levels of representation. These properties arise because the TRACE model is a **connectionist model** (or, as such models are sometimes termed, a **neural network model**). Parallel processing and interactivity are an essential part of how models of this sort function. Connectionist models in general are composed of very simple representational units, called **nodes** or simply **units**, that

What's in a (node) name? There is nothing special about a node that makes it represent one word or another, or one phonological unit or another. The way the nodes are connected, how they correspond to the input speech signal, and in general how the researcher designs the network, is what allows us to say that a node represents something. The interpretation of the model is in our minds, not in the machine, but the model allows us to make predictions about human behavior given a fixed interpretation of its parts.

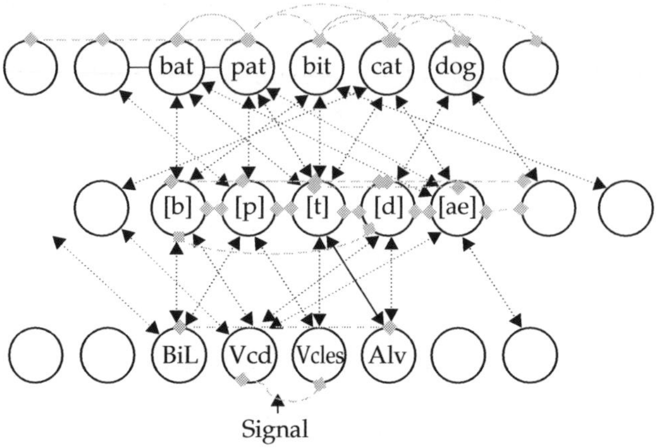

Figure 6.2 Example of the organization of the TRACE model. "BiL" = *bilabial*, "Vcd" = *voiced*, "Vcles" = *voiceless*, "Alv" = *alveolar*.

become active (or inactive) as processing occurs. These units are designed by the researcher to represent something, such as a phonological unit or a word. Units are linked to other units through **connections** (hence the name of the models), and a unit becomes active when the units it is connected to become active. Generally speaking, the activity of a unit is **proportional to** the activity of the units connected to it: The more active the connected units are, the more active the unit in question will become. Figure 6.2 demonstrates in schematic form how a small sample of words and phonological units are connected in the TRACE model. This example shows nodes for several words, and the phonological units that are connected to them.

The nodes and connections in the TRACE model were set up to reflect the levels of processing thought to be involved in human word recognition: phonetic units on one level, phonological units on the next level up, and word units on the highest level. Any unit on a given level was connected to all the units at the other levels that were associated with it. For example, the phonological unit representing [k] was connected to all the units at the word level that contained a [k] (e.g., *cat, act, craft, cart*), and at the phonetic level to all the phonetic properties that contributed

Do we have different representations for words at different times? Probably not. Computational modeling always involves simplifications for convenience. In this case, the duplication of units is a convenience for dealing with the issue of time; it is not a claim about the human representational system. A question researchers always have to consider is whether the desired behavior of an implemented model comes from the components that are related to the cognitive theory (e.g., different levels of representation and their interaction) or from the unrealistic but sometimes necessary simplifications. This issue can become a point of debate for researchers with different theoretical views.

to the perception of [k], voiceless, velar, (perhaps) aspirated, stop. (The features used in TRACE were slightly different from the ones discussed in this book.) Time was represented "spatially" or discretely in the TRACE model, so that, in fact, there were separate units for [k] at time 1, [k] at time 2, and so on, and likewise for all the units at every level of representation.

Another important component of the TRACE model's design is the interactive competition among representations at the same level. In the cohort model, the notion of competition is simply that if there are multiple words active in the cohort, the competitors delay recognition of the target until their activation level is sufficiently low (because of increasing incompatibility with the top-down or bottom-up information). In this sense, the competition among words is *passive*. In the TRACE model, words *actively* compete for recognition through **inhibitory connections** – connections that lower a unit's activation in proportion to the rise in a connected unit's activation. Each word unit has inhibitory connections to all the other word units (for the corresponding time window), such that when one word unit is active, it sends a proportionate amount of inhibitory activation to all the other words, which decreases their activation. This is a way of building into the model the idea that a sample of speech does not give rise to the simultaneous perception of two distinct words. In a sense, this operates as a third kind of information in addition to bottom-up and top-down (side-across?). So, rather than having to wait for all the competitors to sufficiently decrease their activation, as in the cohort model, in the TRACE model, an active target word can speed up the process by lowering the activation of its competitors. The TRACE model implements this notion of within-level inhibition at each of the three levels of representation.

To show how the TRACE model functions, using Figure 6.2 we will walk through the steps that would occur when processing the word *bat*. First, as the [b] is processed, the features corresponding to *bilabial* and *voiced* become active (again, the features in the actual TRACE model are slightly different; we will use the ones you're familiar with for clarity). The activation of these phonetic units then sends inhibitory activation to incompatible units (such as *voiceless* and the other places of articulation). At the same time, it sends activation through the connections to the phonological units, in particular [b] and [p]. The unit [b] receives activation from both *bilabial* and *voiced*, so its activity will be relatively high. In contrast, [p] only receives activation from *bilabial*, so it will be active, but not as much as [b]. (Vowels will also be somewhat active, since they receive activation from *voiced*, but for now we will concern ourselves with the consonants.) If we were to stop processing the input at this point, and ignored the word level, after a little time the unit for [p] would become inactive, in part because of inhibitory signals from the more active [b], so that [b] would be the only active phonological unit.

Following the activation to the word level, all the words beginning with [b] would become active, as would all the words beginning with [p], since both phonological units are active. But here too, not all word units would be equally active since the activation from [b] will be stronger than from [p]; so *bat* and *bit* will each be more active than *pat*.

At this point in processing, the words active in the TRACE model are different from those that would be active in the cohort model. In the cohort model, only words that begin with [b] would be active, since the initial cohort must match the bottom-up information at the level of phonological units; words beginning with [p] do not match, because the first sound in the word was indeed [b]. In the TRACE model, a partial overlap of features in the first sound is sufficient to activate all words consistent with that phonetic property.

Part of the interactive nature of the TRACE model is that activation is not restricted to flow only from the lower levels to higher levels. Rather, activation of high level word units can affect the activation of lower level units, like the phonological units. For example, when *bat* and *pat* become active, they send activation *down* to the phonological units. Of course, that particular top-down information is in agreement with the bottom-up information, so it's not particularly interesting. What's more interesting is what happens when the top-down and bottom-up information "disagree," which happens as more of the signal is processed. To see how, consider what happens when the rest of the word *bat*, the [æ] and the [t], are processed. When the [æ] is processed, the associated phonetic features are activated, which in turn activates units at the phonological level, in particular [æ]. The unit [æ] in turn sends activation to all the words that have [æ] in the second position. Remember that *bat* and *pat* are already active, so their activation is augmented because of their connections to [æ]. But in addition, the word *cat* now becomes somewhat active because of the bottom-up input from [æ], even though it wasn't active before. Again, this would never be predicted by the cohort model; in the cohort model, words that are not initially active cannot become active later as the word is processed. The activation of *cat* then has a top-down effect on the phonological level, providing slight activation for [k] even though nothing in the bottom-up signal initially activated [k]. As the [t] is processed, the activation of *cat* increases (of course, so does the activation for *bat* and *pat*), which further activates [k], from top-down information.

There are several important take-home points from this discussion. First, as we noted before, in the cohort model any word that does not match the initial portion of the signal would never become active. Related to that, words that are not initially active would not later become active in the cohort model. In the TRACE model, both of these phenomena are possible. Lastly, the later activation of words in the TRACE model, combined with the top-down activation from the word level, means that phonological units can become active without support from the speech signal. (In the "bat" example above, after processing the initial phonetic features, [k] was not active at the phonological level, but after the rest of the word activated *cat*, the [k] was then active as a candidate for the first sound of the word, as if in retrospect.)

How do you think the TRACE model can provide an account for, or explain, the phoneme restoration effect and the Ganong effect?

This last property of the TRACE model has been cited by its proponents as a benefit because, among other things, it provides an account of the phoneme restoration effect. It also provides a natural explanation of the Ganong effect, since word status affects the perception of phonological units.

Tests for the activation of rhymes

There are similarities between the word recognition models we've discussed, but there are important differences as well. A considerable amount of research has been focused on developing experiments that can provide evidence for one theory over another. As in science in general, an informative experiment is one that yields results that are consistent with the prediction of one theory, but not of another. In that respect, rhyming words have been a focus in the research on word recognition. In the TRACE model, when recognizing *bat*, words like *cat* that only received partial bottom-up support from the speech signal would only momentarily be active because of inhibition from the more active (because more supported) sound. But the TRACE model nonetheless makes clear predictions that words that rhyme with the target word – like *cat* for *bat* – will be active in the mind of the listener at some point, to some degree. This prediction, although not shared with the cohort model, is shared to some degree with the neighborhood-activation model, since some rhyming words are phonological neighbors, hence competitors. What evidence is there about the activation of rhymes in *human* listeners?

Using experimental techniques like the ones we've discussed, researchers have come to differing conclusions about the activation of rhymes as competitors in word recognition. Part of the problem may come from the fact that many of the techniques for probing the activity of nontarget words, such as cross-modal priming, are indirect: there are many extra processes that the information from active words must go through before it is apparent in the behavior being measured. Subtle and temporary activations might not be discernable using many of these techniques. The unnaturalness of some of these tasks may also contribute to difficulty in detecting activation.

However, a relatively recent technique has been developed that might provide more direct access to the words active in a listener's mind as he or she listens to a word unfold in time. It turns out that listeners' eyes can be informative as to what's going on in their minds from moment to moment as they listen to speech. In everyday conversations, when a talker mentions an object that is present, the listener's eyes rapidly and momentarily fixate on the mentioned object. These very rapid eye movements, called **saccades**, happen without conscious control or often even awareness. Researchers hypothesized that they might be a window into the mind, indicating what words are active as individuals listen to speech. This has led to a body of research using **eye tracking** as a technique for studying word recognition. The experimental setups used to track eye movements vary with the demands of the experiment – for example, whether the subject looks at a scene depicted on a video monitor, or actual objects on a workspace. In either case, the data collected consist of the image of the overall scene in front of the subject, along with the precise location in the scene where the subject's gaze is directed, moment-to-moment during the experiment. This data is usually collected every 33 milliseconds, resulting in a fine-grained measure of where the subject is looking as words unfold over time.

One advantage of eye tracking is that it measures a natural behavior of the listener, rather than requiring an unnatural response, as in lexical decision tasks. Scientists can thus measure eye gaze in situations where listeners are attending to speech in much more natural situations. One influential study by Paul Allopenna and his colleagues set out explicitly to test whether, as the TRACE model predicts, rhyme words are active during word recognition. Specifically, if a subject heard the instruction, "Pick up the beaker," the researchers wanted to probe whether a rhyme like *speaker* would also be active during the processing of *beaker*. The experiment consisted of an array of objects on a video screen in front of the subject, as depicted in Figure 6.3. (Subjects performed the "picking up" task by clicking on the object with a computer mouse.) In this example the critical objects are pictures of the speaker, the beaker, the beetle, and the carriage. *Beaker* is the **referent** word, *beetle* is called the **cohort** (because it would be active in the cohort with the referent until the [k] in *beaker* is encountered), *speaker* is called the **rhyme**, and *carriage* is **unrelated** – its purpose is to establish a baseline measure of how much subjects look at the items that do not correspond in some way to the acoustic signal.

As far as the subjects knew, they were just listening to and carrying out instructions like "Pick up the beaker," at which point they would click on the object and then would be instructed where to place it, "now place it over the square." This exercise involved a relatively normal listening situation for the subjects (although the tasks they were performing were somewhat unusual). But as target words like *beaker* were spoken, the researchers were recording subjects' eye movements relative to the four kinds of objects on the screen: referent, cohort, rhyme, and unrelated. The

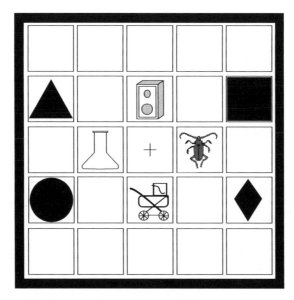

Figure 6.3 Sample display depicting the referent object (beaker), the cohort (beetle), the rhyme (speaker), and the unrelated object (carriage). The other objects provide target locations for the movement instructions. Reprinted from *Journal of Memory and Language*, 38, Allopenna, P. D., Magnuson, J. S., and Tanenhaus, M. H., Tracking the time course of spoken word recognition using eye movements: Evidence for continuous mapping models, 419–439, Copyright (1998), with permission from Elsevier.

graphs in Figure 6.4 show the results for the eye-tracking study and the predicted results from performing a similar computational "experiment" with the TRACE model. On both graphs, the *x*-axis shows time in milliseconds, and the *y*-axis shows the proportion of time listeners' eyes were fixated on a particular object in the human experiment, and the prediction of the human behavior by the TRACE model.

The first thing to notice is that the graphs look very similar, suggesting that the TRACE model is quite good at predicting the details of human behavior. Not surprisingly, they both show fixation to the referent increasing over time, until it is basically the only thing the subjects look at. But at the same time that fixations to the referent increase, so do fixations to the cohort, as both the cohort and TRACE theories predict; fixations to the cohort start to decline as the bottom-up information starts to diverge from that word. However, as more of the word is heard, subjects increasingly look at the rhyme object, indicating that the rhyme word is becoming an active competitor. This is not something the cohort model would predict. However, as the graphs show, the TRACE model predicts the degree and timing of fixations to the rhyme object remarkably well. Interestingly,

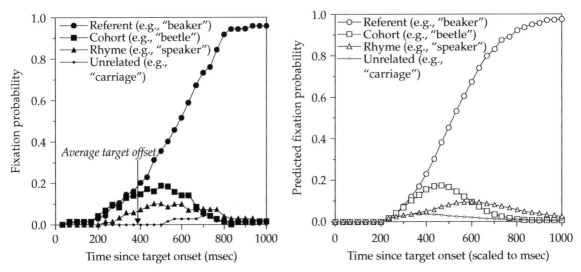

Figure 6.4 Graphs showing actual fixation probabilities from an eye-tracking experiment (left) and predicted fixations from the Trace model (right). Reprinted from Journal of Memory and Language, 38, Allopenna, P. D., Magnuson, J. S., and Tanenhaus, M. H., Tracking the time course of spoken word recognition using eye movements: Evidence for continuous mapping models, 419–439, Copyright (1998), with permission from Elsevier.

Why do fixations not occur until about 200 milliseconds? This is the approximate amount of time it takes to **program** an eye movement. The fact that there are discernible fixations to the referent and cohort at about 200 milliseconds suggests that subjects are starting to make (unconscious) conjectures about the word's identity as soon as they hear just the *very* beginning of a word, consistent with all the models of word recognition we've discussed.

the TRACE model predicts that, over time, fixations to the rhyme object should be slightly higher than fixations to the cohort object, presumably because of the increasing bottom-up support for the rhyme and decreasing bottom-up support for the cohort; the human data seem to be somewhat consistent with that as well.

Eye tracking has become an important experimental tool in psycholinguistics research. It provides another way of tapping into mental representations as their activation fluctuates during normal sentence processing. The experiment we just worked through provided compelling evidence in favor of theories that allow for words to be competitors for recognition even if they are not initially supported by bottom-up information from the speech signal.

Summary

In this chapter, we have looked at a number of variables that influence word recognition: top-down information from context, word frequency, competitor frequency, and competitor neighborhood density. We also discussed a variety of "online" psycholinguistic methods for probing the activation of candidate words as listeners hear spoken words unfolding in time. This chapter also introduced the notion of computational models, and how implementations of theories within these models allow for precise predictions about human behavior. Finally, we examined several theories of word recognition that attempt to explain the findings from experiments. As in many areas of science, the theories were not entirely in agreement about the facts that need to be explained. We saw how computational modeling can be used to evaluate theoretical proposals of human word recognition and ultimately guide scientists toward an ever more sophisticated understanding of how humans discern and identify words in language.

Further Reading

Altmann, Gerry T. M. (1990). *Cognitive Models of Speech Processing: Psycholinguistics and Computational Perspectives*. Cambridge, MA: MIT Press.

Chapter 7

Phonological Units and Phonological Patterning

What do we know when we know a word? We know some fairly complex details of what a word means – we know that "cat" is not only an animal, but that it is alive, furry with four legs and a tail, a potential pet, something some people are allergic to, and so on. We also know how a word can be used in the sentences of our language – we know that "cat" is a noun and, as such, can be a subject or object for many kinds of verbs. These only scratch the surface of our semantic and syntactic knowledge of words. There is, however, one more very important aspect of knowledge that we have about words; we know their building blocks or cognitive units. For "cat" we know that we must form a velar closure with our tongue rear and open our glottis to make a [kʰ] sound, open our mouth and create a pharyngeal constriction to make an [æ] sound, and form a closure with our tongue tip at the alveolar ridge to make a [t] sound. Each of these actions and their resulting sounds have no inherent meaning of their own, but when organized appropriately in time, they can build the word "cat." The same building blocks could be called on in a different word with a different arrangement, like in "tack" [tæk] or "act" [ækt]. We call these cognitive building blocks of words **phonological units**.

Do you remember the term **compositionality** from Chapter 1? This describes the property of human language that complex messages are built from smaller discrete and manipulable parts. Sentences are built from structured combinations of meaningful parts – words, and words are built from structured combinations of nonmeaningful parts – phonological units. Knowing a language means knowing its phonological units and how they pattern both within words and across the lexicon, that is, across the totality of word forms of a language. This aspect of linguistic knowledge is called **phonology**.

How does a linguist investigate this phonological knowledge? A linguist is interested in a variety of sources of evidence for the linguistic units that any particular language may call on or the set of such possible units across all human languages. A linguist will want to investigate what people know about how phonological units in their language are organized and the details of how these units surface in the words of the language. In this chapter we will be walking through some different kinds of linguistic evidence for phonological units. These units range from small building blocks of words to larger cognitive building blocks of words. In each case, scientists of language have reason to believe that these units are "psychologically real" in some sense. This means that speakers and listeners of a language are aware of and can manipulate phonological units. This knowledge and skill is generally something we exploit without even realizing it. Sometimes, we do have access to linguistic intuitions that provide evidence of phonological units – for example, in the case of poets creating verse, of language games, or in the invention of writing systems. But most of the time, phonological knowledge about the internal structuring of words is subconscious or implicit knowledge, not overt or explicit or taught knowledge. Nevertheless, it is very real knowledge that all human language users have and exploit.

In order to study phonological units, we will start with the smallest cognitive building block and move to larger ones. For each case, we will present some language data demonstrating a linguistic process that crucially relies on the existence of that particular building block. Thus we will simultaneously be studying **phonological units** and the **phonological processes** or **phonological patterning** that linguists have found to utilize or exploit those units.

The Gesture or Feature: The Phonological Building Block We Combine to Make Words

Gestures

What is the smallest *atomic* building block of words? In the example of "cat" above, we saw that in order to utter or understand the word "cat," the constriction place and degree of the various constrictions and their ordering in time are key pieces of phonological knowledge. Linguists have developed two ways to talk about these. We happily entertain both here, as they are quite similar.

One way of conceptualizing the atoms of phonological knowledge is in terms of articulatory **gestures**. These are movements of the vocal tract achieving some linguistically important goal, like the formation of a constriction.

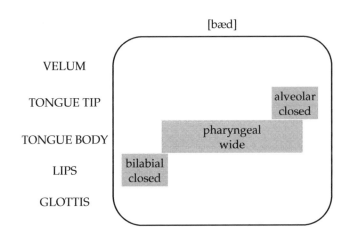

Figure 7.1 Gestural score of "bad".

For example, a **lip closure gesture** is a phonological unit at the beginning of the word "bad." It is what the words "bad," "beauty," and "bingo" all have in common at their onset. At the beginning of these words, the upper lip, lower lip, and jaw all move in concert or in a **coordinative structure** to achieve the lip closure gesture. The gesture lasts over an interval of time: one can think of this in terms of the gesture turning on, and a small amount of time later, turning off again. Sometimes it is useful to imagine this like an on–off switch – a gesture is present when it is on and absent when it is off. Other times it is useful to think of a gesture's activation being more like a dimmer switch – it gets more and more active as the constriction is achieved and then gets less and less active until it is completely finished. Figure 7.1 is a diagram called a gestural score, showing the *on* intervals for the gestures in the word "bad." Each of the horizontal panels indicates which vocal tract subsystem is called on to achieve a particular gesture. We already saw that the lip system that uses the upper lip, lower lip, and jaw is called on for the first vocal tract action.

The independently controllable vocal tract subsystems that gestures can call on are shared across all human languages because they are determined by the structural and functional anatomy of the human vocal tract. They include the lip aperture system; the tongue tip, body, and root systems; the velum system; and the glottal system. How an individual language makes use of these possibilities – what subsystems they use and how they use them – differs from language to language, although all languages seem to have some severe constrictions, which we call consonants, and some markedly less severe constrictions, which we call vowels.

Features

Sometimes linguists may not be concerned with when a gesture begins or ends in time, but it may be important for them to understand simply what

Table 7.1   An overview of some phonological features

Articulatory quality being categorized	Feature name	Feature description
Vocal tract constrictor system and/or Gestural constriction location	[labial]	involving the lips
	[coronal]	involving the tongue tip or blade
	[dorsal]	involving the tongue body/rear
	[nasal]	involving velum lowering ([+nasal] is the opposite of "oral")
	[lateral]	involving tongue narrowing that allows air to flow down one or both sides of the tongue ([+lateral] is the opposite of "central")
	[back]	small distance between F1 and F2 ([+back] is the opposite of "front")
Gestural constriction degree and/or its acoustic/aerodynamic consequences	[continuant]	not a full closure
	[consonantal]	not a vowel
	[sonorant]	having a wide constriction and smooth airflow ([+sonorant] is the opposite of "obstruent")
	[high]	a low F1 produced by a fairly narrow vocalic constriction ([+high] is the opposite of "low")
Gestural constriction shapes and orientations or their acoustic/ aerodynamic consequences	[strident] (or sometimes [sibilant])	having high amplitude frication noise created by turbulent airflow, especially greater high-frequency noise than found in adjacent vowels
State of the glottis	[voice]	having vocal fold vibration for normal voicing
Coordination of constriction and glottal opening actions	[aspirated]	having a positive VOT

the phonetic properties of a word's gestures are. These properties are called **features**. The beginning of the word "bad" has the properties or features of being [bilabial], [noncontinuant] (i.e., a closure), and [voiced]. Featural units can refer to the presence or absence of various gestural properties or their aerodynamic or acoustic consequences. Often these feature values are expressed as binary, which means that that feature is considered to either characterize or fail to characterize a particular sound. So, for example, a sound that has voicing is referred to as having the feature value [+voice], and a sound that does not have voicing is referred to as having the feature value [−voice]. Table 7.1 summarizes some of the features or phonetic properties that linguists believe to be cognitively important in describing the structure of words.

We will be adopting two graphical conventions in this chapter. First, we will use capital C for consonant and capital V for vowel. Secondly, we will use an asterisk (*) to indicate a word that is *not allowed* in a language, that is, a word that is ungrammatical in the linguistic sense.

Some linguists believe that there is one universal set of phonological features used in all languages. Others dispute this view. Regardless of the position taken on this question, phonological features have two uses for linguists. First, they describe articulatory or acoustic properties of sounds. Second, they can be used, alone or in combination, to define qualities that play a systematic role in the language. That is, we can analyze the phonological patterns of words in one language or in many languages by examining which features are seen to work in some common fashion.

Language patterns that demonstrate the gesture or feature

Let's turn to a specific language pattern that is one of many that convince linguists that gestures or features are cognitive units that participate in defining the properties and patterns of words. You probably never noticed that in English there is a restriction on words of the shape *s-consonant-vowel-consonant* (or [sCVC]) such that the two consonants can't both involve the *same* (nonglottal) constrictor system. So these two consonants can't both be nasal, can't both be labial, can't both be velar. Compare the following (* means that a form is ungrammatical and does not occur):

snip (which is an OK word)   versus the following, which are not OK words:
    *snim
    *snom
    *smung
    *sning
    all have two nasals

spot (which is an OK word)   versus the following, which are not OK words:
    *spob
    *smaf
    *sphefe
    all have two labials

Scott (which is an OK word)   versus the following, which are not OK words:
    *scock
    *skig
    *skong
    all have two velars

Indeed, the words on the right-hand side of the table above probably sound "wrong" to you in some way that you might have trouble stating; if asked whether they sound like a possible word in English, you would likely say no. (In the whole English language, only a handful of exceptions occur, such as *skunk*, *spoof*, and *spiffy*, and the more marginal: *skank*, *skag*, and *spam*.)

In order to explain this pattern, a linguist would have to describe what phonetic quality the second and final consonant may *not* have in common. It's not a straightforward case of identity; many of the impossible words like *smaf and *snim have nonidentical consonants. For an adequate explanation, linguists must appeal to a small *atomic* unit or property to describe this pattern of English – the gesture or feature. (Remember that, for the most part, we are not concerned with the distinction between the action-based *gesture* and the category descriptor *feature*. We will use the term **gesture** here, but your instructor might instead use a feature description.)

The *sCVC constraint in English requires that the consonants may not share a constriction gesture. The two consonants may not both have a velum-lowering gesture (i.e., be [+nasal]); may not both have a tongue dorsum constriction gesture; may not both have a lip-constriction gesture. It is the repetition of an identical *small atomic unit* in the sCVC word context that is critical to describing this linguistic pattern. **Phonotactic constraints** on word forms like this one occur in many languages and are one source of evidence for the cognitive importance of the phonological unit of gesture or feature in the phonological system of human language.

Let's look at another phonological pattern found in many languages that requires small atomic units for a suitable linguistic description. **Harmony** refers to a constraint on a word form that requires all of a word or a certain part of a word to *agree* in the presence of some particular gesture. Let's consider an example from Malay, spoken in Southeast Asia, in which words are harmonic for – agree in having – a velum-lowering gesture, which yields nasal airflow. (Remember that we could alternatively refer to this as agreement in the feature [+nasal].) The specific pattern for this language requires that if a nasal sound (i.e., a sound with a velum-lowering gesture) occurs in a word, all sounds after it in the word must also be nasal (i.e. have velum-lowering), until either the end of a word is reached *or* until another gesture with a narrow or closed constriction degree occurs (i.e., a liquid, stop, or fricative). Find this pattern in the following Malay words (remember that the ˜ symbol transcribes nasalization on vowels)[1]:

baɲõn	to rise
mə̃ratappi	to cause to cry
pəɲãw̃ãsan	supervision
mĩnõm	to drink

[1] Malay words from Farid M. Onn (1980). *Aspects of Malay Phonology and Morphology.* Bangi: Penerbit Universiti Kebangsaan Malaysia; cited in Rachel Walker (2000). *Nasalization, Neutral Segments and Opacity Effects.* New York: Garland.

The underlined parts of the words are heard as nasal, so are presumed to have the velum in a lowered position.

A word that didn't obey Malay's harmony pattern would be an ungrammatical or impossible word in Malay because speakers of Malay have internalized knowledge of this pattern in their language. We see that, in order to describe the knowledge of this harmony pattern, we again need to make reference to an atomic vocal tract action or phonetic quality. Examples of various kinds of harmony exist in many languages – Turkish, for example, and many African languages. In order to explain speakers' knowledge of their language-specific harmony patterns, phonological gestures (or features in the sense used above) must be "real" or functional cognitive units since this is the object of agreement in the harmony pattern.

Finally, let's look at one last pattern that demonstrates the activity of the gesture or feature in shaping word forms. **Assimilation** is the pattern in which one sound becomes like an adjacent sound in some specific property. You can think of assimilation as a kind of harmony limited to be strictly local to adjacent sounds. Sometimes assimilation has occurred in a historically earlier time in a language, and we simply see its "frozen" results in our current words. For example, we know that there is an English prefix *in-* which means roughly *not*, as in words like *inconvenient* or *intolerant*. Yet we see in the current frozen spelling of English that adjectives beginning with a labial consonant are often written (and pronounced) with a labial nasal in this prefix – such as *imperfect, impossible*. The final [n] of the prefix has become **assimilated** in its place of articulation so that it has taken on the labial place of the adjacent sound in the beginning of *perfect* and *possible*. To describe such variations we must refer to a labial gesture or feature as being the property which the final sound of the prefix "adopts" from the initial sound of the adjective; it becomes like or assimilates to the initial labial of the main word. You can notice other examples of assimilation in your own speech. Think about how you pronounce the phrase "this show" if you put it casually in a sentence. It is very likely that you say [ðɪʃoʊ], without an [s] at the end of "this." This is another example of assimilation of place of articulation, only this time it occurs across a word boundary.

> Assimilation can be regressive (anticipatory) in which a sound becomes more like an upcoming sound, or it can be progressive (preservative) in which a sound becomes more like a preceding sound.

In sum, we have seen three types of phonological patterns whose analysis requires that the gesture or feature – the smallest or most atomic element of sound structure – play a critical role: phonotactics constraints, harmony, and assimilation. These are observed across language after language and appear to be regular and common properties of language structure. Thus we can conclude that the elemental sound building blocks that specify a sound's constriction location, constriction degree, voicing, and aerodynamic properties are critical to how the mind represents and organizes sounds in language.

Segments

In nature, and in cognition, larger structures emerge from the combination and interaction of smaller structures. This is also a property of human language. We can consider the segment to be a cognitive phonological unit for structuring words that emerges from a regular pattern of combination across the lexicon of our small atomic building blocks. In any given language, linguistic actions of the vocal tract can combine in certain (language-specific) patterns to create larger units. Segments are one such unit. Segments are roughly the unit we've been describing with an IPA symbol, or can be thought of roughly as an alphabetic character in writing systems that have a very transparent orthography, like those of some Romance languages or Icelandic or Finnish.

For example, a [p] is a segment that combines a bilabial closing gesture and a glottal widening gesture. In a given language that has a [p], these two gestures will appear in many words and always recur with a particular pattern of temporal overlap. It is this gestural **molecule** that we refer to as the segment [p]. Other segments may include one to several gestures, always cohering in a special way to form a unit. In fact, experiments have shown that if a scientist "perturbs" (physically bumps or disrupts) the articulation of one component gesture of a segmental molecule, the other gestures in that segment or molecule automatically and extremely rapidly compensate for the perturbation to make sure that the segment is spoken as accurately as possible under the circumstances. Some examples of how segments emerge from combining atomic phonological building blocks are shown in Table 7.2.

Table 7.2 Segments produced by different gestural combinations

	Alone	*Combined with a velum-lowering gesture for nasality*	*Combined with a glottal widening gesture for voicelessness*
Labial closing gesture	[b]	[m]	[p]
Tongue tip closing gesture	[d]	[n]	[t]
Tongue body closing gesture	[g]	[ŋ]	[k]

Note that English does not allow for a combination of a closing gesture with *both* a velum-lowering gesture and a glottal widening gesture – but other languages do. Can you think what kind of segment this would create? It would create a voiceless nasal. Such segments or gestural combinations do occur in some languages, like Burmese. Each language has its own ways of combining its atomic building blocks. Of course there are universal constraints on these combinations – the resulting sound must be able to be identified by a listener. If it weren't, how would any baby or child be able to learn the particular combination in the course of language acquisition!

Many linguists feel that in creating the phonological patterns found in the world's languages two forces are at work – the force for **perceptual recoverability** by listeners competes with a speaker-driven force for **ease of articulation**. However, we linguists actually understand relatively little about what makes some vocal tract actions or combinations "easier" than others, how this "ease" might depend on larger scale organizational factors, or about the perceptual skills listeners bring to bear in identifying the components of words.

Language patterns that demonstrate the segment

Just as we considered some examples of phonological patterns to demonstrate how atomic building blocks must be cognitively active in the patterning of languages, we can similarly consider examples of phonological patterns in language that require reference to a segment-sized unit. In fact, one simple metalinguistic experience of humans makes explicit reference to segments – this is the invention of the alphabetic writing system. Even if such a system has been invented only once by humans – as indeed appears likely to be the case – it would require the inventor, and the learners, to have had cognitive access to the segment.

Some patterns found in the way people speak languages also point to the cognitive validity of the segmental unit. The phonological process of **deletion** can critically make reference to the segment. In some dialects of French, for example, certain word-final consonants are omitted or *deleted* before a consonant or before a pause but are spoken when they occur before a vowel or glide. (The exact circumstances in which deletion may, must, or must not occur are somewhat more complicated than that which we'll undertake describing here). Consider the word "très" (very); in the prevocalic string "très élégant" this is pronounced [trɛzelegã], *but* "très" is pronounced [trɛ] in the preconsonant context "très chic" [trɛʃik].

"très" (very)   →   "très élégant" [trɛzelegã] vs. "très chic" [trɛʃik]

Or consider the phrase "mon ancien collègue" ("my old colleague," pro-nounced [mɔ̃nɑ̃sjẽkɔlɛg]) in which an [n] is pronounced before the vowel-initial word but not before "collègue." In order to describe the phonological unit targeted in these and similar examples from French, reference must be made to the unit **segment**. It is not just a gesture or feature that is pronounced or fails to be pronounced; for example, the [n] shown in the second example above involves two gestures that partici-pate as a unit. (Can you figure out what they are?) The segments [z], [t], [ʀ], and [n] are all common consonants to participate in this pattern in French, and most of them are multigesture segments. There would be no way to explain the linguistic relation between the short (with-deletion) form of a word, like [trɛ] for "très," and its long (without-deletion) form, like [trɛz], if speakers didn't have cognitive access to a segment-sized unit, and *clearly* speakers do know that both realizations of the word are, in terms of meaning, the *same* word. A linguist is interested in capturing the basis for this knowledge.

A second example of a phonological process or pattern that involves seg-ments is **metathesis**. You may remember that we discussed metathesis in Chapter 3. **Metathesis** is a reversal in the temporal order of two segments so that two segments that appear in a particular order in one form of a word occur in the reverse order in another form of the word. A linguist named Elizabeth Hume has created an interesting web database of many examples of metathesis in the world's language (*www.ling.ohio-state.edu/ ~ehume/metathesis*). You can see many examples there of how sequences of two consonants or a consonant and a vowel alternate in their ordering in a variety of languages depending on the particular contexts in which they occur. For example, Elizabeth Hume describes how in the language Leti spoken on the island of Leti near the Indonesian–East Timorese border, the linear ordering of the final consonant and vowel of a word can vary. For example, the combination of "finger + bachelor" for "index finger" is pronounced "uk<u>ra</u> ppalu," but the same word for finger is pronounced "uk<u>ar</u>" in the sequence "uk<u>ar</u> lavan" "finger + big" meaning "thumb or big toe." Segments are generally the phonological unit participating in metathesis. Other metathesis examples that Hume has collected are shown below. Can you identify the segments involved in the metathesis?

From Sidamo spoken in Ethiopia
Word + suffix beginning with [n]

gud+nonni	gundonni	they finished
has+nemmo	hansemmo	we look for
hab+nemmo	hambemmo	we forget
ag+no	aŋgo	let's drink

Why do you think the nasal is pronounced as labial in the word meaning "we forget" and as velar in the word meaning "let's drink"? (Hint: look for one of the phonological patterns we discussed above.)

A third example of the phonological status of segments can be viewed in the way verbs are formed in Semitic languages like Arabic and Hebrew. In these languages, related forms of a word are differentiated by using a common set of consonants (often three) and interleaving them in different ways with vowels to encode different word meanings.

kʃr (to tie)

Present:	*Past:*	*Future:*
koʃer (sing., masculine (m.))	kaʃarti (I tied)	ʔekʃor (I will tie)
	kaʃarta (you tied, m.)	tikʃor (you will tie, m.)
koʃeret (sing., feminine (f.))	kaʃart (you tied, f.)	tikʃeri (you will tie, f.)
	kaʃar (he tied)	jikʃor (he will tie)
koʃrim (plural, m.)	kaʃra (she tied)	tikʃor (she will tie)
koʃrot (plural, f.)	kaʃarnu (we tied)	nikʃor (we will tie)
	kaʃartem (you tied, m.)	tikʃeru (you will tie, pl.)
	kaʃarten (you tied, f.)	jikʃeru (they will tie)
	kaʃru (they tied)	

Clearly, what a language learner of Hebrew and similar languages must learn, and what a proficient speaker of such a language must know, is that there are segment units that can be and are manipulated in words in a meaningful way.

In sum, so far in this chapter we have seen evidence for small atomic phonological building blocks – gestures/features – and larger molecular structures emerging from the combination of the atomic building blocks – segments. We have seen that a variety of phonological processes or patterns including phonotactic constraints, harmony, deletion, metathesis, and Semitic morphology provide evidence to linguists of the cognitive significance of these units. Next, we will consider larger phonological units and evidence for their psychological reality for humans using language.

Syllable and Subsyllable Units

A larger unit of linguistic structure composed of organized gestures and segments is the syllable. The syllable generally contains a vowel preceded and followed by zero or more consonants with which it is associated or coordinated, though some languages can have syllables that consist only of certain consonants like [l], [r], or nasals where these particular consonants

$$C_n V C_n \quad n \geq 0$$

Figure 7.2 A shorthand summary of a typical syllable composition.

It's interesting to note that even though most of the time people easily agree on the number of syllables in a word (though sometimes people may disagree – consider "our" and "real"), from a speech acoustics point of view, linguists have never found a satisfactory identifying characteristic of the syllable, even though they have looked for a long time at a lot of different acoustic and even respiratory possibilities. But from a phonological point of view, the syllable seems to be an essential unit of organization. We can also see evidence for the cognitive relevance of the syllable by virtue of the many syllabic writing systems in existence, such as in Japanese. How do we reconcile these two observations of phonological importance of the syllable but no unique identifying characteristics in the acoustic signal? Some phoneticians believe that syllable structure is best defined by fundamental temporal coordination patterns between articulatory gestures, and that these may not have a direct or obvious reflection in the resulting acoustic signal.

However, it is worth noting that in some languages, including English, speakers may disagree about where some syllable boundaries are; and knowledge of spelling also complicates these judgments.

"take the place" of the requisite vowel. We can schematize the syllable as in Figure 7.2.

Every word in a language consists of at least one syllable; sometimes this syllable may be composed of only one segment – like in the word "a" – and sometimes it may be composed of multiple segments – like in the word "strengths." People almost always agree on how many syllables a word has, so it seems that we have relatively common and sure instincts about what a syllable is.

Language patterns that demonstrate the syllable

Languages also provide us with linguistic evidence that the syllable is an important cognitive unit in organizing words. Let's look next at a phonological process that can involve the participation of syllable units. **Reduplication** refers to the repetition of a whole word or of some part of a word in the formation of a related word. As we will see shortly, sometimes the part of the word which is repeated is a syllable. Many of the world's languages use reduplication as a way of making new words. English only does this in special circumstances, putting contrastive emphasis on a word (or sometimes a phrase): *In your latte, do you want soy-milk, or milk-milk?* But in other languages, reduplication plays a very common and productive role in phonologically relating words that share some component of meaning. Consider, for example, Tagalog, a language spoken in the Philippines, that creates the future tense of its verbs by the phonological process of reduplication. Take a look at the following related verbs in Tagalog[2]:

sumulat	"to write"	sulat	"writing"	<u>su</u>sulat	"will write"
kumanta	"to sing"	kanta	"song"	<u>ka</u>kanta	"will sing"
pumasok	"to enter"	pasok	"entry"	<u>pa</u>pasok	"will enter"
magtrabaho	"to work"	trabaho	"work"	mag<u>tra</u>trabaho	"will work"

If the Tagalog word for "passenger" is *sakay*, how do you think "will ride" is said? Right! It's *sasakay*. Reduplication in different languages creates a partial or whole copy of a word, and that copy will have its shape determined by phonological structure. You probably already see that the Tagalog example provides evidence where the copy is the size of a syllable. This provides linguistic evidence that the syllable unit is an important cognitive unit since it is critical to specifying the Tagalog reduplication process used to make the future tense.

Here is another example of reduplication. This is from a language called Yidin^y, an Australian aboriginal language.[3]

ḍimuru	"house"	ḍimu-ḍimuru	"houses"
gindalba	"lizard species"	gindal-gindalba	"lizards"
ḍaḍama-n	"jump"	ḍaḍa-ḍaḍama-n	"jump a lot"
ḏugarba-n	"have an unsettled mind"	ḏugar-ḏugarba-n	
		"have an unsettled mind for a long period"	

How would you describe the phonological "size" of the copied part (called the **reduplicant**) in terms of phonological units for these related words in Yidin^y?

---

[2] Data from Teresita V. Ramos (1985). *Conversational Tagalog: A Functional-Situational Approach.* Honolulu: University of Hawaii Press, and Kie Zuraw.
[3] Data from R. M. W. Dixon (1977). *A Grammar of Yidiny.* Cambridge, UK: Cambridge University Press; cited in A. Marantz (1982) Re Reduplication. *Linguistic Inquiry*, 13, pp. 435–82.

Subsyllabic structure

Though we have said that syllables are made up of smaller units such as segments, it also seems to be the case that the syllable, since it is typically a conglomeration of consonants and vowels, may group these consonants and vowels into subsyllabic units or constituents that are smaller than the syllable but potentially larger than a segment. That is, the syllable may be broken down into component parts that are active in language.

These subsyllable parts are given names. The **nucleus** refers to the vowel (or, if there is no vowel, the sound in the syllable having the most open vocal tract). The **onset** refers to the consonants before vowel or nucleus; this may be one consonant or more than one. The **coda** refers to the consonants after vowel or nucleus; this may be one consonant or more than one. And the **rime** refers to the nucleus and the coda together. (When two words contain final syllables that have identical rimes, we hear them as rhyming.) Schematically, we can picture the syllable parts as shown in Figure 7.3. Or, in order to show the nested relationship of rime and coda, sometimes this structure is shown as in Figure 7.4.

Can you figure out the syllable onset in the word "space?" What about in the word "train?" "Food?" Did you answer [sp], [tr], and [f]?

> It's interesting to note that poetry differs from language to language in what counts as a sufficiently near-identical rhyme, or in the type of identity that is allowed as a poetic rhyme. You have perhaps heard of "slant rhymes" or "half rhymes" in English that are nonidentical rhymes.

Language patterns that demonstrate the syllable onset

Of course, many words (at least in English) have more than one syllable. That means we might find sequences of the sort V_1CV_2 or V_1CCV_2. How do the consonants in these sequences pattern into syllables? Do the consonants

ONSET RIME CODA

Figure 7.3 Components of the syllable.

sprat

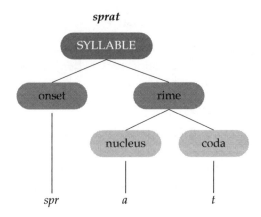

Figure 7.4   A hierarchical depiction of syllable structure.

function as a coda to the earlier syllable with V_1 as the nucleus, or do they function as an onset to the later syllable with V_2 as the nucleus, or, in the case of two consonants in sequence, do they split up between the syllables? As it turns out, languages don't handle this in an arbitrary or random way. Rather, across the world's languages, a systematic preference for how consonants pattern syllabically is observed. Consonants prefer to syllabify with the later syllable (i.e., "rightward") as syllable onsets. This is the case generally as long as the language permits words to begin with those particular segments or sequences of segments. So in English, the sequence [apa], for example in "papa" will syllabify [pa.pa] (where we use a full point [.]

Alliteration in poetry provides another sort of evidence for the syllable onset unit. You may have learned that alliteration in poetry is the device of using two or more words that start with the same (or similar) sound. However, there is evidence (notably from the work of linguist Donka Minkova) that poetry of various types also may alliterate like onset clusters. For example, in the Old English poem *Beowulf* we find: "ond on **sp**ēd wrecan / **sp**el gerāde" ("and on success create / a skillful tale").

to signify a syllable boundary). However, in English the sequence [aŋa] may not syllabify [a.ŋa] since English words and syllables may not start with [ŋ]. So we get "sing.a.long" not "si.nga.long." When multiple consonants are permissible as a possible onset, they indeed form one. Most English speakers would agree that "asparagus" is syllabified "a.spa.ra.gus" and not "as.pa.ra.gus," but that "grandpa" is syllabified "gran.pa" (or "gram.pa") but not "gra.mpa" because [sp] is a permissible onset (as in, say, *spa*) but [mp] is not.

In sum, a source of evidence for subsyllabic units is cross-linguistic **constraints** on syllable structure. One of the most universal constraints or patterns regarding syllable structure is that words with syllable onsets are more common (preferred) over those without – this is the rightward preference we just discussed. A second common cross-linguistic constraint is that words with single-consonant syllable onsets are more common (preferred) over those with multiconsonant onsets. Finally, we learned above about phonotactic constraints. Reference to the constituents of a syllable is often necessary to accurately express these constraints, as phonotactics in syllable onsets and codas may differ from one another.

In order to state that languages of all different sorts have these patterns or preferences, then the subsyllabic unit **onset** must be relevant to the language's structure. That is, human language makes reference to the structural unit of syllable **onset**. There are other linguistic behaviors that make reference to other subsyllabic units – what unit comes to mind when you think of poetry in verse? The rime, of course! *Jack Sprat would eat no fat*.

Let's turn next to a different type of phonological evidence that can be brought to bear in evaluating how the human mind structures words. This is **language games**. These are fun activities that (usually young) people use to create a sense of community or an "in-group," because an individual must know how to play the game to be understood (young people often assuming that the older people don't know how to play the language game). In fact, similar activities occur in some adult communities – in this case they are sometimes called "secret languages" – though again the main purpose is to segregate communities and messages exchanged within those communities from others not counted as belonging to the community.

One language game that most American children learn is Pig Latin. If you are a native player (or former player) of this game, you know that to say "speak pig latin" in Pig Latin you would say "eakspay igpay atinlay." Can you state the pattern for playing this game? At first try, you might suggest: *Move each syllable onset to the end of the syllable and add "ay."* But notice that "latin" becomes "atinlay." If the process of *onset movement + "ay"* actually applied to syllable onsets across the board, for "latin" you would get "alayintay" because there are two syllables (so two onsets) in "latin." Thus our first statement formulation is not sufficiently precise. It seems that in the English, the Pig Latin process applies to only the first syllable onset of the word and moves it to the end of the word. So we could restate the pattern more accurately as: *Move the first syllable onset in the word to end of the word and add "ay."*

Some of you may have learned a game called Ubbi Dubbi from the PBS children's show *Zoom*. This language game would say the phrase "Speak Pig Latin" as "spubeak pubig lubatubin." The pattern can be stated: *Insert [ub] after each syllable onset.* Can you say "Speak Ubbi Dubbi" in Ubbi Dubbi? Try – "spubeak ububbi dububbi." Some kids (and former kids) are amazingly fast and proficient at Ubbi Dubbi; as the *Zoom* website says, they "Jubust Dubo Ubit!" So, in summary, language games or secret languages

---

A further look at Pig Latin

How would you say the following in Pig Latin: "every," "aim," "apply"? It might be a good idea to use your IPA transcription to look at these patterns. (If you are not a native speaker of English, ask someone who is; nearly everyone knows how to play this game). What is different about these words than those in the text that led us to our statement of the pattern? How would you have to elaborate the description in the text, if at all, to capture the complete pattern including words such as these?

Further, how would you say in Pig Latin: "twin," "you," "cute," "few," "twinkle," "which?" What do the patterns suggest (for your own personal version of Pig Latin) for whether a consonant+glide sequence is affiliated with the syllable onset or with the syllable nucleus? Are the patterns the same for both English glides? If you ask a handful of other people, are their answers the same as yours? Ⓦ

---

are another type of evidence for cognitive units that language users are sensitive to, and can even overtly manipulate.

Table 7.3 summarizes to this point in the chapter the various phonological units we have discussed as being important in the structuring of the words. On the right-hand side of the table is a list of a number of phonological phenomena or patterns that linguists feel yield important evidence to suggest the cognitive reality or significance of particular phonological units.

Table 7.3   Phonological units and patterning discussed so far

Phonological units	*Phonological patterning examined as evidence for various phonological units*
Gestures/Features	Phonotactic constraints
	Harmony
	Assimilation
Segments	Deletion
	Metathesis
Syllables	Reduplication
Onsets & rimes	Syllable-structure universals
(and also nuclei and codas)	Poetic devices
	Language games

We will continue with an examination of an additional large phonological unit, and revise this table to be a more complete summary at the end of the chapter.

The Stress Foot

In order to examine how syllables cohere into larger units, we must first take a look at word stress. Stress refers to the "beat" of the word, which falls on one, or sometimes more than one, syllable of the word. One can think of stress as the property of being a rhythmically strong syllable in a word. We've already seen that stress is implicated in how the brain manages word segmentation, and we want to understand here the role that stress plays in the phonological structuring of a word.

When more than one syllable in a word is stressed, we call the stronger stress the primary stress and the weaker one(s) secondary stress(es). In English, the following words have stress on the underlined syllables; nonunderlined syllables are stressless and generally (for English) have their vowels pronounced as schwa [ə].

Lena
Anna
banana
Benjamin
fruit
Minnesota

Phonetically, these syllables of relative prominence are likely to have greater acoustic intensity, higher relative pitch, and more extreme and longer acoustic properties due to larger and longer articulatory movements. When words are put together into utterances, some stresses are more prominent than others. So while the word "into" spoken alone has stress on its first syllable, in the following sentence spoken aloud – *Toby lifted the suitcase into the taxi* – the syllable "in" is much less prominent than the stressed first syllables in "suitcase" and "taxi."

Some languages don't make use of differing stress among syllables, but many languages do. For the ones that do, stress can be conceived of as the linguistic use of rhythm in language. Stressed syllables in some sense correspond with the beat, though the beat-pattern favored by languages differs. Some languages have a very regular beat pattern and little vowel reduction (i.e., vowels are generally realized fully, not as schwas). Other languages favor an alternating beat pattern such that strong and weak beats are intermixed in a fairly regular way – like *strong–weak–strong–weak*, or *weak–strong–weak–strong*, or *strong–weak–weak–strong–weak–weak*, and so on.

In still other languages, stress always falls on a particular syllable within a word, often the first (as in Czech or Finnish) or the next to last (as in Polish or Swahili). Finally, languages may not have a predictable stress pattern; in these languages, such as Russian and Spanish, stress is used contrastively to create meaning differences.

In Spanish:	*hablo*	"I speak"	*habló*	"he/she spoke"
	plato	"dish/plate"	*plató*	"(film) set"
	ingles	"groins"	*inglés*	"English"

Some languages have hybrids of these systems. For example, stress may be partially predictable. In such cases, the stress placement is often influenced by the segmental composition of syllables, perhaps in combination with syllable position in the word.

English stress is actually a relatively complicated system – a system about which whole books have been written. It is partially predictable with very complex patterning. Certain stress facts are quite predictable in English – for example, for semantically related, two-syllable noun–verb pairs, the noun always has first syllable stress and the verb has second syllable stress: record (n) versus record (v), impact (n) versus impact (v). But English stress can also vary unpredictably in minimal pairs such as:

discus (noun)	*discuss (verb)*
Louie's	*Louise*
misery	*Missouri*

(this last is a minimal pair at least for Western US speakers – is it for you?)

We will not try to understand the ins and outs of the English stress system, but we will assume at this point that you can distinguish the stressed syllable(s) in an English word.

We are now ready to turn to the final phonological unit to be introduced in this chapter – the **stress foot**, often just called the **foot**. Stress feet are groupings of syllables defined by the stress pattern of a word. We will only work on understanding the stress foot using English, but in general, languages that have regular repeating stress patterns have foot structure of either the sort strong–weak or weak–strong.

In English, a foot (or, equivalently, stress foot) is a group starting with a stressed syllable and including the following syllable if it is unstressed. (It's helpful to remember that stressless syllables often are pronounced with a schwa vowel.) A single "unfooted" syllable may occur as the first syllable in a word, if that first syllable is stressless (and elsewhere in certain circumstances too complex for us to tackle here). In the following examples, brackets have been used to denote stress feet, with underlining showing where the stresses in the words are.

1 foot	**2 feet**	**3 feet**
(Lena)	*(Sacra)(mento)*	*(Tim)(buk)(tu)*
(rider)	*(Benja)(min)*	*(trans)(liter)(ated)*
(fruit)	*(hang)(over)*	
ba(nana)	*(men)(tor)*	
a(mount)		
de(licious)		

You may not have consciously noticed how many feet are in a word or phrase, but feet are used frequently and naturally as an organizing unit in language. If you have ever studied poetry, you might remember that verse often follows a foot pattern. Simple children's poems, for example, typically contain four feet per line. Can you clap out the four feet per line in the following nursery rhyme – your clap will fall naturally on the first syllable of foot:

Find a penny, pick it up;
All day long you'll have good luck.

(Find a) (penny) (pick it) (up)
(All day) (long you'll) (have good) (luck)

In many sorts of poetry, it is the number of feet that constrain the verse, while the number of syllables is irrelevant. Consider:

(London) (Bridge is) (falling) (down),	7 syllables; 4 feet
(Falling) (down), (falling) (down),	6 syllables; 4 feet
(London) (Bridge is) (falling) (down),	7 syllables; 4 feet
(My) (fair) (lady).	4 syllables; 3 feet plus a beat

The use of stress feet in verse has been much studied not just by linguists but by those interested in poetry from a variety of perspectives.[4]

A linguistic word formation process in English that demonstrates the cognitive reality of the stress foot as a phonological unit is expletive infixation. This is a fancy term for something that might at first seem scandalous but which has been presented in scholarly journals in linguistics for the elegant scientific picture it paints of the cognitive role of the foot in structuring words. In fact, the phonologist John McCarthy

---

[4] For those of you who remember iambic pentameters from high school, it's important to note that feet in verse are not identical to linguistic feet – you can have a foot in verse that is unstressed–stressed in English, even though this is not a possible phonological foot.

presented a study of this process in a 1982 article in the flagship journal of the Linguistic Society of America. Expletive infixation is the insertion in American English of the word "fucking" (or sometimes in British or Australian English of the word "bloody") to indicate emphasis or incredulity, such as in *fan-fucking-tastic* and *abso-fucking-lutely* and *engi-fucking-neering*.

You might, just looking at these three examples, think that the expletive gets inserted in the middle of the word or immediately before a stressed syllable. What additional data could be brought to bear to evaluate this hypothesis? What happens in monosyllabic words? At word edges? Consider the examples below (we've used *freakin* for the expletive); remember that * indicates an impossible word form.

*flat-freakin
*fl-freakin-at
de-freakin-licious BUT NOT *deli-freakin-cious
*rider-freakin ("der" is considered stressless)
*r-freakin-ider
*ri-freakin-der
men-freakin-tor (noun)
Timbuk-freakin-tu OR Tim-freakin-buktu
Sacra-freakin-mento BUT NOT *Sa-freakin-cramento or *Sacramen-freakin-to

On examining these possible and impossible word forms, you might have formed a new hypothesis. If you are thinking that expletive insertion is possible *only between feet*, you are correct!

> While the use of profanity might offend some, there are valid scientific reasons for examining this phenomenon that have been nicely outlined by the linguist Michael Hammond. The general phenomenon of infixation occurs in many languages (with nontaboo words) but can only be shown in English in this usage. It also shows that casual speech exhibits the same structural complexity of more standard styles of speech. Finally, even people who do not use these word forms have quite certain judgments, when asked, about where the expletive may and may not occur in a word. This indicates the cognitive robustness of the foot structure as part of our inventory of phonological structures.

Another linguist, Alan Yu, more recently has investigated a pop-culture example of infixation dubbed Homer infixation after the television character Homer Simpson, who popularized it. Take a look at the following word forms with Homer infixation and see if you can determine the pattern based on the footing at the right:

saxophone	*saxa-ma-phone*	*(saxo)(phone)*
secretary	*secre-ma-tary*	*(secre)(tary)*
education	*edu-ma-cation*	*(edu)(cation)*
sophisticated	*sophista-ma-cated*	*so(phisti)(cated)*
But also		
lonely	*lon-ə-ma-ly*	*(lone)(ly)*
grapefruit	*grape-ə-ma-fruit*	*(grape)(fruit)*

While Homer infixation is in fact a tad more complicated than this (which some of you who watch the show may realize)[5], we can describe the data above by noting that Homer infixation must be between feet, with the qualification that the foot preceding the *ma* infix must be bisyllabic. When the foot before *ma* is monosyllabic, this situation can be "repaired" by inserting a syllable and thereby allowing Homer to infix.

Another Simpson character, Ned Flanders, has a different infixation, described by linguists Emily Elfner and Wendell Kimper. Take a look at the following data and see if you can formulate a succinct linguistic description of Ned Flanders's infixation.

welcome → wel-diddly-elcome

action → ac-diddly-action

murder → mur-diddly-urder

order → or-diddly-order

Clue: Flanders does not do this infixation in words that do not have initial stress.

---

[5] The complication arises with words with a medial unstressed syllable that doesn't "fit well" into a foot: like [multi]pli[cation] and [deli]ca[cy]. For these, Homer could say "multipli-ma-cation" but not *"multi-ma-plication" and "delica-ma-cy" but not *"deli-ma-cacy." Linguist Alan Yu argues that this supports a conception of foot organization that incorporates the medial syllable into the preceding foot and still views that foot as having two branches (e.g., "multi+pli").

When children are learning a language they often explore or linger in phonologies that are not (yet) adult-like. This means that the patterning of sounds in the children's words may yield word forms that do not match their adult counterparts. Linguist Sharon Inkelas reports, for example, data from a child that, from age one year old until slightly over age two, produced word forms in which the adult velar stops ([k], [g]) were pronounced as tongue-tip stops ([t], [d]). Interestingly, this wasn't a complete alteration for all [k]s and [g]s nor was it random alterations here and there. In fact, this child used his particular phonological pattern precisely when the velar stop was in *foot-initial* position only. Thus for a period of about a year, this child learned and used a phonology in which foot-structure played an active role in how he pronounced lingual stop consonants.

	Adult word:	Child pronunciation:
	(cup)	[təp]
	a(gain)	[ədɪn]
but		
	(bucket)	[bəkɪt]
	(big)	[bɪg]

After this time, he quickly settled into a more adult-like phonology in which velar stops were pronounced in an adult-like pattern.

Summary

Table 7.4 presents a summary of the phonological units and types of phonological patterning we have surveyed in this chapter.

These collections of units and of patterns is by no means complete; humans are capable of organizing words into a rich granularity of structure, and the thousands of world languages offer many fascinating examples of how this structure is utilized in word formation and defining the relations among words. However, there is, upon closer examination, a fascinating degree of similarity among the structural elements evidenced across the world's languages. This must be due to the fact that we are all, regardless of what language "family" we are born into, humans with a human brain that develops in a characteristic way in a society of interacting and communicating humans. One of the primary interests of the field of linguistics is understanding the fundamental principles of how the sounds and articulations of words are not just randomly concatenated or mixed "beads on a string," but are rather organized into structures with systematic properties and functions in language.

Table 7.4 Summary of phonological units and patterning discussed in Chapter 7

Phonological units	*Phonological patterning examined as evidence for various phonological units*
Gestures/Features	Phonotactic constraints
	Harmony
	Assimilation
Segments	Deletion
	Metathesis
Syllables	Reduplication
Onsets & rimes	Syllable-structure universals
(and also nuclei and codas)	Language games
Stress Feet	Verse
	Infixation

Further Reading

Browman, C. P., and L. Goldstein (1992). Articulatory Phonology: An Overview. *Phonetica*, 49, pp. 155–180.

Flemming, Edward (2005). Deriving Natural Classes in Phonology. *Lingua*, 115, pp. 287–309.

Liberman, Mark (1998). Linguistic form in art and play: language games, song, verse: *http://www.ling.upenn.edu/courses/Fall_1998/ling001/games.htm*

Chapter 8
Word Form and Function

It probably comes as a bit of a shock – perhaps disconcerting – to pick up a textbook called *Discovering Speech, Words, and Mind* only to be told that the **word** is a rather dubious unit of language. But unfortunately there are great difficulties in defining what a word actually is. Perhaps one might say that it is the thing that is written on this page with a space before and often after it. But many of the languages of the world are not written languages, and some written languages don't put spaces between words. A statement as to the nature of the **word** won't be able to rely on orthography. Even in orthography, there are inconsistencies both within and between languages. One might write: *takeout* or *take-out*, but only *without*, not *with-out*. And what is spelled without a space as *Rauchverbot* in German is spelled with a space as *smoking ban* in English. For our purposes of learning language science, we appeal to a partial characterization of a word as a three-way mapping or relationship between a (somewhat) consistent speech form and a (somewhat) consistent language function and a (somewhat) consistent meaning.

If you remember the term **arbitrariness** from Chapter 1, you will recall that the particular association of a meaning with a phonological or spoken form is arbitrary in language. That is, there is no required association of certain vocal tract actions with certain meanings. We humans must learn this association. Once we have learned, for our particular language, a relationship (or connection or mapping) between a phonological form, its linguistic function, and its meaning, we can be said to have that word as a **lexical entry** in our **mental lexicon**. **Mental lexicon** refers to the whole set of such mappings or relationships that we know, and **lexical entry** refers to a single such grouping of form, function, and meaning.

While it is often the case that a word is composed of several meaningful pieces, a word can also be composed of pieces that have no clear or consistent meaning. For example, in the word *reset*, most people would agree that there are two meaningful pieces – the first part *re-*, which means roughly "(do) again," and the second part *set*. However, in the word *receive* or *reject*, it is not at all clear that *re-*, *-ject*, and *-ceive* have particular meanings; yet we still would be likely to say that these are word parts that

> It's not in fact always obvious whether a word can be analyzed into smaller pieces. What about *relate*? *relay*? Do you think there is a meaningful *re-* part in these words?

English speakers would be likely to identify since, for example, they know that there is a relationship between the words *receive* and *reception*.

Sometimes it is clear that people recognize and use pieces of words in a way independent from a specific lexical entry. We will adopt the term **morpheme** as a cover term for the parts of words that may join to create meaning. When a speaker can use an individual word part or morpheme to make new words, that morpheme is said to be **productive**. The prefix *re-* is quite productive in English. For example, when my husband sorts the laundry, this is usually shortly followed by me *resorting* the laundry. What about the suffix *-able*; is this productive for you? Most people could take a verb that they had never heard used with the suffix *-able* and turn it into an adjective by adding that suffix *-able*: *blogable*, *SMSable*, and so on. In fact, I can be happy that the laundry is *resortable* before it hits the washer. Can you think of other productive word pieces that you can make new words with?

When a word part is productive for an individual, we have good reason to think that it can play a role in that individual's cognition of language.

> Children will sometimes use productive morphemes in novel ways. For example, one of our daughters has used as an infix the morpheme "single" (recall that we discussed infixes in Chapter 7) in the word "everysinglebody." The term a linguist might use for an individual's invented word is **neologism**. This same child also seemed to be comfortable using "neath" productively, as seen in her neologism "overneath," on analogy, of course, with "underneath." In this case, this neologism, like most children's, makes sense in that its meaning can be compositionally discerned from the independent morphemes. It also demonstrates a phenomenon called **overregularization** because it shows that a wide variety of location prepositions can be used productively by this child in forms like this. This commonly happens with children using tense endings on verbs, like "goed" instead of "went." Other neologisms, such as those we will discuss in a later chapter, formed by patients with certain brain abnormalities, may not be sensible words at all.

However, as linguists we often analyze words into structural components even in the absence of evidence for productivity on the part of individual language users. Indeed, speakers may have little or no intuitions about word parts that linguists notice (although these morphemes might have been productive at an earlier point in the history of the language). For example, a linguist might remark that there is a morpheme *-th* that creates an abstract noun – *warmth, health, width*. But this is clearly not a productive morpheme (*coldth, blogth*?). So it is important to remember that while linguists might talk about a word having a structural composition, psychologists would want to establish independently that individuals are sensitive to this composition in their cognitive processing of word. In reality, the distinction between productive and nonproductive is not black-and-white; word parts are quite commonly somewhat productive, having certain restrictions on their use in and extension to new words.

We said above that a lexical entry or word is an intersection of form, grammatical function, and meaning. In particular, the relationship between form and function can be at a level smaller than an entire word. To understand this, we must be clear on the differences between phonological structure and morphological structure and words.

You may have already figured out that a word can have exactly one morpheme. Can you think of some examples? Some words that are only one functional piece are *blog, bangle, potato, piano*, even though some of these words have more than one syllable. Clearly a single morpheme may be one, two, or more syllables long. The syllable count of a word has no necessary relation to how many morphemes may be in a word. A morpheme may be more than one syllable long (like *piano* or *-able*) or exactly one syllable long (like *child* or *re-*) or even less than one syllable long (like *-th*). In sum, morphological structure is a separate and different kind of structure than phonological structure. Phonological structure tells us about the spoken form of a word and how that is organized. Morphological structure tells us what linguistic function and use that phonological form has.

Sometimes a specific word part has basically the same form and the same meaning every time it occurs. However, there are many situations in which we need to think in slightly more abstract terms. Consider for example, the word part that encodes plurality in English; this is generally a suffix. You may recall from the discussion in Chapter 1 that this suffix can actually be pronounced in three ways depending on the final sounds in the noun it is attaching to: for example, *cats [-s], dogs [-z], witches [-əz]*. In addition, on rare occasions the plural can even be marked with change internal to the word rather than at its edge: *geese, feet, teeth, mice, lice*; or with unusual word endings: *children, oxen*; or with no change: *fish, sheep*. We would want to recognize that all these words in some abstract sense are marked as being plural, although the form used to encode that plural marking is pronounced somewhat differently (or even not pronounced).

Stem and Function Morphemes

Word parts come in two varieties: **stem morphemes** and **function morphemes**. **Stems** can be understood as the part of the word that denotes or refers to creatures, objects, actions, concepts, or states. Simple stems in English include, for example, *cat*,

> The **root** is the main or most basic part of the stem, stripped of any functional components.

sweet, run, quick, idea. Other terms you might encounter for a stem morpheme are a base, a content morpheme, or a root; but we are not going to dwell on refining the term further. **Function** morphemes can be understood as the part of a word that combines with the stem to create new lexical categories (parts of speech), inflect words (such as marking tense and agreement in case or number), or otherwise serve grammatical or logical functions of relating words in a sentence (such as marking negation and topical focus). Articles and (some) prepositions are generally considered function morphemes. Because each language differs in what it requires to be overtly marked as a part of a word, languages will differ in the particular function morphemes they have. In English some examples of function morphemes include the plural morpheme, words marking tense such as *will*, and verbal endings such as *-ing*. Some function morphemes can be used as a **clitic**, a small partial word that attaches (in a relatively fixed form, unlike many other function morphemes) to another word, like *'ll* for *will*, *'ve* for *have*.

One interesting property of clitics that differentiates them from other affixes is that while an affix will be limited to attaching to a stem that is a particular type of lexical category, such as a verb, a clitic is not so limited. It can attach to entire phrases or even words with other clitics. Consider the English possessive clitic *'s* and verbal clitic *'ve* in the following examples (which indicate things that can be said, even if they wouldn't necessarily be captured this way in orthography):

The student's assignment
The student of psychology's assignment
The student that we invited's assignment
The student dressed in red's assignment
The student who went out's assignment
The men's assignments have been done, but the women's've not.

Can you think of other clitics? Can they attach to multiple lexical categories? To phrases? To other cliticized words? Can you think of clitics in other languages you may know?

A spoken word must always include a spoken stem. Functional morphemes, however, may sometimes lack a spoken form. We saw above the example of the plural word *fish* in which the plurality marking has no overt form. As another example, the function morpheme *-er* can be suffixed to many words to indicate *someone who does X*, but there are some words that lack this pronounced morpheme – we have *singer* but not *filmer*. We'll return to this possibility of fixed function without a fixed form for function words in our consideration of reduplication below.

Free and bound morphemes

It might look at first as if stems can always stand alone and that function morphemes never can, but that is not accurate. Consider Table 8.1, which shows stems and function morphemes.

Stems can be "less than" an entire word and function morphemes may in fact be an entire word. There is no necessary relationship here, though there are certainly tendencies.

We call morphemes that are required to occur as part of a larger word **bound morphemes**. In English, function morphemes are often but not always required to be part of a larger word; that is, they are often bound. We call morphemes that can occur as stand-alone words **free morphemes**. In English, most stems can generally occur as stand-alone words. However, notice in Table 8.1 that there are some English stems that are required to be bound morphemes. We will spend the remainder of this chapter characterizing the different ways in which bound morphemes are fixed to their stems.

Table 8.1 Examples of types of morphemes

	Stem morphemes	*Function morphemes*
Free	blog cat witch able	of not will
Bound	fel- (as in feline) dent- (as in dental) electr- (as in electricity) hydr- (as in hydrology) bio- (as in biometrics) cran- (as in cranberry) -kempt (as in unkempt) -sheveled (as in disheveled)	-s re- -able -ize, -ily, -ous, -ive, en- . . . -en (as in enlighten, embolden)

Open-class and closed-class morphemes

Novel stems can easily be added to an individual's lexicon, or to the lexicon of the language as a whole, through borrowing from other languages or through invention. New stems are always being invented: *smurf, byte, blog, splenda*. We say that stems are **open-class** to indicate this ability to be able to freely add to a class of word parts. In contrast, one cannot freely add function morphemes to a language; thus, due to this status, they are called **closed-class**.

Many languages have a noun number system of singular, plural, and dual, such as Slovene as seen in Table 8.2. But despite the fact that it is perfectly possible for a human language to have a dual affix, I couldn't wake up one morning and decide to add a dual affix to English, as number affixes are closed-class. Such developments in functional morphology only occur over long epochs of historical time in language history. As another example, people have commented that they would like there to be a gender-neutral animate pronoun in English: *his, her*, X ("*its*" is nonanimate of course); yet proposals to add a new function word to uniquely serve this purpose of being singular, gender-neutral have not gained traction. We are confined, at least in our lifetimes, with our 100–200 function words in English.

> Do you think pronouns are stems or function morphemes? What might be some arguments for and against each possibility? What about adverbs like *here* and *there*? *Then* and *now*? Numerals like *two* and *three*?

> Interestingly, while we can't add a gender-neutral pronoun, we *can* adapt an existing one to add a new use. The pronoun *they* is often used in place of such a singular pronoun: *If anyone is thinking of going to the class picnic, they are going to need to bring a potluck dish.* The pronoun *they* stands in for the awkward and overly formal "*he or she*" singular, even though it continues to agree with the verb *are* in plurality.

Table 8.2 Slovene noun number system demonstrating the singular, dual and plural morphemes

Singular	Dual	Plural
rib-a	rib-i	trib-e
"a/one fish"	"two fish"	"three or more fish"
rac-a	rac-i	rac-e
"a/one duck"	"two ducks"	"three or more ducks"
miz-a	miz-i	miz-e
"a/one chair"	"two chairs"	"three or more chairs"

Table 8.3   Properties of stem and function morphemes

- **Stem morphemes:**
  - Refer, denote
  - Are potentially infinite in number (open class)
  - May be inflected, for example for number and case
  - May be derived to form new lexical categories
  - Do not cliticize
- **Function morphemes:**
  - Have grammatical function
  - Belong to a small closed class
  - Can inflect and derive
  - May contract, cliticize, affix

Table 8.3 summarizes some of the properties of stem and function morphemes that we have discussed.

The distinction between stem and function morphemes is thought by scientists to be a cognitively relevant distinction. Children learn stem morphemes first, well before function morphemes are used. This is not to say that children are insensitive to the use and meaning of function morphemes, but rather that their rich use within a child's grammar comes later than such use of stems. Some scientists feel that intelligent non-human mammals can learn some morphemes that refer to objects and perhaps more abstract meanings but that they may not be able to learn function morphemes. Adults' cognitive processing of function words also show some signs of being different than their processing of content words. Various experiments have shown that listeners are slower to react to and make decisions about function words, even when both types are of equal frequency and duration. Surrounding sentence material also seems to have a strong impact on the lexical access of function morphemes in a way that does not seem to be as strongly the case as for referential words. Finally, there are specific kinds of brain damage or disorders that seem to more profoundly impair function words than referential words. This can be taken to indicate a different cognitive status of the two types of words.

Constituent structure

Because morphemes contribute to the total meaning of a word, there are situations in which differing internal organizations of a word's morphemes can yield different meanings of the same word. We call this **constituent structure** or **hierarchical structure**. Linguists view multimorphemic words as having such internal structuring or geometry. Such geometric structural

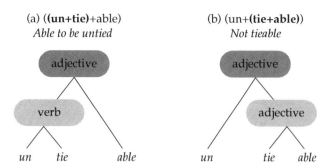

Figure 8.1 The word-internal hierarchical morphological structure for the two forms of the word *untieable*. In (a) *untieable* means *able to be untied* and can be represented by the suffix *-able* modifying the verb *untie*. In (b) *untieable* means *not tieable* because it is the adjective *tieable* that is modified by the prefix *un-*.

organization is considered to be one of the hallmarks of human language. We often graphically represent these relations among word parts with a tree structure, or equivalently with bracketing. Further, linguists generally assume that such structure is **binary branching** which means that each node in a tree has exactly two daughter nodes. (This introductory text is not the place to tackle why linguists make this assumption; we will simply state it as an axiom and invite you to take a course in linguistic theory!)

Consider the word *untieable* – as in *The rope was untieable*. Do you see that this word can have two meanings? It can mean *able to be untied* (i.e., a loose knot), or it can mean *not able to be tied*. Graphically, as in Figure 8.1, we can notate these two different structures in a tree or with bracketing that indicates the different meanings. Another way to say this is that for the meaning *able to be untied*, *-able* modifies *untie* and for the meaning *not able to be tied*, *un-* modifies *tieable*.

The function of a particular word – for example, whether it is an adjective or a verb – is determined by a particularly designated morpheme of that word, which we call the **head**. In most instances, the rightmost element in a (binary branching) morphological string determines the type of node dominating that binary branch. So in Figure 8.1a, because *tie* is a verb and is the rightmost element in its subtree, the entire subtree acts as a verb. In both (a) and (b), *-able* is the rightmost element of the highest tree and, as the head, determines that both meanings of *untieable* are adjectival, since *-able* is an adjectival affix. Why don't you try to draw the morphological tree structure for the word *sensibility*; we'll help by starting you off with the parse: *sense-able-ity*.

New lexical entries can often be made by combining other lexical entries – this is called **compounding** and is one of the most common type

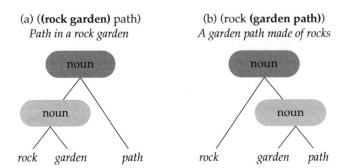

(a) ((**rock garden**) path)
Path in a rock garden

(b) (rock (**garden path**))
A garden path made of rocks

Figure 8.2 The word-internal hierarchical morphological structure for the two forms of the word *rock-garden-path*. The different structures account for the two different meanings. In structure (a) *rock-garden* modifies *path*; thus the expression refers to a path in a rock garden (and makes no reference to what the path is made of). In (b) *rock* modifies *garden-path* and therefore refers to a path that is in a garden, and the path must be made of rocks.

of word formation processes found in many languages. Compounds name objects, qualities, or actions rather than describing them per se. We can also see the geometric or structural aspect of word formation in the formation of compound words (which sometimes may be written with hyphens, spaces, or no spaces, depending on convention). The compound *rock-garden-path* can have two possible structures, each of which is consistent with a different meaning of the compound. Similarly, consider *French-history-professor* or *new-world-slavery*. In each of these examples, the rightmost element of the highest tree – the **head** – is a noun, so the entire compound is a noun.

Lastly, another important property of the internal structure of words is called **recursion**. This is basically the nesting of like binary-branching structures and is considered to be a hallmark structural property of human language. So, for example, we know the compound word *counter-intelligence*. We can also understand the meaning of *counter-counter-intelligence*, and so on. Or imagine there is a pill that makes the birth control pill ineffective; this could be called the *anti-Pill pill*. You could go on imagining another pill that renders the *anti-Pill pill* ineffective and thereby returning protection against pregnancy – this would be the *anti-anti-Pill pill pill*, and so on. While of course the cognitive processing of highly recursive or nested structure becomes unwieldy, human language seems to be special in allowing such structures to exist in its communication system. Indeed there is no example in an animal communication system that is analogous to the *rock-garden-path* example in that the same string of signal has two possible meanings depending on a structural parse of [[A B] C] versus [A [B C]].

In many compounds, such as the ones given in the text here, the meaning of the compound specifies some particular type or kind of instance of the **head**. So we had a type of professor, a type of path, and a type of slavery. Here are some examples of compounds drawn from Laurie Bauer's excellent book *Introducing Linguistic Morphology*. Note that the head, depending on the language, need not be the last element; in the French example below it is the first element.

Finnish	*kirje-kuori*	letter-cover	envelope
Maori	*puku-aroha*	belly-love	sympathetic
French	*oiseau-mouche*	bird-fly (noun)	hummingbird
Vietnamese	*hoa-xe*	fire-vehicle	train
Yoruba	*í-gbà-lé*	noun-sweep-ground	broom
English	*blackboard*		a black board
English	*table tennis*		ping-pong

In a different and interesting type of compound, neither part is clearly the head as the meaning is not a type of either element.

English	*highbrow*	one who possesses or affects culture/learning	
English	*egghead*		a studious nerd
French	*bleu-blanc-rouge*	blue-white-red	the French flag
Tamil	*appaa-v-amma*	father-mother	parents

There are also phrases that behave interestingly like these headless compounds. Think about *kick the bucket*, in which neither *bucket* nor *kick* is the head – the meaning is an independent one, not determined by the meaning of any of the individual parts.

How Are Morphemes Bound?

Affixation

Since we now know that there are some morphemes that must be bound or incorporated into words in order to be used by speakers, it makes sense to turn next to the question of the different ways in which languages can do this. As speakers of English, you are already familiar, perhaps from elementary school, with suffixes and prefixes, and we have already been using these terms in this chapter. More generally, this type of morpheme concatenation is called **affixation**. The term **affix** does not designate whether a morpheme is bound to the left or right edge of a stem; we use more specific terms for affixes to indicate that. **Suffixes** are bound to the right edge of a stem, and **prefixes** are bound to the left edge of a stem. Below we see, for English, an example of prefixes occurring before a stem and suffixes occurring after a stem.

Prefixes	Suffixes	Stem
re-do	do-able	do
pre-view	view-ing	view

Many languages use prefixes and suffixes, and these affixes can encode an enormous variety of morphemes. In Turkish there is a suffix meaning "each other." So the Turkish verb "to see" *gör* will be used with the suffix *-üs* in *gör-üs* to mean "see each other." In fact, a common Turkish expression is *görüsürüz*, which means roughly "see ya" or "toodles" (*ürüz* is the first person plural suffix). Affixation is the most common way of making new words in human language, and suffixation is the most frequent type of affixation.

One interesting area of linguistics is how word representations of different sorts interact with one another. There are, for example, interactions of morphological structure and phonological structure. Any particular word formation process cannot apply to each and every word in a language; there are restrictions on productivity, and these restrictions may include phonological, morphological, syntactic, or semantic (meaning) restrictions. Consider the suffix *-en*. Linguist Renate Raffelsiefen has discussed how this suffix can be bound to adjectives like *blacken*, *redden*, and *whiten* but not to **purplen* or **orangen*. (Remember that * means that a form is ungrammatical and does not occur.) As an exercise, consider what phonological properties of these stems might determine whether *-en* can be used to form a verb from an adjective. What if you now consider that **greyen* and **greenen* are also not possible; what additional phonological restriction do these words suggest? Can you think of other examples that would test your hypothesis? Raffelsiefen also discusses the suffix *-teer* as in *musketeer*. Consider that it would be possible to say *profiteer* but not **gaineer* and *racketeer* but not **fraudeer*. This suffix is productive with words that end in [t] and that have the form of a stressed syllable followed by an unstressed syllable. Is this an absolute restriction or can you think of any exceptions?

In English most affixes have the same phonological form whenever they occur (though there are certainly variations in some, particularly at the edges of function morphemes – consider *inaccurate* versus *imperfect*). For example, whenever -ing is used at the end of a word, it always sounds like [ɪŋ] (or [ɪn] in some dialects of English). We say in this circumstance that the morpheme is **prespecified** in its phonological form. The alternative to an affix being prespecified or relatively stable in its phonological form is for an affix's form to be **stem-dependent**. This means that the sounds that are used for an affix having some particular meaning will depend on the sounds in the stem to which the affix is being bound. In fact, we already have seen examples of this when we talked about reduplication in Chapter 7, and now we are simply framing the phenomenon in a slightly different way in our discussion of morphology.

In Tagalog we saw a prefix whose form is stem-dependent. This is the future tense morpheme. It doesn't make sense to identify a specific form for that morpheme without knowing the verb it is attaching to, so we can simply refer to it as *futuremorph*. Recall that when the Tagalog future-morph is used with the verb *bili* (to buy), the resulting word is *bi-bili* (will buy) and the futuremorph has the form [bi], which can be predicted from or is dependent on the stem verb. But when futuremorph is bound to the stem *sulat* (to write), it has the form *su-*, yielding *susulat*. Suffixes can also be stem-dependent in form. We can see this in the Marshallese suffix for intensification (perhaps we'd want to refer to this as *intensemorph*), spoken on the Marshall Islands in the Pacific.

enno (delicious); *enno-no* (very delicious)
ennon (aroused); *ennon-no*n (sexually aroused)

Can you determine the stem-dependent pattern that this suffix follows? The Marshallese word for "to make full" is *ebbok*; what do you think the word for "puffy," which uses the intensemorph suffix, is? It is *ebbokbok*.

There are two other types of affixes. In Chapter 7 we examined **infixes**. Recall that infixes appear inside a stem. Another way to say this is that the infix is surrounded both before and after by a portion of the stem. In Leti, an Austronesian language spoken on an island east of Timor, there is an infix (in several forms actually) that makes nouns from verbs:

kakri	"to cry"	*k-ni-akri*	"act of crying"
kasi	"to dig"	*k-ni-asi*	"act of digging"
paari	"to pay"	*p-ni-aari*	"act of paying"
soli	"to dwell, live"	*s-ni-oli*	"way of living, tradition, custom"
teti	"to chop"	*t-ni-eti*	"chop, chopping"
vaka	"to ask (for)"	*v-ni-aka*	"act of asking, request"[1]

[1] Leti nominalization from Juliette Blevins (1999), Untangling Leti Infixation. *Oceanic Linguistics*, 38(2), pp. 383–403.

One note: don't be misled into thinking that when multiple prefixes or multiple suffixes occur, the more interior one is an infix. For example, in the word *intentional* the *-tion* is a suffix not an infix; *-al* is of course also a suffix. An infix only appears interior to the root, the primary meaningful part of the stem.

Finally, there is an affix type called a **circumfix**. A circumfix behaves like a prefix and a suffix used together to encode a single meaning. Importantly, a circumfix is often characterized as a single affix because its meaning is dependent on *both* pieces being bound to the stem, and oftentimes the individual pieces of a circumfix don't carry an independent meaning, or have an unrelated or remotely related meaning when used as a simple prefix or suffix. Sometimes circumfixes, for obvious reasons, are also called discontinuous affixes. In English we can point to only the circumfix *eN-X-en* (where N means a nasal that assimilates in place to the following consonant), as found for example in *embolden* and *enlighten*. Circumfixes are more easily exemplified in some other languages. Chickasaw is an Indigenous American language now spoken in Oklahoma, and it uses a circumfix for negation in which ik- and -o are bound to the stem.[2]

chokma	"he is good"	*ik-chokm-o*	"he is not good"
lakna	"it is yellow"	*ik-lakn-o*	"it is not yellow"

German uses a circumfix to form one type of past tense for many verbs; this circumfix places a *ge-* before the stem and a *t-* after:

rauch-en	to smoke	*ge-rauch-t*	smoked
spiel-en	to play	*ge-spiel-t*	played
koch-en	to cook	*ge-koch-t*	cooked

Just as we cautioned against misunderstanding a sequence of affixes as an infix, we must also be sure not to confuse a stem that has both a prefix and a suffix with stems having a true circumfix. There are many words with both a prefix and a suffix in English, such as *preconceived*, which has the prefix *pre-* and the past tense suffix *-d*. We know that these are independent prefixes and suffixes because each can occur singly with many words and each has its own meaning, unlike the pieces of a circumfix. But it is worth noting that, just like a circumfix, multiple affixes at *one* edge may sometimes have a single meaning such that each affix doesn't have an independent function; consider for example, *electrical* for which it doesn't particularly make sense to say that *-ic* and *-al* have any separate function, yet they are both adjectival suffixes. So it may be that circumfixes

---

[2] From Arrell M. Gibson (1971). *The Chickasaws.* Norman: University of Oklahoma Press.

are not particularly different in their function than some other instances of multiple affixation, but rather only somewhat unusual in that they are discontinuous. Even that quality of discontinuity can be found in other morphological structures. We will turn to this below when we discuss Semitic morphology.

Prosodic morphemes

Prosodic morphemes have no specified segmental content. Instead they are speech events "added" or in simultaneous combination with the segmental material that composes a word. These prosodic morphemes can take a variety of forms including: **stress**, **nasalization**, **phonation type** (manner of vocal fold vibration), and **tone** (use of particular regions of a speaker's pitch range).

One of the ways that Spanish, for example, encodes past tense is by shifting stress to the final vowel. Nasalization can be used similarly. In the Creek language spoken in Oklahoma and the Southern US, nasalization is used on a (particular) vowel in the verb stem to indicate that the action took place over a long period or was repeated (in linguistic jargon this can be called the imperfective aspect). We can refer to the morpheme encoding the imperfective function as being vowel nasalization in Creek. So the verb "to tie" *wənəyetə* is spoken as *wənãyes* to mean "he/she keeps tying it."[3]

Similarly, phonation type or the manner of vocal fold vibration can be a type of prosodic morpheme. The now nearly extinct language Udihe, spoken in the Russian Far East, is reported to have used creaky voice (transcribed with a ˷ under the vowel) as a marker of the third person perfect verb form[4]:

Present stem		**Perfect**	
bunde	add	*bundḛ*	has added
zawa	take	*zawa̰*	has taken

In many languages of Africa and also elsewhere, tone is used to mark verb tense. In Bamileke Dschang, spoken in Cameroon, the following sentences in the present and past tense are differentiated

> Professor Steven Bird on his website has an audio demonstration of this use of tone for encoding tense in the Cameroonian language he studies, Bamileke Dschang: *http://www.ldc.upenn.edu/sb/fieldwork/*

---

[3] From Martin, Mauldin, & McCarty, *Pum Opunvkv Pun Yvhiketv Pun Fulletv*; available at *http://web.wm.edu/linguistics/creek/learning_creek.php*.

[4] From Irina Nikolaeva and Maria Tolskaya (2001). *A Grammar of Udihe*. Berlin: Mouton De Gruyter.

by tone only; the location of the pitch differences for the past tense as compared to the present tense is underlined. The past tense has a high tone on the underlined vowel while the present tense has a low tone.

    ə̀fɔ̀ ɔ̀ kə̀mtè mə̀mbhʉ́   "the chief buries dogs" (simple present)
    ə̀fɔ̀ ɔ́ kə̀mtè mə́mbhʉ́   "the chief buried dogs" (immediate past)[5]
    the mark over ɔ̀ indicates a low tone; the mark over ɔ́ indicates a high tone

Stem mutation

Now that we are getting used to thinking about the notion of function morphemes as not having a fixed phonological form, we can turn to another way of "binding" abstract morphemes to stems. In **stem mutation**, some phonological change (or changes) in the stem itself encodes the function morpheme. Stem mutation is one way of binding the past tense function in English. In many English verbs, such as those in Table 8.4, the past is formed not by the suffixation of *-ed* but rather by changing a vowel in the verb stem.

These patterns of stem mutation are neither perfectly predictable, nor completely random. As you can see, there are patterns that recur for

Table 8.4 Stem Mutation in the English Past Tenses

Present	*Simple past (preterit)*	*Past perfect*
strike	struck	struck
teach	taught	taught
drive	drove	driven
ring	rang	rung
drink	drank	drunk
sing	sang	sung
spit	spat	spat
fling	flung	flung
win	won	won
run	ran	run
wear	wore	worn
blow	blew	blown
grow	grew	grown
throw	threw	thrown

[5]   From Steven Bird (1999). Multidimensional exploration of online linguistic field data. *NELS*, 29, pp. 33–50.

English speakers are sensitive to these verbal past-tense stem mutation patterns, and while children are learning to master the complexity of this system, they often make mistakes, but reasonable ones. They will sometimes use the regular *-ed* ending on verbs that, for adults, bind the past tense function using stem mutation, before they have thoroughly learned how to form the English past tense – so a child might say *teached* instead of *taught*. Or you could, for example, hear an elementary-school-age child say *brang* instead of *brought*. Why do you think the child might use that form? When one word form is realized in a way driven by its similarity to other word forms, we say this is the process of **analogy**. Sometimes even adults aren't sure of whether certain past tense forms take the *-ed* suffix or create a past tense via stem mutation. What is the past tense of *dive*? If you answered with the more innovative *dove* rather than *dived*, what form in Table 8.4 might be driving the analogy-based answer you gave? Many linguists think that morphological **overregularization** (see earlier in this chapter) and **analogy** are fundamentally the same cognitive process.

similar sounding stem verbs, so one wouldn't be wholly inaccurate in seeing this English pattern as a subtle type of stem dependency.

Verbs that do not encode past tense in the most common way – in English by adding *-ed* – are called **irregular verbs**. Most of the verbs that use stem mutation to form the past tense in English are monosyllabic, frequent words, but not all of them are; consider *forget/forgot, begin/begun*. There are about 250 such verbs in English that do not form their past tense with regular suffixation. How children learn both the regular and irregular verb forms has been a topic of great interest to psycholinguists trying to understand how the human mind organizes language. Some scientists emphasize the importance of statistical patterns across all the verb forms the child hears, while others emphasize the reliance on the common or regular pattern *-ed* as a default system or "rule," viewing each irregular form as requiring memorization as exceptional.

Interlacing

The final form of morphological binding that we will review is **interlacing** of vowels and consonants. We've already worked through this in Chapter 7, but let's recall that in Semitic languages, such as Arabic and Hebrew, different vowel sequences serve as function morphemes by interlacing with consonants of stems to encode, for example, verb tense.

kʃr – the root for "to tie" (Hebrew)
Present:
koʃer   I tie (sing., m.)
Past:
kaʃarti   I tied
kaʃarta   you tied (m.)
kaʃart   you tied (f.)
Future:
ʔekʃor   I will tie
tikʃor   you will tie (m.)
tikʃeri   you will tie (f.)

The language speaker knows both the phonological form(s) of the function morpheme – which vowels – and also where or how they should be interlaced with the stem. On further consideration, this is not particularly different from the other types of morphological binding. The speaker must know both the phonological form of the function morpheme and the temporal location relative to the stem for that function morpheme to occur. In the case of affixation, this location may be before, after, intermediate, or both before and after the stem. In the case of prosodic morphemes, the speaker knows that some particular element(s) of the stem co-occurs with the prosodic or suprasegmental event. In the case of (English verbal) stem mutation, the alternating segment is the stressed vowel of the stem. Notice that when looked at from this perspective the Semitic interlaced morphology does not look dramatically different from English stem mutation.

Summary

In this chapter we have discussed why the notion of the word is difficult to define in a formal way, and indeed we prefer the term **lexical entry** to refer to the set of relationships that exist between a particular phonological form, a particular meaning, and the grammatical category and function that define use in phrases. We adopted the term **morpheme** as a cover term for the parts of words that may join to create meaning. When a speaker can freely use a morpheme to make new words, that morpheme is said to be productive; morphemes can be considered to be more or less productive, rather than completely productive or not. In particular, we identified stem and function morphemes as being an important distinction in the morphological structure of words. We noted the distinction between open and closed class, and described how the function morphemes of a language are a closed and relatively fixed set, unlike stems, which may be freely added to a language.

Next we turned to the distinction between free and bound morphemes. Many, though not all, function morphemes must be bound or occur as part of a larger lexical entry. In the second half of this chapter we examined a number of different ways that function morphemes can be bound to stems, including prespecified and stem-dependent affixation of various sorts, prosodic morphemes of various sorts, stem mutation, and interlacing in Semitic languages.

Further Reading and Resources

Baker, Mark (2001). *The Atoms of Language*. New York: Basic Books.

Bauer, Laurie (2003). *Introducing Linguistic Morphology*. Washington, DC: Georgetown University Press.

Koopman, Hilda, Dominique Sportiche, and Edward Stabler (2008). *An Introduction to Syntactic Analysis and Theory*. At: *http://www.linguistics.ucla.edu/people/stabler/isat.pdf*

Chapter 9
Sign Languages

Introduction

Up until this chapter, this book has been about spoken language. This is not too surprising given the prominence of *speech* in language communication (and hence in the title of this book). Although speech is, indeed, the focus of this book, in order to fully appreciate the *mind* (another prominent concept in the title) and its capacity for language, it's critical to consider languages that are transmitted in other **modalities**. We therefore turn in this chapter to discussing sign languages.

Sign Languages Are Natural Languages

Until the last half of the twentieth century, sign languages were not very well understood and were marginalized as rudimentary, primitive, unstructured, pantomime-like communication systems. Even today, as the status of sign languages as full-fledged languages has become more visible in the popular media and in educational settings, many students in our introductory classes still have misconceptions about sign languages. Common among these is the belief that sign languages are primitive and cannot convey the same thoughts and nuances as spoken languages, that all deaf individuals can understand each other through sign language, that signs are pantomimes without linguistic structure, or that sign languages are simply gestured forms of the spoken language of the community. You will learn in this chapter that these and some other commonly held beliefs about sign languages are inaccurate.

A comprehensive linguistic analyses of sign languages began in the 1960s with work by William Stokoe, who was the first to systematically analyze

American Sign Language (ASL). One of his discoveries was that, in fact, ASL signs are made up of a relatively small set of discrete, recurring parts (e.g., hand-shapes, movements), that are put together in different ways, to convey different meanings; the components of signs need have no intrinsic meaning on their own but contribute to conveying meaning in specific combinations with other components. Recall from Chapter 1 that two hallmarks of human languages are the related notions of **compositionality** and **duality of patterning**, whereby linguistic messages are formed by combining elements in a structured way. So Stokoe's findings provided the first scientific evidence that ASL – and perhaps any sign language – was a bona fide natural language.

The psycholinguists who were probably the most responsible for widening the scientific acceptance of ASL as a natural human language were Edward Klima and Ursula Bellugi at the Salk Institute for Biological Studies. In 1979, they published a comprehensive analysis of the structural, historical, and social properties of ASL in a volume called *The Signs of Language* that was the culmination of years of research. Most of the discoveries about ASL presented in this chapter come from that source or from later work that their initial discoveries inspired.

What do we mean when we say sign languages are natural languages? We discuss some key aspects of the grammatical structure of American Sign Language (ASL) later, but now we will outline some of the more general ways in which ASL and other sign languages (there are many) are identical to spoken languages.

Grammatical functions

Rather than being pantomimes, sign languages have syntax (sentence structure) and morphology, just like spoken languages, and the kinds of grammatical functions that exist in spoken language are found in sign language (e.g., verbal and nominative morphology, the grammatical marking of subject and object, person and number agreement), and the kinds of meanings that are conveyed by grammatical morphemes are the same (e.g., number, tense, negation). In short, the grammars of all long-standing sign languages appear to be composed of the same underlying components and organizational principles as the grammars of spoken languages.

Acquisition

Like children learning a spoken language, deaf children who are exposed to a sign language early in their life will acquire it automatically and without explicit instruction. In fact, hearing children who are acquiring a spoken language will acquire a sign language as well, given sufficient exposure (e.g., if one or both of their parents sign and do not communicate with spoken language). The acquisition of established sign languages by children follows the same patterns as spoken language, including babbling with the hands (manual babbling) before the first year of life. At around one year of age, children produce a few single signs, then at around 18 months they start to combine signs into rudimentary sentences. As with spoken language, children do not at first produce grammatical morphemes productively, suggesting that, early on, they do not fully decompose signs into their component grammatical parts. In addition, at an abstract level, the kinds of errors children make learning sign languages (e.g., see the box in Chapter 8, p. 00 on overregularizations) are similar to errors children make learning spoken languages. Taken together, the evidence on the acquisition of sign languages strongly support the idea that signed and spoken languages share core cognitive learning mechanisms. This, in turn, is further evidence that sign languages are natural human languages.

Expressive capacity

If sign languages were indeed primitive pantomime-like communication systems, then one wouldn't expect them to be able to express the full range of thoughts, ideas, and emotions that can be expressed in spoken languages. However, as in the other properties we've overviewed, all the evidence shows that sign languages are equivalent to spoken languages in terms of what can be conveyed, and in terms of the possibilities for subtlety and nuance in the messages. Related to this point, in the United States the deaf signing community has a strong cultural history in the language arts, including poetry and theater.

And, just as in spoken languages, when a new concept enters the public discourse for which the language lacks a word, sign languages can coin new terms, adding a word to the language. In short, sign languages are **open-ended** and **generative**, which, as you learned in Chapter 1, are two additional hallmarks of human language. In their expressive capacity, sign languages and spoken languages simply do not differ.

Communicative efficiency

Signed and spoken languages both employ gestures, or action units, as the source of the information signal. However, the size and mass of the articulators are very different – relatively small and light for spoken language (tongue, lips, jaw, etc.), and large and heavy for sign language (fingers, hands, arms, torso, head). Not surprisingly, this has an effect on the rate at which gestures can be generated across modalities. Linguists have discovered that normal conversational speech contains approximately twice as many words per second as sign language contains signs per second. This would seem at first glance to confer a communicative advantage to spoken language. However, comparing signs and spoken words might not be the best comparison. As you will see later in the chapter, in many signs a number of linguistic elements are communicated *simultaneously*, transmitting as much information as might be done in multiple words in English. For example, one sign for a verb of motion might contain a subject and direct-object pronoun as part of the sign of the verb – for example, *He asks you* is one complex sign in ASL. Another measure of the rate of communication linguists use is **propositions** per second. A proposition is roughly a complete idea, or thought: *I eat*, rather than *I* or *eat* alone. If one compares signed and spoken languages on the measure of propositions per second, then they are identical. The slowing down that occurs due to the nature of the articulators is apparently offset by the extra **bandwidth** provided by a three-dimensional, **visuospatial modality**. The end result is that sign languages are just as efficient at communicating information as spoken languages.

Arbitrariness

Another property of human language – but also of some other communication systems – that we discussed in Chapter 1 is **arbitrariness**. Words in spoken language do not resemble in any way what they mean. This property would seem, on the surface, to be the most likely not to be shared by sign languages. Even if sign languages have syntax, morphology, and the other properties of spoken language we've mentioned, don't signs look like what they mean?

While it is true historically that signs that *enter* a sign language tend to have an **iconic** component – that is, resemble what they stand for – the majority of signs have completely lost their originating iconicity. This can be seen in the examples in Figure 9.2a on p. 232, which show the ASL sign for *child* and for *thing*. It is hard to argue that there is anything iconic about them. In addition, many signs are almost identical (and to a naïve observer may even be seen as identical), yet refer to unrelated concepts (e.g., the ASL signs in Figure 9.2b differ only on where they are signed on the body); if signs were not arbitrary, one would expect the meanings to be similar as well.

> The property of arbitrariness is one reason that speakers of different sign languages cannot understand each other: the vocabularies are different. (There are also grammatical differences between sign languages.)

Summary

In summary, for every hallmark property of natural language that has been analyzed, sign languages have been shown to be equivalent to spoken languages. This shows us that the human capacity for language does not depend on speech, but rather is **modality-independent**. This does not mean that human language can exist in any format – a communication system that conveyed messages by the stamping of feet or by tapping one's companion on the nose could probably never have the characteristics necessary for human language. But if the modality can provide the right raw materials – a set of discrete elements that can be recombined and sequenced, and that can be efficiently produced, transmitted, and perceived – this may be sufficient to activate the cognitive mechanisms and processes of human language.

Despite the overwhelming similarities between signed and spoken languages, there are also important differences that result from the difference in modalities. One difference was alluded to above: sign languages generally convey much linguistic information – specifically morphological information – *simultaneously*. The modality differences do not alter *what* linguistic information is expressed, but rather *how* it is expressed. The effects of modality on the form of language is interesting scientifically in its own right, but it also has important implications in a number of areas, including the education of deaf individuals. Effects of modality are also important for understanding the scientific discoveries regarding language acquisition and language evolution to which the study of sign languages have contributed. These are topics that we cover in this chapter, so after a brief discussion of the history of ASL, we discuss some of the important aspects of *how* syntax and morphology are realized in sign languages.

A Brief History of American Sign Language

The origins of ASL can be traced to mid-eighteenth century Paris, where the priest Charles-Michel de l'Épée founded the Institution Nationale des Sourds-Muets à Paris (National Institute for Deaf-Mutes), a school for deaf children. His method of instruction was somewhat revolutionary for the time. Rather than attempt to teach the children French through the use of pictures and spoken words, l'Épée used a system of signs. His motivation to do so came from observing members of a deaf community conversing among themselves with gesture. L'Épée learned their signs (now called **Old French Sign Language, OFSL**) and adapted them to reflect the grammar of French. This became the primary means of instruction in his school, although l'Épée's own modifications were not used by the students when conversing among themselves. The school flourished and became quite well known abroad for its successes in educating deaf children, and l'Épée set up a program to train other teachers in his technique.

Although l'Épée viewed OFSL as a useful communication system and tool, he did not regard it as a language. He modified many of the signs to incorporate manual version of French morphology and tried to impose French syntax on the ordering of signs, believing that OFSL lacked a grammar. One of the deaf graduates of his school, Laurent Clerc, later wrote that l'Épée's modifications didn't stick; the students found them cumbersome, and over time they were largely abandoned in the school. Interestingly, similar methods of imposing spoken language grammar resurfaced in deaf education in the twentieth century (see "Artificial manual communications systems that aren't natural languages" below).

As you will see throughout this chapter, sign languages have the same underlying grammatical organization as spoken languages, but the way grammatical elements are combined and sequenced is somewhat different than in spoken languages. There is little documentation about the structure of OFSL, but what little there is (much of it written by former deaf students of the school) suggests that it had many of the grammatical components of fully developed natural sign languages.

Meanwhile, in Hartford, Connecticut, a recent Yale graduate and seminary student, Thomas Gallaudet, became occupied with the situation of a neighbor's daughter. Alice Cogswell became deaf after contracting a form of meningitis as a toddler. Her father (an influential doctor), Gallaudet, and others in the area became interested in establishing a school for deaf people in Hartford. (At that time, there were no such institutions. Parents who could afford it had to send their children abroad to receive an education.) Having heard good things about the Paris school, Gallaudet sailed for France in 1815. (He went by way of London and Edinburgh to visit deaf schools there but was not impressed with their methods or their successes.) Gallaudet studied the school's methods for a year and returned to the United States with a former graduate of the school who was then a teacher, Laurent Clerc. With Clerc, Gallaudet established the American Asylum for the Deaf and Dumb in Hartford, which is still in operation as the American School for the Deaf. The school duplicated the methods employed in Paris, educating deaf children version of the sign system from the National Institute in Paris that was modified to reflect aspects of English grammar. (As with l'Épée's modifications of OFSL, the modifications modeled on English grammar were not adopted by deaf users.) Gallaudet and Clerc also provided education for instructors, so that the techniques could be replicated elsewhere in the United States.

While manual communication systems develop wherever there are deaf people, the early forms of such systems usually lack some of the key components of natural languages (in some ways, they are more like **pidgins**, communication that develops when multiple spoken languages interact without a common language). But the establishment of schools brings large numbers of deaf people into contact. In schools where signing is encouraged, the effect is to accelerate the evolution of the communication system into a full-fledged language (see "The evolution of a language" below). This is what happened at the National Institute in Paris, and then again at the American Asylum, producing what we now call American Sign Language.

Grammar and Structure of Signed Languages

Words

One of the first important discoveries about the structure of ASL (and sign languages in general) was that it has discrete words. While this perhaps seems obvious, it is worth mentioning because, going back to l'Épée, the predominant view of sign languages was that they were pantomime-like – that is, signs and gestures were thought to be iconic depictions of things in the world, not word-like symbols with arbitrary connections to concepts. However, as we discussed above, the signs of sign languages are, in fact, abstract symbols. Furthermore, the words in sign languages have the same grammatical categories (like noun, verb, and adjective) as words in spoken languages.

Phonology

Having established that sign languages have words, in a truly linguistic sense, it becomes possible to ask whether those words are composed in a similar way as they are in spoken language. As we discussed in the first chapters of this book, in spoken language words are composed of phonological units, each of which can be described by a property on a variety of phonetic dimensions: for example, place of articulation and manner of articulation. What about words in sign languages? Are they all composed of a basic set of building blocks that can be combined in different ways to make different words? The answer is a resounding *yes*! The signs that constitute words can be described by several basic dimensions: for example, hand shape, hand orientation, place of articulation (on the body), and type of movement. (These dimensions have further subdimensions, but those details are not important for our discussion here.) Because of the parallelism of having combinatorial features in sign language and in spoken language phonology, the area of study concerning the formal building blocks of signs is called phonology. Figure 9.1 shows the categories for the articulatory dimension of place of articulation (of a sign on the body). These

Figure 9.1 Dotted sections show places of articulation – locations on the signer's body where hand shapes can be located. A change in location results in a different sign. From Klima, E. S. and Bellugi, U. (1979). *The Signs of Language*. Cambridge, MA: Harvard University Press. Copyright © 1979 by the President and Fellows of Harvard College.

can be viewed as parallel to articulatory categories such as alveolar and velar: they have no meaning in and of themselves, but they contribute contrastive properties to the formation of words.

To summarize, the compositional structure of spoken and signed words is strikingly similar. They both are constructed from units that can be described by a small set of articulatory dimensions, and each dimension has a restricted set of values to choose from. In spoken language, these properties give rise to **minimal pairs**, in which a change of value along any dimension (say, from a bilabial to an alveolar place of articulation) changes from one word to another (say, from *bowl* [bol] to *dole* [dol]). This is the case in sign languages as well. Figure 9.2 shows three sets of minimal pairs in ASL. In Figure 9.2a, the difference between *child* and *thing* is in the orientation of the hand, with movement and hand configuration staying constant. As shown in Figure 9.2b, *summer*, *ugly*, and *dry* vary only in the place of articulation on the body, with all other dimensions held constant. Finally, in Figure 9.2c, only the movement path varies to distinguish *tape*, *chair*, and *train*, with all other dimensions held constant. In each example, a categorical shift along a single dimension produces a new sign with a new meaning.

The signing space and simultaneous morphology

Not surprisingly, many of the differences between signed and spoken languages arise from the fact that they use different **mediums** to convey information. In spoken language, information is encoded (mostly) sequentially, with one phonological unit following the other. Consequently, *sequencing* is an important organizing dimension in spoken language – a major difference between *stoke* ([stok]) and *coats* ([kots]) is in the **temporal**

(a)   CHILD   THING

SUMMER   UGLY   DRY

(b)   Signs contrasting only in Place of Articulation

TAPE   CHAIR   TRAIN

(c)   Signs contrasting only in Movement

Figure 9.2   Examples of minimal pairs in ASL: (a) changes only hand orientation, (b) changes only place of articulation, (c) changes only movement path. From Klima, E. S. and Bellugi, U. (1979). *The Signs of Language.* Cambridge, MA: Harvard University Press. Copyright © 1979 by the President and Fellows of Harvard College.

sequencing or precedence of the phonological units. Of course, sign languages also make use of sequencing in time to convey information, and spoken languages do make use of space in forming constrictions along the vocal tract. That said, the visual-spatial nature of sign language makes the use of **location in space** a salient organizing dimension in a way somewhat different than vocal tract space is used for actions in spoken language. There are two concepts relating to the use of space that are important for understanding general structural principles of all natural sign languages: **simultaneous morphology** and the **signing space**.

Simultaneous morphology
In our overview of sign languages as natural languages, we mentioned that sign languages make use of morphology to perform the same grammatical and semantic functions as in spoken languages. But while the linguistic functions of morphemes in sign languages and spoken languages are the same, the **formal properties** of morphology – how stems and inflections are

> Note that interlacing in Semitic morphology (see Chapter 8) shares some similarities to simultaneous morphology in sign language.

realized in the linguistic signal – are different across the two modalities. In particular, in sign languages, morphemes don't generally occur as a sequence of affixes, as they often do in spoken languages. Instead, many grammatical morphemes are signed *simultaneously* with the stem, as a systematic and grammatically driven modification of the root form of the sign.

An example of simultaneous morphology is the **classifier** system in ASL verbs of motion. A classifier is a grammatical morpheme that is associated with a noun and describes some property of the entity it refers to, such as whether it is animate, human, or vehicle. Classifiers also can convey something about the noun's shape (e.g., cylindrical), its size, or other properties. Although English does not have a grammatical classifier system, many spoken languages (such as Mandarin Chinese) do, and the kinds of properties expressed by classifiers in spoken languages are the same as those expressed in sign languages – having classifier morphemes does *not* distinguish sign languages from spoken languages. As in spoken languages that have them, the use of classifiers is obligatory and part of the regular grammar of the language. But unlike in spoken languages, where a classifier might be an affix or a separate function word (see Chapter 8), in sign languages classifiers are signed *simultaneously* with the relevant verb. For example, in ASL the distinct classifiers for humans or vehicles are organized to co-occur in time with signs communicating behavior of the nouns. A signer who was talking about a car moving would produce the vehicle classifier hand shape while moving the hand from one location in space to another. If, instead, the sentence was about a *person* moving, the classifier hand shape for person would be signed instead, with the same movement path. Therefore the noun classifier is signed simultaneously with the verb.

Classifiers are just one example of simultaneous morphology in signed languages. But they demonstrate the important point that while a grammatical device and the linguistic function it serves may be similar across language modalities, the form it takes (e.g., whether sequential or simultaneous) can differ dramatically.

The signing space

There are additional modality-related differences that surface in the grammar of signed languages. In particular, for many verbs, location in space is used for the grammatical function of *agreement*, for example, marking person and number of the subject and object on the verb – as in *I go* versus *he goes* (person) and *I am* versus *we are* (number) in English. In the cases where subjects and objects are individuals or entities present in the vicinity of the signer (especially the signer or addressee themselves), the location in signing space designating the individual or entity will define the starting point of the verb if it's playing the role of subject or the endpoint if it's playing the role of object. For example, Figure 9.3 shows various forms of the ASL verb *ask*. Note that the form in (c) that marks a third-person indirect object uses a location in space that is neither the signer nor the addressee. These are examples of how spatial locations are used as symbolic references to absent entities. In an actual discourse, the signer would designate a specific location in space to refer to an entity. Verbs in a discourse for which that entity plays a role of subject, object, or indirect object would incorporate that location to carry out agreement functions when verbs (or adjectives) involving that entity are produced. Not to do so would constitute a grammatical error in ASL, akin to saying **I asks John a question*. The signing space, then, plays a critical grammatical role in sign languages.

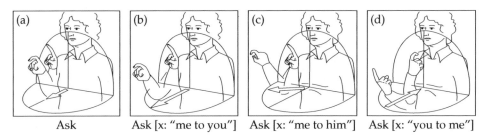

| (a) | (b) | (c) | (d) |
| Ask | Ask [x: "me to you"] | Ask [x: "me to him"] | Ask [x: "you to me"] |

Figure 9.3   Several inflected forms of the ASL verb *ask*: (a) uninflected citation form, (b) first-person subject, second-person indirect object (hand is extended farther than in citation form), (c) first-person subject, third-person indirect object, (d) second-person subject, first-person indirect object. From Klima, E. S. and Bellugi, U. (1979). *The Signs of Language*. Cambridge, MA: Harvard University Press. Copyright © 1979 by the President and Fellows of Harvard College.

Unique Scientific Insights Into Language and Mind

The scientific study of sign languages that began in the latter half of the twentieth century has generated a wealth of information on the linguistic structure of ASL and other sign languages, and it was crucial for the recognition of sign languages as natural languages. The discoveries that came out of this research, some of which we have introduced here, then allowed for broader scientific questions to be asked about language and the human mind. In general terms, the very existence of manual languages demonstrates that many of the underlying processes and representations that are responsible for the structure of language are not restricted to speech and spoken languages. Beyond that, there are some questions that could not have been answered without studying language used by communities of deaf people. One question concerns the acquisition of language.

Learning a first language after childhood – the critical period hypothesis

Within 36 hours after hatching, geese and some other birds normally **imprint** on their mother: they form a strong bond, following her around, and generally try to stay close and connected. But geese will, in fact, imprint on anything that meets some minimal criterion – basically, anything that moves! – as long as it is encountered near the gosling during a certain window of time, called a **critical period** or **sensitive period**. If the mother is not present during this period, the gosling may imprint on another goose, a human, or even something that isn't a living being. The critical, or sensitive period, then, refers to a window of time when an animal must receive a certain kind of input in order to develop a skill or capacity; the input will not have the same effect if presented outside that window of time. So, if the mother is present after the window is closed, no imprinting will take place. It turns out that many capacities in different animals can be described this way, including the development of **binocular vision** in mammals.

Many scientists think that there is a critical period, or sensitive period, for language acquisition. We will review evidence for this when we discuss recovery from **aphasia** – language impairment brought on by brain damage – in Chapter 10, but evidence also comes from studies comparing children's and adults' acquisition of a second language. In several studies, Elissa Newport and colleagues investigated the grammatical competence (see Chapter 1) of learners of English as a second language who were all adults when tested, but who had learned English either in childhood (early learners) or adulthood (late learners). They found that late learners were far more variable in their ultimate mastery of the grammar. They also found

The difference between *critical* and *sensitive* period is generally just a matter of degree, with critical periods having more abrupt and well-defined beginnings and ends. In many cases, some learning and adaptation can take place outside the critical or sensitive period, but effects of the environment will be weaker than changes that take place within the period. The kinds of environmental stimuli that can give rise to changes are also generally much more restricted outside the critical/sensitive period.

The claim that there is a critical period for learning language is not inconsistent with the fact that adults can indeed learn language. Rather it is the case that the processes by which adults learn language and their ultimate attainment will be different and overall poorer than learning within a child's critical period.

that there was much more variability in ultimate language ability among later learners than among early learners, with some late learners ending up mastering nearly all aspects of the second language grammar, and some doing quite poorly. These results held true regardless of how long the learners had been speaking the second language. These kinds of findings constitute one piece of evidence that the human brain is specially prepared for learning language during childhood – that there is a critical period for acquiring a language.

The limitation of those findings, however, was that the second-language learners already had a native (first) language – they had already been exposed to and mastered one language during childhood. So the apparent critical/sensitive period that seemed to be implicated might have been relevant only for learning a second language, but not a first language. That's where deaf learners of sign language (in this case ASL) became a unique source of information about this issue.

Even today, with the tremendous scientific evidence that ASL is a natural human language, many well-meaning educators believe that learning and conversing in ASL inhibits students from learning how to read and write in English, and in general how to navigate a predominantly spoken-language world. (In fact, the evidence suggests that just the opposite is true.) Hence, in many schools, parents of deaf children are discouraged from exposing their children to ASL. The schools focus instead on lip-reading, spoken language training, and literacy. Unfortunately, students in such programs generally attain poor English language abilities. As a result, there are many deaf children who enter adulthood without a native language. But some of them will later become exposed to ASL and acquire the language to varying degrees. A battery of language tests, similar to the ones for second language learning, were devised by Newport and colleagues to compare the language competence of early learners and late learners of ASL *as their first language*. The results looked remarkably similar to the analysis of late versus early learning of a second spoken language: late learners were overall poorer and more variable than early learners, even with comparable time exposed to the language. Moreover, the age at which these maturational changes seem to take place was the same across the studies (about 10 years of age). The studies also found striking similarities in the kinds of grammatical rules late learners of a second language and of a first language tended to have difficulty mastering.

Since the study just described concerned age of exposure to a *first* language, the issue (confound) of having already learned a prior language was not relevant. The findings, then, provided further evidence for a critical period for language learning.

We will see in a later chapter that the situation of a deaf child not being exposed to any natural language is becoming less frequent in the developed world due to the increase in the use of cochlear implants, particularly beginning in young childhood, to create hearing sensation and a bootstrap into learning a spoken language. You should now have a sense of why it would be important that access to such technology, if it is to be used, take place early in life. It is strongly preferred that the introduction of a cochlear implant to create hearing sensation be done before age three and a half.

The experiments would not have been possible were it not for prior research demonstrating that ASL was a natural language. It also would not have been possible to carry out a similar study in a spoken language, as situations in which individuals are not exposed to their first language in childhood are rare, and usually occur when there are other highly abnormal social and environmental factors that could themselves have adverse effects on cognition and learning. In contrast, the late-exposed ASL learners had otherwise normal upbringings.

Artificial manual communication systems that aren't natural languages

As we mentioned above, some schools for the deaf in the United States discourage signing entirely and do not use any kind of sign system for instruction. Others use manual communication systems that, while they might incorporate some signs from ASL, are *not* natural languages. There are several versions of these artificial signing systems, which are versions of **manually coded English (MCE)**. These systems, which were designed by committee, duplicate the syntax and morphology of English, going so far as having separate signs for bound morphemes, like *–ing*. One of the reasons for developing a sign system that mirrors English was to make the spoken language accessible in gestural form. It was thought that this

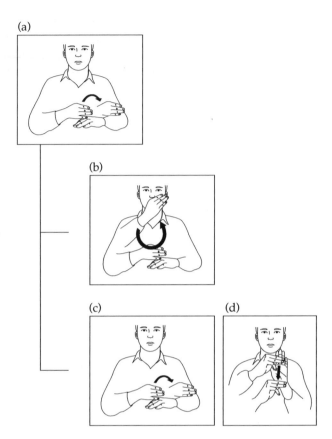

Figure 9.4 The top figure shows the ASL sign *improve*. The middle row depicts the ASL derived noun *improvement*. The final row shows the MCE sign(s) for *improvement*: the ASL verb form plus the MCE affix *-ment*. From Supalla, S. J. (1991). Manually coded English: The modality question in signed language development. In P. Siple and S. D. Fisher (Eds.), *Theoretical Issues in Sign Language Research Volume 2: Psychology*. Chicago: University of Chicago Press. Copyright © 1991 by the University of Chicago.

would make learning to read easier, as well as learning to lip-read or even speak, by making the spoken language visible.

However, duplicating English in manual form produces a sign system that has a very different character from naturally occurring sign languages. For example, when morphemes are sequential affixes, as in MCE, then words that have any kind of bound morpheme in English require multiple signs, whereas the equivalent ASL word would involve only one (see Figure 9.4 for the formation of the derived noun *improvement* in ASL and MCE). Recall that in sign languages simultaneous morphology is prevalent, which allows for a greater proposition rate compared to word rate. Measures of the proposition rate of MCE show that it is half that of natural signed and spoken languages. In addition, the concept of signing space is absent in spoken language, and it doesn't enter into the designs of manual codings of spoken languages. This also reduces the amount of linguistic information that can be conveyed efficiently; we might say that MCE has **reduced bandwidth** compared to naturally occurring sign languages.

You may recall that similar attempts at mirroring spoken language were made at the National Institute in Paris and in the American Asylum in Hartford. And now, as then, students do not adopt these artificial sign systems for their own use. But students, of course, want to communicate, and scientific analysis of how students in these schools communicate led to the following interesting finding. In schools where most students did not know ASL, and MCE was used in classroom instruction, students adopted the basic MCE vocabulary when communicating with each other, but they *modified* the form of the syntax and morphology to bring it more in line with natural sign languages. For example, the sequential English-like morphology would become simultaneous, and some grammatical functions would be conveyed by the use of the signing space, rather than sequential morphemes. These modifications were apparently not conscious, and they involved students who didn't know a natural sign language. Yet the modifications were consistent with the structures of known sign languages.

The apparent inability of children to acquire and use MCE as they would a sign language, combined with their self-imposed and automatic restructuring of MCE systems, is informative for several reasons. First, it suggests that imposing the sequential structure of spoken language onto a sign system does not produce a natural sign language, and is relatively inefficient for communication. Second, it provides evidence to linguists about the properties of sign languages that arise because of **modality constraints**. Lastly, it shows how learners spontaneously (and unconsciously) add linguistic elements to communication systems that lack them, pointing to the properties of language that might arise from internal constraints on the language learner. Below we describe a related situation, in which a new sign language is in the process of being formed.

The evolution of a language: Nicaraguan Sign Language

In this chapter, we've mentioned two points in history when schools for the deaf were established, bringing many young deaf students together and providing a "critical mass" for the growth of a sign language: l'Épée's National School for Deaf-Mutes, in the late eighteenth century for FSL, and the American Asylum in the early nineteenth century for ASL. A similar situation has arisen in more recent times, in Nicaragua (and elsewhere), and provides a unique laboratory for studying the birth and evolution of a language.

Before the late 1970s, few deaf children in Nicaragua had access to any kind of special schools or educational programs that were designed for the deaf. There were also no widely available opportunities for groups of deaf people to come into contact with each other. That changed in 1979, when the Sandinistas came into power. Over the next few years in Managua, several schools for deaf students were established, and existing schools were made more accessible. The schools served different ages, and brought a large number of deaf children and adolescents together, forming an active deaf social community.

The schools did not use any kind of sign system for instruction and did not attempt to teach a signing system, focusing instead on lip-reading and speaking. Like similar attempts elsewhere, this was not very effective. However, manual communication was not discouraged, and children were free to converse among themselves using gestures. Of course, there was initially no common language among the children, but deaf children with no language develop rudimentary communication systems called **home signs** – sign systems that deaf children develop as a way of communicating with their hearing family members. Home sign systems lack much of the complexity of full-fledged languages, but some communication is possible. Of course, every child entering school in Managua had his or her own home sign system, each with their own idiosyncratic signs. However, the intensive interaction of the first students to enter the schools gave rise to a more conventionalized system of shared signs. But grammatically, this system was not much more language-like than home sign systems.

Home signs in different cultures have been extensively analyzed, and found to all share some basic characteristics: There are signs for actions and objects; utterances are generally short, just a few signs long on average in younger children; home sign systems lack morphology and generally use word order to convey grammatical functions; home signs do not use the signing space in the way sign languages do. Not surprisingly, the signs are generally iconic.

This first-generation signing system did not last long. As a new generation of young students entered school, they were immediately exposed to a much more conventionalized signing system than their predecessors. They quickly adopted the system, but they also changed it. One striking change was the gradual incorporation of the signing space in consistent and rule-governed ways. This property was not present in first-generation signing, and the introduction of it by the later students came closer to the use of the signing space in more established sign languages. Another significant change was that children entering in the second generation were more "fluent," in that they produced many more signs per minute than the signers who were their linguistic models.

Although this may seem to be more a fact about the signers than the developing language, an increase in fluency would probably not be possible if aspects of the language were not becoming less haphazard and more "grammatical."

It is important to note, in addition, that these changes were not simply due to a "new set of eyes" observing the first-generation language. The *age* of the second-generation learners turned out to be a critical part of the modifications. In addition to young children coming into the school system in the second generation, older individuals entered as well. They were in virtually the same situation as the children with respect to their experience with the language, but they did not show increased signing rates, and they did not show a greater tendency to use the signing space in a more consistent manner. In short, only the young children were responsible for the development of the language.

Not surprisingly, Nicaraguan Sign Language (NSL) continues to undergo transformations as new learners are exposed to it, and these processes continue to be analyzed by linguists and psychologists. The findings have important implications for theories of language evolution and change, of language acquisition in children, and of the evolution and structural properties of sign languages in particular. In short, studying the evolution of a sign language within deaf communities provides unique insights into the mind's capacity for language that would otherwise be unattainable.

Another case of a sign language that is in the process of development is the Al-Sayyid Bedouin Sign Language (ABSL). The Al-Sayyid Bedouin community started approximately 200 years ago in the Negev region of present-day Israel. There is a relatively high incidence of congenital deafness in the tightly knit population, and within the last 70 years, over several generations, a sign language has developed. The social situation is unique in that deaf individuals always marry hearing members of the community, and a significant portion of the hearing community communicate with sign language. So, unlike the case of Nicaraguan sign language, where new generations are exposed to the language only after arriving at the school, deaf infants born into this community are exposed to ABSL from their earliest days. Linguists who have studied this language and its development report that a grammatical word order (subject-object-verb) developed within a generation. Interestingly, the particular word order is different from any of the languages used by the hearing signers (e.g., Arabic or Hebrew) and from Israeli Sign Language. Thus the structure of ABSL (like NSL) seems to have sprung from internal properties of the minds of the users and learners of the language and the demands of communication, not from other languages.

Summary

This chapter emphasized that sign languages are natural languages, with the same expressive power and underlying structure as spoken languages. Yet differences in modality necessarily lead to differences in the ways grammatical functions are realized in spoken versus signed language. In particular, sign languages make extensive use of simultaneous morphological marking, and they incorporate location in the signing space to carry out grammatical functions.

Education of deaf individuals is an important topic throughout this chapter, as it played a role in the very formation of ASL in the United States, and also in providing unique scientific opportunities to address fundamental questions about language acquisition, language evolution, and in general the human mind's capacity for language.

Further Reading and Resources

Helmuth, Laura (2001). From the Mouths (and Hands) of Babes. *Science Magazine*, 293, pp. 1758–9.

Hickok, Gregory, Ursula Bellugi, and Edward Klima (2001). Sign Language in the Brain. *Scientific American*, 284, pp. 58–65.

Klima, Edward and Ursula Bellugi (1998). *The Signs of Language* 1988. Cambridge, MA: Harvard University Press.

Newport, E. L. (2002). Critical Periods in Language Development. In L. Nadel (Ed.), *Encyclopedia of Cognitive Science*. London: Macmillan Publishers Ltd/Nature Publishing Group. Available at http://www.bcs.rochester.edu/people/newport/Newport-ECS-A0506.PDF

Sandler, W., Meir, I., Padden, C., & Aronoff, M. (2005). The emergence of grammar: Systematic structure in a new language. *Proceedings of the National Academy of Sciences, 102* (7), 2661–2665.

Senghas, Ann, Sotaro Kita, and Asli Ozyurek (2004). Children Creating Core Properties of Language: Evidence from an Emerging Sign Language in Nicaragua. *Science*, 305 (5691), pp. 1779–82.

American Sign Language Browser, Michigan State University Communication Technology Laboratory: http://commtechlab.msu.edu/sites/aslweb/browser.htm

Chapter 10

Language and the Brain

Introduction

Back in Chapter 1 we introduced the idea of a *functional* theory of a cognitive system – the nature of the computation, the nature of the representations and processes, and so on. The linguistic analyses and psycholinguistic experiments you've been reading about all contributed to developing a functional understanding of linguistic structure across the world's languages, speech perception and production, and word recognition. As to what goes on inside the brain, a functional theory of speech and language is basically a theory at the computational and algorithmic levels (recall Marr's levels of analysis, p. 17). We touched on the implementational level when we discussed the physical means of production and sensing language. A further understanding of speech and language at a functional level, we argued, is necessary if one ever hopes to understand how the neural circuits of the brain process language – we likened the situation to trying to understand how a computer works simply by measuring its internal electrical activity without understand what it was *doing*. But now that you do have some background about the functional properties of language, we devote this chapter to overviewing what is known about how language is implemented in the brain.

Before continuing, it's worth contemplating why we should care about studying the brain at all. If it's possible to make good progress in understanding language and the mind using traditional linguistic and psycholinguistic techniques (what most of this book has been about), can we learn anything new by "looking inside" the brain? We believe the answer is *yes*, and that there are a number of reasons why understanding the neural implementation of language is valuable.

First, there is intrinsic scientific interest in understanding how the brain does what it does: how does it compute things we care about understanding, like language? For many scientists, this is sufficient reason alone. Others think that the insights we can glean from understanding how the brain implements language could be useful in designing machines that can communicate with spoken language. Another major reason to study brain function is to be able to intervene when language is impaired for some neurological reason. Understanding how affected brain regions play a role in language could, if not help provide a cure for the impairment, at least inform us how best to manage it to improve a patient's ability to communicate. Finally, we are now at a point in time in the advancement of **neuroimaging** techniques, as well as in the sophistication of our linguistic and psycholinguistic (functional) theories, that studying the organization of language in the brain can actually influence those theories; we might change or deepen our functional models based on what we find by "looking inside" the brain.

The Locations of Language in the Brain

An early guiding interest in **neurolinguistic** research was understanding whether various linguistic functions are *located* in distinct areas in the brain, and if so, where. Where are words stored? Where are phonological segments processed? Where are morphological processes carried out? The term used to describe the scenario where certain kinds of representations and processes are located in specific areas is **modular organization**. Of course, there was always the understanding that the organization of language in the brain might not be entirely modular, and that some representations and processes might be **distributed** – where a given function is processed by multiple different regions in the brain. After all, it's been recognized for over 100 years that the brain is highly interconnected, so there is much reason to believe that many regions could be involved with a given function. Nevertheless, there has been a strong tendency to seek out physical areas of the brain that correspond to functional components of theories of language representation and processing. And, indeed, there is evidence from nonlinguistic domains in mammals, and in humans in particular, that certain areas of **cortex** are selectively responsible for certain motor or sensory functions (see accompanying box). For

The cortex is the "grey matter" that constitutes the outer layers of the brain. It is evolutionarily the most "modern" part of the brain. It contributes to abstract reasoning, perception, and motor planning. **Topologically** it is complex, in that much of its surface area is hidden in many folds and wrinkles in the **sulci** (plural of **sulcus**).

example, tactile information from a particular part of the body is processed in a particular local region of **somatasensory** cortex, and a particular part of the body is control by a local area of **motor cortex**. Localization of function carries over to more complex perceptual systems. The mammalian visual system is highly compartmentalized in the early stages of processing, when the visual signal enters the cortex, and successive stages of processing in different physical areas correspond to the bottom-up organization of simple features to higher level representations. So it is certainly reasonable to entertain the hypothesis that language processing might be similarly organized: first the extraction of phonetic features, then the activation of phonological units, then word recognition (as in the TRACE or cohort models from Chapter 6).

Interestingly, the idea that distinct language functions might be carried out in distinct neural regions was held even before much was known about the mammalian visual system, and before modern theories of language. In the late 1800s two important discoveries were made separately by two neurologists, the Frenchman Paul Broca and the German Carl Wernicke, that influenced the field's conception of language and the brain for over a century, and their general discoveries are still relevant today.

Aphasia

The general term for a language impairment that is due to some form of trauma to the brain – for example, a stroke, a blow to the head, or penetration by a foreign object – is **aphasia**. Trauma resulting in aphasia is almost always to the left side of the brain. Broca and Wernicke independently treated patients who had **lesions** (damage) in different parts of the left side of the brain, and who each suffered

A **stroke** is caused by a rupture or a blood clot in an artery that supplies blood to the brain. The neural tissue that is deprived of blood (and the necessary oxygen it carries) dies and does not regenerate.

very different sorts of language impairment. These symptom patterns became associated with the names of the scientists who discovered them, giving us the labels for patients who exhibit these symptoms: patients with **Broca's aphasia** and with **Wernicke's aphasia**.

Broca's aphasia
Broca's patient was nicknamed Tan, because that was the only syllable he could reliably produce. Yet he appeared to be able to understand what people were saying to him. So although the lesion impaired his ability to speak, it did not seem to have a profound effect on his comprehension. Broca interpreted the impairments caused by the lesion as evidence that the affected cortical area was the seat of language. This

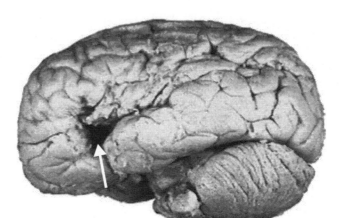

Figure 10.1   Photograph of the brain of Paul Broca's famous patient, Tan. The site of the lesion is now known as "Broca's area." Adapted by permission from Macmillan Publishers Ltd: *Nature Reviews Neuroscience*, Rorden, C., & Karnath, H., pp. 812–819, copyright 2004.

area became known as Broca's area. Figure 10.1 shows a photograph of Tan's brain.

Subsequent study of patients with lesions in the same general area revealed a similar pattern of deficits with language production. Most Broca's aphasics – as patients with lesions to Broca's area are called – are more verbal than Tan, but their speech is very effortful, with lots of **disfluencies** – pauses, "ums" and "ahs" – and a striking lack of function words and inflectional morphology – in other words, the morphemes having critical grammatical functions. This has led to the term **agrammaticism** to describe this cluster of symptoms, and these patients are also called **agrammatic aphasics**. Below is a sample of speech from an agrammatic aphasic:

Broca's aphasic response to "Describe your job":
Lower Falls . . . Maine . . . Paper. Four hundred tons a day! and ah . . . sulphur machines, and ah . . . wood . . . Two weeks and eight hours. Eight hours . . . no! Twelve hours, fifteen hours . . . workin . . . workin . . . workin! Yes, and ah . . . sulphur and . . . Ah wood. Ah . . . handlin! And ah sick, four years ago.

While comprehension in patients with Broca's aphasia is not perfect, it allows for communication. One can have a conversation with a Broca's aphasic in the sense that they generally understand what you say, and their responses, although effortful and not grammatically well formed, are logically related to your utterances and to the discourse. There is some suggestion that Broca's aphasics have comprehension problems when faced with utterances that have an atypical sentence structure. For example, in typical **transitive** sentences in English, the *doer* of an action is the subject, as in *Simone kicked the ball*. But in a **passive** sentence, the *doer* is the indirect object, and might not even appear in the sentence: *The ball was kicked (by Simone)*. While Broca's aphasics may not have trouble understanding a passive like the last one, where world knowledge makes it clear that *the ball* is not the kicker, they can have problems understanding so-called **reversible passives**, like *Simone was hugged by Albert*, where each participant is equally likely to be a hugger. They apparently cannot process the function words *was* and *by* in the way that normal listeners would to identify the reversal in roles. In general, sentences in which the meanings are not recoverable from a typical interpretation of the content words (e.g., nouns, verbs, adjectives) and that require syntactic processing pose comprehension problems for *some* Broca's aphasics. We stress *some* to emphasize the fact that comprehension deficits in Broca's aphasics are not uniform. The comprehension of reversible sentences is one area in which patients vary.

The problems in producing grammatical words and morphemes, and the apparent problem in some **morphosyntactic processing** in comprehension, makes it compelling to view Broca's area as the *grammar area*. While it certainly is clear that processing grammar is hindered in these patients, it is not entirely clear exactly what the nature of the deficits are, and this is further complicated by the fact that, as we just mentioned, patients with Broca's aphasia do differ from one another in the details of their impairments. Nevertheless, Broca's area is certainly involved in grammatical processing in some way.

It is worth noting that Broca's area is very near the area of motor cortex that is responsible for controlling the mouth and face (see Figure 10.2). Broca's aphasics with large lesions might exhibit general motor impairments in other parts of the body as well, depending on the size of the lesion. Could the difficulty in production simply be due to motor difficulties in producing speech? Although facial motor areas might be affected, some problems seem to be specific to speech production and language. For example, Broca's aphasics are able to produce similar kinds of articulations as required for the grammatical items in speech when they produce them in a nonspeech domain. In addition, a simple motor problem wouldn't explain why the production deficits would be especially apparent for grammatical morphemes. In sum, the symptoms of Broca's aphasia appear to involve some kind of impairment(s) to linguistic functions.

Wernicke's aphasia

The symptoms of Wernicke's aphasia are in many respects complementary to those of Broca's aphasics. Patients with damage to Wernicke's area generally have no problem producing speech at a normal speaking rate,

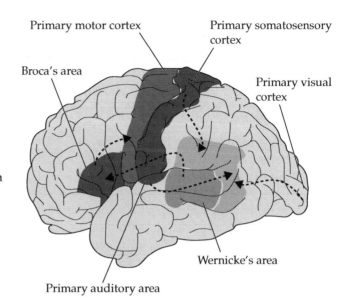

Figure 10.2 Depiction of Broca's and Wernicke's areas, as well as sensory and motor areas. Adapted with permission from Bruno Dubuc (www.thebrain.mcgill.ca).

with normal prosody and intonation. In fact, someone listening to a Wernicke's aphasic, who didn't know the language, would probably not think anything was wrong, as the speech seems, on the surface, *fluent*. However, in examining the *content* of the speech it becomes immediately clear that the speech being produced is highly abnormal. It consists of a jumble of disconnected ideas that bear no discernable relation to each other and no relation to what a conversational partner says. In short, unlike Broca's aphasics, who maintain a logical, coherent conversation, Wernicke's aphasics do not. But, also unlike Broca's aphasics, Wernicke's aphasics do not suffer from severe problems in speech articulation, nor in producing grammatical morphemes. Because of the character of their speech, Wernicke's aphasics are sometimes called **fluent aphasics**. Also, because their speech contains many **neologisms** – made-up words – they are also called **jargon aphasics**. Here is a sample of speech from a patient with damage to Wernicke's area:

> Wernicke's aphasic response to: "What brings you to the hospital?"
> Boy, I'm sweating, I'm awful nervous, you know, once in a while I get caught up, I can't mention the tarripoi, a month ago, quite a little, I've done a lot well, I impose a lot, while, on the other hand, you know what I mean, I have to run around, look it over, trebbin and all that sort of stuff.

Aside from the obvious lack of coherent meaning, patients with Wernicke's aphasia also seem to be impaired in comprehension. For example, in a neuropsychological evaluation, aphasic patients might be asked to pick up a specific object, say, a comb, given four or five objects in front of them. Although they might understand the request to pick up an object, there can be significant deficits in their understanding of *which* object to pick up.

While it may be tempting to conclude that Broca's area is the seat of syntax and Wernicke's area the seat of semantics, or meaning representations, in the brain, that would probably be overly simplistic. For one thing, it's not clear that the syntax of Wernicke's aphasics is entirely unaffected: because their comprehension is so poor, it's hard to determine if they really understand the function of the grammatical morphemes they produce. For instance, it's hard to test if they understand the syntactic cues to passive sentences if they don't correctly understand active sentences. In general, the fact that there is impairment at the lexical level makes it hard to assess whether syntactic competence has been affected. What does seem to be clear is that Wernicke's aphasics have deficits in the mapping between phonological forms and meanings, both in comprehension and production. The deficit seems to apply at least to the lexical level.

It's also interesting to note that while Broca's aphasics are intensely aware of their deficit and the effort involved in communicating, Wernicke's aphasics appear to be unaware that they have a significant problem communicating. We will return to Broca's and Wernicke's areas later in this chapter.

> Aphasia in general and the difference in symptoms between Broca's and Wernicke's aphasia is not restricted to spoken language. Deaf signers who incur brain damage exhibit the same location-dependent deficits in the production and comprehension of sign language. Of course, this is further evidence that sign languages are natural languages. But it could have turned out that, although functionally similar, the neural pathways involved in processing language in the two modalities was different. The evidence from deaf aphasic patients suggests that much of the neural hardware responsible for processing signed and spoke languages is the same. Similar conclusions come from neuroimaging studies, which show substantial (though not complete) overlap in the brain regions activated for signed and spoken languages.

Contemporary views of aphasia and localization

As just described, the symptoms of Broca's aphasia and Wernicke's aphasias are clearly different, and in the history of the study of aphasia, there are indeed many patients who display one or the other of these distinct sets of symptoms. However, what has also been discovered is that the correlation between the location of the lesion and the type of symptoms are not as strong as once thought. For example, there are patients who have lesions in Broca's area who do not display typical symptoms of Broca's aphasia (and sometimes no aphasic symptoms at all). Conversely, there are patients whose aphasic symptoms are characteristic of Broca's aphasics who do not have damage to Broca's area. Similar decoupling of symptoms and location of damage have been found with respect to Wernicke's aphasics and Wernicke's area as well. While these exceptions may not be the majority of cases, they have been encountered often enough that scientists have been moving away from the notions of strict localization of function for which aphasia was an original source of evidence.

Recovery from aphasia

Recovering language after brain damage is possible. Some adults do recover some or all of the linguistic abilities they lost due to brain damage, but any recovery occurs within the first six months after the brain trauma.

The situation for children with acquired language impairments – that is, impairments due to brain trauma – is much better. Children generally have a good prognosis for improvement. If children are very young and have acquired little to no productive language, there's not much to lose; they generally pick up from the point they were at before the trauma. Older children might have a more noticeable language decline, but they then seem to "reacquire" what they lost, resulting in a short-term delay in language learning, but overall a normal outcome. In some extreme cases, for medical reasons an entire hemisphere must be removed from a child's brain; if the left hemisphere is removed, it invariably results in aphasia (see "Lateralization" below). But amazingly, then the right hemisphere takes on the function of acquiring and processing language. In typical situations, when these individuals are older there may be not obvious signs of having only one hemisphere, although subtle impairments might be evident in situations when processing resources are taxed.

In general, the ability of children to recover from aphasia is taken as evidence of the inherent **plasticity** of children's brains. Plasticity refers to the ability of cortical regions to take on functions that they normally would not. This is an area of intense interest in cognitive neuroscience, as it is important to cognitive functions such as learning, but also to understanding cognitive development. Plasticity is critical to **functional organization** in the brain – how and why particular cortical regions come to be responsible for processing particular kinds of information.

Lateralization

An important generalization about aphasia is that brain trauma that results in aphasia is almost always limited to trauma in the left cerebral hemisphere. Right hemisphere lesions do not lead to the same patterns of deficits in most patients and are generally not so obviously disruptive to language. This has led to one of the most widely held scientific views of language localization, which is that the left hemisphere is the domain of language.

There are a number of sources of evidence, other than brain damage, that point to a critical role for the left hemisphere in language representation and processing. We overview some of the central ones here.

Split-brain patients

One source of evidence for language lateralization comes from so-called **split-brain patients**. These are individuals who, for medical reasons, had their **corpus callosum** severed. The corpus callosum is a dense band of neural fibers connecting the two hemispheres of the brain; it is the major communication pathway between the left and right hemispheres. Severing of the corpus callosum is sometimes prescribed for patients suffering from epilepsy. "Disconnecting" the two hemispheres from each other has a beneficial effect of reducing epileptic seizures for some patients. And while the procedure does not otherwise drastically alter the patient's behavior and daily life, there are some observable differences in these patients, particularly involving language, compared to normal individuals.

Before appreciating the phenomenon, you need to know a few facts about the organization of the **sensory-motor pathways**, which refers to the nerve pathways between parts of the body and sensory and motor areas of the brain. The generalization is that sensations (input) and motor commands (output) that involve the right side of the body are processed by the left brain hemisphere, and sensations and motor commands involving the left side of the body are processed by the right brain hemisphere. The sensory-motor pathways are therefore said to involve **contralateral connections** – the hemisphere involved is *opposite* to the side of the body in question.

In the case of vision, the important distinction with respect to contralateral connections is not between the left eye and the right eye, but rather between the **left visual field** and the **right visual field**. The visual field, roughly, refers to the side of a perceiver's body from which the visual signal is coming. The position of the eyes in humans is such that information

The left hemisphere dominance for language seems to be linked to handedness. Of the approximately 85 percent of individuals who are right-handed, estimates are that 97 percent of them have a left hemisphere dominance for language. Of the 15 percent of left-handers, just under 70 percent also have left hemisphere language dominance. The remaining portion of the population appear to have a more **bilateral** distribution of language areas, rather than having a right hemisphere dominance for language.

from either visual field impinges on the retina of *both eyes*. But the retina in each eye is actually split, sending information from the *right visual-field* to the left hemisphere, and from the *left visual-field* to the right hemisphere. This is true of the neural pathways *from both eyes*. In other words, the contralateral connections in the visual system distinguish left and right visual fields, not left and right eyeballs.

What does all this have to do with language? Well, in experiments where scientists can control exactly what information is available to each visual field (and therefore each hemisphere), it's been found that in split brain patients, information that is only accessible to the right hemisphere is *inaccessible* to language. That is, patients cannot talk about things in their left visual field. Figure 10.3 shows a typical experimental setup. In this depiction, if the patient is fixating at the central point, the bird is in her left visual field and the fork is in her right visual field. When asked to identify the objects she sees, she will only be able to talk about the fork,

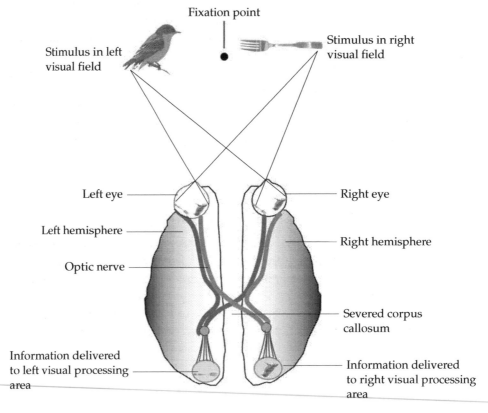

Figure 10.3   Depiction of flow of visual information when patient is fixating towards a central location. The right hemisphere processes information from the left visual field and vice versa. Most patients with a severed corpus callosum cannot talk about what is in their left visual field.

as the part of her brain primarily responsible for language will not have access to the visual information in the right hemisphere. However, she *would* be able to manipulate the objects seen by the right hemisphere if using her left hand (controlled by the right hemisphere), indicating that the information is present in the brain and in an accessible format. It's just not accessible to the language areas.

The reason why this phenomenon is only clearly noticeable in controlled experiments is that – fortunately for these patients – in daily life, when you're moving your head, or even just shifting your gaze, images go back and forth into each visual field, so generally a particular piece of visual information will still enter both hemispheres.

The Wada test
Before severing a patient's corpus callosum (or before other types of brain surgery), doctors want to understand the contribution of each hemisphere to various cognitive tasks for each individual patient. Doctors can essentially put one hemisphere to sleep for a while and see how the patient's behavior in a variety of tasks is affected. One way to do this is with what is known as the **Wada test**, named after its inventor, Dr. Juhn Wada. In this procedure, sodium amobarbital, or a similar barbiturate, is injected into either the patient's left or right carotid artery. The effect is to "knock out" the corresponding hemisphere until the drug wears off. During this time, the patient is essentially functioning with half of a brain. For most patients, when their left hemisphere is sedated, their ability to comprehend and produce language is impaired, but not when the right hemisphere is.

Dichotic listening
We just overviewed two **invasive** techniques – the Wada test and the split-brain procedure – for testing for left-hemisphere dominance of language. Dichotic listening techniques are noninvasive, and also quite revealing. We discussed the general dichotic listening methodology in Chapter 5, in the context of duplex perception. The general technique is to present a different sound to each ear, through headphones. The technique can be informative for questions of lateralization of function, even for individuals with normal, fully intact brains. This is because the representation of the auditory information received from one ear is stronger in the contralateral hemisphere than in the **ipsilateral** – same side – hemisphere. Although there are ipsilateral auditory connections, they are weaker and sparser than the contralateral connections. In addition, when both ears are processing sounds (whether the same sounds or different sounds), the ipsilateral connections are **attenuated** – they pass less information – than when only one ear is exposed to sound. All of this means that if one hemisphere is more dominant in processing a certain type of sound – for example, speech – than the other, sounds of that type played to the contralateral ear should have

a processing advantage compared to sounds presented to the ipsilateral ear. We now describe several experiments that used dichotic listening techniques to test for a hemisphere dominance, or lateralization, in language.

In one experiment, subjects heard different syllables played dichotically, such that in one ear they might hear a [da] while hearing [bi] in the other. Subjects' task on each trial – a presentation of a pair of syllables – was to report both syllables. What scientists found was that subjects were much more accurate at reporting syllables presented to the right ear (initially processed by the left hemisphere) than to the left ear, demonstrating a left hemisphere dominance for processing linguistic material. Of course, it could be that the left hemisphere is, for whatever reason, better at processing all kinds of auditory stimuli, not just linguistic material. Other experiments tested just that. In one experiment, musical melodies were presented dichotically, and subjects had to identify them. In contrast to speech, subjects did not show a right ear advantage to music – in fact, they showed a *left* ear advantage.

The apparent right hemisphere dominance for melodies is interesting, because in some ways music and speech are similar: They are both acoustic signals, they vary over time, they involve discrete units that are recombined and sequenced over time, and they both have **hierarchical structure**. One might have expected that they would be preferentially processed by the same hemisphere. In fact, in a similar study with expert musicians there was indeed a left hemisphere advantage for processing melodies. This makes sense if one considers that expert musicians would be more likely than novices to extract all the rich structural information from music. So, **depth of processing** might be an important factor that determines hemisphere dominance; the fact that material is highly structured might not be relevant if listeners don't process the structure in its rich complexity.

This idea was confirmed in another dichotic listening study involving **Morse code** – sequences of tones with the same pitch and two different durations (short "dots" and long "dashes") that encode letters of the alphabet (e.g., *a* is · –, *b* is – · · ·). For novices, these tone sequences have no particular structure or interpretation. But expert Morse code operators are highly practiced at recognizing patterns in the sequences and mapping them to letters. When Morse code was used in dichotic listening experiments, both experts and novices showed a right ear/left hemisphere advantage for brief sequences. But for longer sequences, novices showed a right hemisphere advantage, while experts maintained their left hemisphere advantage. So part of what may be special about the left hemisphere is a greater ability to assemble pieces into larger parts – so-called **analytic processing**. For novices, remembering the sequence of individual parts was possible if there were a small number. But longer sequences were processed differently between novice and expert.

Thus a number of different methods converge on the idea that for the majority of individuals, the left hemisphere is the primary seat of language. Some of the evidence we've just presented, particularly from dichotic listening studies, suggests some reasons *why* the left hemisphere may be well suited for processing language. One of the advantages may be a propensity for **combinatorial processing** – putting together structures from smaller parts. Along these lines, there are some proposals that Broca's area may be implicated in grammatical processing because of a more general function of this area in analytic and combinatorial processing, linguistic or otherwise.

One set of methods we have not yet discussed is functional brain imaging techniques – methods for actually observing activity in the brain while it's processing language. If anything could tell us about the localization of function, couldn't brain imaging?

Imaging the Brain and What We Can Learn

Imaging methods are getting better every year, both in terms of the precision of the technology, but also in our ability to effectively analyze the data in meaningful ways. Nonetheless, there are a number of challenges and downsides to every brain imaging method. We will briefly overview several prominent imaging techniques, discussing their pluses and minuses, and then describe several insights into language processing that they have given us – some classic in the field, some relatively new.

Cerebral blood flow

As the activity of neurons increases, their demand for energy increases, and so the body increases the supply of blood to particularly active areas. If one could detect the increase in blood flow, one could then infer that those are areas with greater neuronal activity. Several techniques have been developed to do this.

An early technique that is still in use, called **positron emission tomography (PET)**, involves injecting a radioactive isotope into the brain. The radioactive fluid can be sensed outside the scalp, and when the blood supply to a region of the brain increases, it results in an increased concentration of radioactivity in that portion of the brain. The technique has a **spatial resolution** of under a centimeter, but because the blood flow increase is

> **Spatial resolution** refers to how fine a distinction one can make in terms of where activity is located in neural tissue. **Temporal resolution** refers to how fine-grained a distinction one can make about the timing of neural events.

delayed after neuronal activation, the **temporal resolution** is very slow relative to language processing – around 30 seconds. This means that the experimental designs have to have long listening sequences that involve the same processes. Of course, a major drawback of this methodology is the injection of radioactive substances.

A blood flow measurement technique that is noninvasive is **functional magnetic resonance imaging (fMRI)**. The MRI scanner uses strong magnetic fields (60,000 times as strong as Earth's magnetic field) and pulses of radio waves to measure changes in the brain that are due to changes in blood flow. One common method of measuring blood flow due to neural activity in fMRI is to measure changes in **blood oxygenation levels** in the brain, called **BOLD** fMRI (blood oxygen level dependent fMRI). The logic is similar to PET, except that BOLD fMRI relies on the fact that the increase in blood flow to active brain areas results in the increase of **oxygenated** blood in active areas. Greater oxygenation levels changes the magnetic resonance properties of blood. As in PET, the spatial resolution is very good, and the temporal resolution is somewhat better (about six seconds), although it is still considerably slower than typical processes underlying speech processing. So again, long sequences of similar stimuli are used, and also clever mathematical techniques have been developed to detect responses to individual stimuli, which allows greater flexibility for scientists. However, it is expensive to set up and maintain an fMRI facility. The machine itself costs several million dollars, and requires a special facility to keep the superconducting magnet near absolute zero in temperature. Furthermore, measuring auditory language processing can be tricky because when measurements are made the device is quite loud, which could interfere with auditory related tasks and measurements.

Near infrared spectroscopy (NIRS) is a technique that is gaining in popularity. It, too, measures blood flow but uses infrared lasers to do so. The lasers are low power and not harmful, and they are very lightweight. A typical device also costs a fraction of MRI technology; it is quiet, and much more flexible in how it can be used. The subject can wear it, rather than having to lie immobile in a tube as in most MRI. The use of this technique has become popular in imaging the brain function of infants and children for these reasons.

EEG and MEG

Electroencephalography (EEG) uses an array of electrodes worn on the scalp that measure the electrical voltages generated by large collections of neurons that are acting collectively. EEG has been very popular in language processing research because it has excellent temporal resolution (on the order of one millisecond). The trade-off is that it has poor spatial resolution, partially because the scalp diffuses the electrical activity. So, although there are electrodes positioned over many parts of the scalp, the source of the activation they detect is not the cortex directly underneath. Still, as you will see, accurate temporal information can be very informative.

Magnetoencephalography (MEG) is similar to EEG except that the sensors measure changes in electromagnetic fields due to activity of large sets of neurons. For various reasons the spatial resolution is greater than EEG but locating the source of activation is still very complicated, and there is debate about how this should be done with respect to imaging language processing. MEG is also more technically demanding than EEG and more expensive.

General challenges in brain imaging

One of the benefits of imaging techniques over traditional behavioral experiments is that we can see what the brain is doing without the subject having to do something special, perhaps unnatural (like a cross-modal priming task), while processing speech. But that's also one of the problems: at any given time we are measuring *everything* the brain is doing – and that's a lot! The brain is constantly processing sensory information at many different levels, and generally performing many covert operations, regardless of what we are consciously thinking about or attending to in an experiment. All those functions involve brain activity, so how do we measure activity that is uniquely associated with language processing?

The problem occurs even if we just consider language activity. In normal language comprehension tasks, processing is presumably occurring at all levels of linguistic analysis, from phonetics to syntax to meaning. And language is not an isolated entity, it **interfaces** with our general concepts and thoughts, linguistic or otherwise. If we're interested in speech perception, how do we measure just the activity related, for example, to phonological units or to words?

There are several strategies that can be taken to improve language-and-brain experiments. One is simplification: as in experiments that require behavioral responses, simplifying the task can eliminate some types of processing. For example, if you're studying word recognition, using isolated words rather than words in sentences would eliminate syntactic processing, and perhaps the activation of broad **semantic networks**. On the other hand, we know from Chapter 6 that word recognition involves top-down processing from meaning, so is such a simplification desirable for understanding word recognition?

Another method is **subtraction**. Generally, this kind of procedure involves a **control task** that superficially resembles the task of interest (the **experimental task**) but differs only on critical properties that you're trying to measure. For example, if you are interested in seeing what areas of the brain are especially active when processing speech, the experimental task might be simply listening to nonsense words (thus activating areas responsible for speech processing but without semantic or syntactic information), while the control task might be listening to the same list played *backwards*. Backwards speech has the same acoustic properties as the forward version, but has no linguistic units. The same areas should be active in both tasks, but speech-related areas should be more active in the experimental task. *Subtracting* the control activity from the experimental activity will identify those areas. (Of course, the speech-related areas might also be active in many other kinds of tasks as well.) The subtraction method is also not without problems. One problem is that it is difficult to design perfect control tasks, so that one could end up subtracting out some of the activity that you are actually interested in. This would have the effect of reducing or eliminating the hypothesized effect.

Another method is to collect data for the same task over a great many trials, and many subjects. This is an approach taken particularly with techniques like EEG and MEG that produce very weak signals for the components of brain activity that are of interest, compared to the "noise" of all the extraneous activity. When activity is averaged over many trials, the noise tends to "wash out," resulting in a stronger signal associated with the task of interest.

Evaluating cognitive/functional models with neuroimaging

One set of findings from EEG electrophysiological research concerns the time-course of various stages in language processing, such as the activation of word meanings and the activation of phonological representations. The typical design in these kinds of experiments is to measure **event-related potentials (ERPs)**. This refers to brain activity that occurs after a specific experimental event, for example, the onset of a word. Event-related activity by itself is not usually what is analyzed. Rather, what is typically measured is differences in activity when processing normal versus **anomalous** events – that is, events that are unexpected or surprising. It turns out that when the brain processes unexpected material, it gives a little electrical "hiccup" that these procedures can detect. In the case of anomalous linguistic events, it is generally thought that the ERP response is a result of the extra processing load in trying to integrate the anomalous material into the linguistic interpretation of the signal at that point. It turns out that the *timing* of these brain responses to anomalous stimuli depends on the nature of the anomaly.

In a famous series of experiments Marta Kutas and Steven Hillyard discovered a specific brain response during reading a sentence when the subject reads a **semantically anomalous** word – a word that is odd in the context of an utterance. For example, *He takes his coffee with cream and* <u>*sand*</u> contains an unexpected word, *sand*, that is nevertheless grammatical, even though nonsensical, in that position in the sentence. Subjects read the sentences one word at a time – the words were displayed on a screen one by one, with a fixed delay – so that the experimenters knew exactly when the critical words were presented. The anomalous words produced a characteristic electrical "signature" that was the strongest about 400 milliseconds after the word was displayed, leading to its name *N400*. (The "N" refers to the fact that the activity has negative polarity.) This general finding has been replicated by different labs, in many different experiments, and it is extremely reliable. It suggests that some kind of **semantic integration** is going on as early at approximately 400 milliseconds after encountering a word. The strength of the N400 signal is thought to correspond to the degree of difficulty or effort involved in integrating the word into the ongoing semantic context. Of course, it should be noted that the first semantic anomaly results involved reading, as opposed to spoken language comprehension. But the findings were later replicated with spoken language.

The N400 findings are consistent with the experimental results on word recognition that show the top-down influence of context on word recognition – the ERP results, like the shadowing experiment results described in Chapter 6, show that comprehenders compute the meaning of an utterance as it unfolds over time, and words are recognized in the context of that meaning. However, does the N400 tap spoken word recognition, or more general lexical processing? The fact that the effects are found for spoken and written language strongly suggest that the N400 does not specifically reflect spoken word recognition. In addition, recall that the close shadowers begin shadowing words as early as 250 milliseconds after word onset. Is there an ERP that reflects early lexical access processing?

In fact, more recent research has shown that when a word onset violates expectations there is an earlier ERP component called the **PMN** (for **phonological mismatch negativity**) that occurs at approximately 250–300 milliseconds after the beginning of a word. In a typical experiment, a subject is shown a picture of an object, say an ice-cream cone. The subject then hears a word that is either *cone* [kon] (a match) or some other word that mismatches in the first sound, such as *fox*. Subtracting ERPs for *fox* from *cone* yields a strong PMN and also a strong N400. The interpretation of such findings is that the photograph of the ice-cream cone sets up an expectation for the word *cone* that is violated, resulting in a semantic anomaly effect as in the previous experiments. However, the PMN is taken as evidence that the expectation is not just semantic but *phonological* as well. When the bottom-up information from the word onset ([f]) doesn't match the expected (or primed) onset ([k]), the mismatch produces a strong negative ERP. The timing of the response is similar to when close shadowers begin to repeat words, so the shadowing results are consistent with the interpretation that PMNs reflect early stages of word selection.

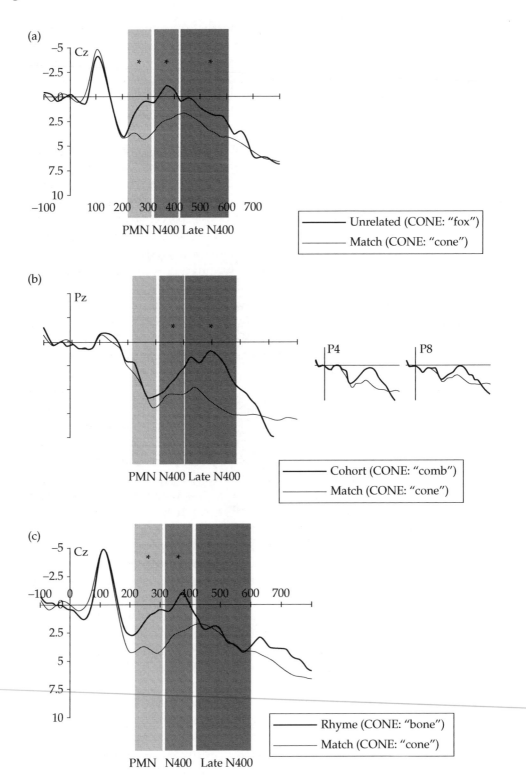

Can ERPs be used to test predictions of different word recognition models, like TRACE and cohort? Perhaps. Some very recent research claims that PMN and N400 responses to particular kinds of words support models of word recognition that allow for the activation of rhymes as well as cohorts as candidates for word recognition (e.g., TRACE, but not cohort). Amy Desroches and colleagues carried out an experiment like the one described above, but in addition to the matched and completely mismatched word, subjects sometimes hear rhyme words, like bone ([bon]), and cohorts, like comb ([kom]) to a target picture of an ice-cream cone. The cohorts did not result in a PMN response. This is consistent with the notion that PMN is a phonological mismatch response and the fact that the cohorts (e.g., [kom]) matched the target (e.g. [kon]) in the initial sounds. However, cohorts did result in an N400, but later in processing the word than with completely mismatched words (Figure 10.4a). This is consistent with the idea that mismatch between the bottom-up signal ([kom]) and the word primed by the top-down visual information from the picture ([kon]) didn't occur until the end of the word. As expected, the rhyme words (e.g., [bon]) resulted in a PMN – because of the phonological mismatch in the initial segment – in addition to an N400 (Figure 10.4b). However, the N400 occurred earlier for the rhymes than for the cohorts (but similar to a totally mismatching word) and the duration of the N400 was much greater for the cohort words than rhyme words (see Figure 10.4). The experimenters interpreted this using concepts from the TRACE model: the phonological units activated by the presentation of the photograph – [k], [o], [n] – activated all the words that overlapped phonologically. Specifically, the [o] and [n] activated [bon] and the [k] and the [o] activated [kom] even before any speech was heard. The duration of the N400 was longer for cohorts than for rhymes because at the point of the cohort mismatch, the target [kon] was highly active from the bottom-up and

Figure 10.4 (*opposite*) An ERP from one electrode channel for a word that matches the priming image and a word that mismatches, but rhymes. The lines are averages over many trials and many subjects. The ERP for the rhyme is more negative in the first region, which corresponds to a phonological mismatch, and the second region, which corresponds to a semantic anomaly. But the divergence from the matching ERP goes away by the third time window. ERPs to cohort and unrelated mismatch words would diverge from the match through the third time window, indicating a greater mismatch with the priming photograph. From Amy Deroches, Randly Lynn Newman, and Marc F. Joanisse, Investigating the Time Course of Spoken Word Recognition: Electrophysiological Evidence for the Influences of Phonological Similarity, *Journal of Cognitive Neuroscience*, 21(10) (October, 2009), pp. 1893–1906. © 2008 by the Massachusetts Institute of Technology. Reprinted with permission from the publisher.

top-down information together, so that at the point of the mismatch at the last phonological unit, [kon] had inhibited [kom] significantly and greater processing effort was required to now suppress [kon] and activate [kom], resulting in a long N400. In contrast, when a rhyme like [bon] was processed, [kon] was never as active as in the cohort cases and therefore inhibited other active words to a lesser degree. The resulting N400 was briefer because the preactivated rhyme was less inhibited by [kon], even though [kon] received top-down activation (from the picture). While the results fit naturally with the TRACE model, the cohort model has no clear explanation of the findings, especially the difference between rhymes and mismatched words (i.e., bone vs. fox). These findings are very recent, and other interpretations are possible. Nevertheless, it gives you a sense of how this neuroimaging technique is used to address questions in speech perception and to help guide how scientists shape their models of these processes.

Revising cognitive/functional models with neuroimaging

The ERP experiment we just discussed is an example of how neuroimaging could, in principle, be used to adjudicate between two cognitive models, just as the behavioral experiments we discussed in previous chapters. We now overview a recent theory of language processing that incorporates insights from neuroimaging data and that adds further nuances to some of the broad generalizations about localization and function that we've discussed up to this point.

Gregory Hickok and David Poeppel, through their own research and from the synthesis of the findings of many other scientists, recently theorized that there are two **pathways** for speech perception – one that is involved only in word recognition (what they call "speech recognition"), and the other that is responsible for speech perception (accessing sublexical units like syllables, phonological units, information about the sequential order of units, etc.). This dual pathway theory claims that there are literally two distinct neural pathways, involving different brain regions, through which information travels and is processed. Moreover, the two neural pathways are proposed to support two distinct functional/computational pathways, such that speech perception and word recognition happen *separately*. This might seem surprising for several reasons: first, all the models of word recognition that we've discussed assume that speech perception occurs at a stage before word recognition. Even the highly interactive TRACE model is explicitly organized so that the signal can only affect word representations *via* phonetic features, then phonological representations – the stuff of speech perception. Second, it might seem logically flawed: how *could* word recognition work without speech perception at a prior stage?

To fully address these issues is beyond the scope of this chapter, but the general idea is the following. The speech signal is first analyzed *bilaterally* – involving both hemispheres – into a phonological code, and that code then bilaterally interfaces with lexical representations. These processes and representations involve Wernicke's area. However, those phonological codes are not representations that are involved when we perform tasks in speech perception experiments. For those, the phonological codes also activate a series of left hemisphere regions; in particular, they activate articulatory motor representations that are associated with the phonological units – perhaps something like the gestural representations in Chapter 7. These representations are proposed to involve Broca's area, among others. According to this theory, these are the representations that are tapped in traditional speech perception experiments, such as tests for categorical perception and detection of syllables in speech. Finally, Hickok and Poeppel propose that the articulatory motor representations also activate lexical representations, so that lexical representations are not only activated directly by the early phonological representations, but also by representations that are mediated through the articulatory-motor pathway.

Given what we've discussed so far about the lateralization of language, it may seem surprising to encounter a theory that claims that some important parts of speech processing are bilateral. But this hypothesis did not come out of the blue. Although many important components of language are typically left-lateralized, the right hemisphere has been known to be able to carry out lexical access to some degree. The dual route theory was motivated in part by unexplained differences across neurolinguistic experiments and in aphasic patient data in speech processing and word recognition. Some experiments and patient data implicated bilateral regions in comprehending words, and some implicated purely left hemisphere regions. Hickok and Poeppel observed that some of the differences might be linked to differences in the tasks involved across experiments. Those that involved sublexical tasks – such as recognizing syllables in words or monitoring speech for particular phonological units – showed strong left hemisphere involvement, whereas simply recognizing words involved both hemispheres. Their dual route theory can account for many of the seemingly paradoxical findings.

In addition, there is some clear fMRI data implicating both hemispheres in lexical access. Bilateral regions near Wernicke's area show activation when subjects listen to words with dense phonological neighborhoods, subtracting out activation when listening to words with sparse neighborhoods. The activation is also dependent on neighborhood density. Words with greater neighborhood density produce more activation, presumably reflecting the activation of more words.

The correlation of the activation patterns with phonological neighborhood density indicate two things: (1) the representations involve lexical access, and (2) the representations involve phonological codes, as the neighborhoods are based on phonological similarity. So this experiment provides strong evidence that at least some aspects of word recognition are bilaterally distributed, and further identify brain regions responsible for lexical-phonological integration.

The more direct, bilateral sound-to-meaning route is advantageous for fast lexical access. There is some evidence that familiar words are processed via this route (in addition to the articulatory-motor route), suggesting that experience might be necessary to set up the sound-to-meaning links in this pathway. Less frequent words and nonwords are processed exclusively through the articulatory-motor pathway, suggesting that it may be the primary pathway for all language processing early on, with the direct bilateral associations being built up through experience. The proposal for a motor pathway for *perceiving* speech is consistent with the motor theory of speech perception, discussed in Chapter 5.

The motor theory of speech perception was conceived before neuroimaging was available. Now we can evaluate some of its predictions regarding the critical use of speech motor representations in speech perception by directly looking at the brain and behavior. Recently, neuroscientists Luciano Fadiga, Alessandro D'Ausilio, and colleagues used a technique that stimulated the motor parts of the brain that control the lip and the tongue; then they asked listeners to identify syllables starting with either a labial consonant ([p] or [b]) or with a tongue tip consonant ([t] or [d]). They found that recognition of lip-produced syllables was faster when the lip motor area was stimulated and likewise for tongue tip syllables when the tongue motor area was stimulated. Also, on hearing [t/da] syllables, listeners were more likely to make an error identifying them as [p/ba] if the lip motor area was stimulated, and, likewise, make more bilabial syllable identification mistakes when the tongue motor area was stimulated. This is compelling evidence that the motor areas deployed in speaking play a critical role in neural pathways used in phonological discrimination.

This theory is by no means accepted by all, but it does account for many discrepancies in the neurolinguistic literature. For our purposes in particular, it provides an example of how neuroimaging research can potentially inform our cognitive/functional theories and cause us to reinterpret the results of previous experiments.

Summary

This chapter has overviewed some of the key concepts and discoveries over approximately the last century concerning the implementation of language in the brain. Many of the generalizations about language localization originally laid out by Broca and Wernicke – including the dominance for language of the left hemisphere – are still useful today. However, with over one hundred years of the further study of aphasia, and with a more sophisticated understanding of the structure of language, the picture has become more complex. Various functional brain imaging techniques have been used to confirm what had been suggested by prior research in language-impaired and in healthy subjects, but neuroimaging has also led to new theories and greater subtlety to cognitive models. As imaging techniques become more precise, the possibility for new discoveries is very exciting. However, it's important to bear in mind that in order to have a framework for interpreting brain imaging data, and in order even to ask scientifically insightful questions, one needs a solid theoretical understanding about language itself and the kinds of representations and processes involved in its comprehension and production.

Further Reading

Hickok, Gregory and David Poeppel (2000). Towards a Functional Neuroanatomy of Speech Perception. *Trends in Cognitive Sciences*, 4(4), pp. 131–8.

Chapter 11

Language, Speech, and Hearing Disorders

Entire fields of medical study are devoted to the wide variety of disorders that relate to the human ability to communicate. These disorders can range from problems with hearing to difficulties with vocal fold vibration to atypicalities of the brain that impact the ability to produce or process speech and/or language. In the last chapter, we discussed aphasia as an example of a communication disorder that arises from the central nervous system. In this chapter, we introduce how language development, speech, and hearing can be atypical in complex ways that we are only beginning to understand.

While this chapter confines itself to a handful of specific disorders of language, speech, and hearing, there are of course many disorders that affect communication more globally as part of neurologically complex syndromes. Such disorders – such as autism spectrum disorder, Down syndrome, fragile X syndrome, and Williams syndrome – are broad in nature, with language communication being only one component. There are many good resources for learning more about these disorders, some of which are listed at the end of this chapter.

Specific Language Impairment

In Chapter 1 we discussed how all healthy children go naturally through a developmental process of learning language. The question arises, however, as to what subtle disorders in the genetic makeup and/or early experience of an individual can give rise to language impairment. Of course, atypicalities in the speech motor system or in the hearing system will likely make speech and language perception atypical. But what about disorders in *language* ability per se that are innate rather than acquired like the aphasia we discussed in the last chapter? Such disorders do exist. One of them is **specific language impairment (SLI)**. At the most simple level of description, children with SLI are significantly behind their peers in both their language production and comprehension, though not in other areas of development. SLI may also be called mixed receptive-expressive language disorder, expressive language disorder, language delay, developmental language disorder, or persistent language impairment. As the preferred name specific language impairment suggests, this impairment is one in which children have problems specifically with certain aspects of language abilities; the disorder need not accompany any problems with articulation, intelligence, social abilities, or hearing, and these children do not have obvious brain lesions or anatomical abnormalities. (However, many children with SLI do end up with reading problems, likely due to the close connection with early language disorders and literacy.) There is evidence suggesting that there is a genetic basis for SLI – albeit a complex one; there appears to be a tendency for SLI to occur in families, within and across generations. Multiple genes seem to be implicated, having a complicated interaction with one another and with the linguistic environment, in determining the time of onset of different language skills and the course of development of those skills.

It is estimated that approximately 7 percent of children meet the definition of SLI as they enter elementary school, with slightly more boys being affected. Many of these children are not identified as having this disorder and unfortunately may be thought to be "slow" or "lazy" in school. Being a late talker is a hallmark characteristic of children with SLI, though only about a quarter of late talkers end up being classified as having SLI at school age.

Specific language impairment has two components that we'd like to draw your attention to. First, children with SLI have persistent delays in their

Mabel Rice, an expert on children's language disabilities, and Joy Simpson describe typical errors in SLI, including:

dropping the -s off present tense verbs and asking questions without the usual "be" or "do" verbs. For example, instead of saying "She rides the horse" the child will say "She ride the horse." Instead of saying "Does he like me?" the child will ask "He like me?" Children with SLI also have trouble communicating that an action is complete because they drop the past tense ending from verbs. They say, "She walk to my house yesterday" instead of "she walked to my house."[1]

---

[1] Quoted from *http://merrill.ku.edu/IntheKnow/sciencearticles/SLIfacts.html*

language abilities relative to their peer groups, including vocabulary size and grammatical abilities. Second, children with SLI show disruptions in the normal trajectory of language abilities in certain areas. Specifically, they have a marked and persistent difficulty with correctly using and understanding verbal morphology such as using morphemes that mark tense and agreement, even while broader sentence structure remains sound. The morphemes that mark tense and agreement with verbs are often omitted well into elementary school, long after age-mates produce these correctly.

The Prevalence of Speech and Hearing Disorders

It is important to know reliable information about speech and hearing disorders, as you will almost certainly encounter individuals with atypical speech and/or hearing in your day-to-day life. The US National Institute on Deafness and Other Communication Disorders, which is part of the National Institutes of Health, estimates that one in six Americans experience a communication disorder of some sort.[2] Communication disorders are wide-ranging and might include anything from a hearing impairment to a voice disorder.

Congenital means present from birth.

About 36 million American adults report a **hearing loss**; this includes 2–8 percent of children and nearly half of people over 75. And while you may not (right now) fall into either of these groups, 90 percent of the children who are born deaf are born to parents who can hear. And hearing loss isn't only **congenital**. Ten to 26 million Americans of all ages have irreversible hearing loss caused by exposure to environmental noise. Hearing loss is prevalent in society for a number of reasons including genetics, aging, disease, and environment.

There are three main types of **speech disorders** – impairments of the voice, speech sound (or articulation), and fluency. Language disorders, which are more linguistic and/or cognitive in nature are another type of disorder; however, we confine our discussion in this chapter to speech and hearing disorders. By the first grade, approximately 5 percent of children have noticeable speech disorders, and generally no known source of these problems can be identified. Difficulties with **voice,** or the effective vibration of the vocal folds necessary for speech, occur for approximately 7.5 million Americans. These problems can have a variety of causes ranging from mundane overuse of the voice to injury, infection, cancer, and a variety of other diseases, and environmental irritants. Speech disorders can also

---

[2] The statistics in this chapter on different types of disorders are taken from the National Institutes of Health estimates.

include **speech sound disorders** such as problems with articulation and phonological processes. The third type of speech disorder is the **fluency** disorder of stuttering. Stuttering is not uncommon in children and does persist into adulthood in a small percentage of individuals.

Finally, birth defects causing **anomalies in craniofacial structure** can, if not surgically corrected, impact speech as well. For example, cleft palate is the fourth most common birth defect, occurring in about 1 in every 700 to 1000 live births, and results in a failure of the palate and/or upper lip to fuse together properly before birth. Cleft palate can be one component of syndromes that include middle ear and heart problems. In addition to leading to speech problems, cleft palate can cause feeding difficulty and severe facial deformity if not corrected. The consequences of craniofacial anomalies such as cleft palate are particularly severe in parts of the world without access to modern surgical care.

You may be interested in the professions that work with and care for individuals with deafness and with communication disorders. These may be medical doctors – often otolaryngologists, who have a surgical specialty – or speech-language pathologists who directly treat the communication aspect of the disorder. Additionally, audiologists work in the field of hearing assessment and remediation, and auditory-verbal therapists (who are also audiologists, speech-language pathologists, or teachers of the deaf by training) work in the field of aural habilitation. In choosing a clinician, it is desirable for audiologists and speech-language pathologists to possess a graduate degree, be certified by the American Speech and Hearing Association, be state-licensed (in those states that regulate the fields), and be specialized in the area of concern.

Deafness and Hearing Loss

In order to understand the causes and kinds of hearing loss, it will be helpful to go back and review the normal hearing process we covered in Chapter 2 if it's not fresh in your mind.

Kinds of hearing loss

Sensorineural hearing loss is produced by abnormalities of the inner ear (cochlea) or its nerve pathways. Sensorineural hearing loss is the most common form of hearing loss and often has a genetic component. At this time, it cannot be medically cured. **Conductive hearing loss** occurs when the middle ear fails to function normally, and it can often be medically or surgically improved. Loss of hearing may be **congenital** or may be **acquired**. It may be in one or both ears (unilateral or bilateral); it may be sudden or gradual; and it may be fluctuating or stable.

Remember how hearing works: when a noise occurs, air pressure fluctu-ations hit the eardrum and move it. This then causes the bones of the middle ear to move as interacting levers to amplify the signal. This in turn sets fluid into motion inside the cochlea causing the basilar membrane to set into motion as a traveling wave. The sensory hair cells on that membrane consequently have their projecting stereocilia bent or tilted against another projecting membrane. This initiates chemical events in the cell, resulting ultimately in an electrical signal that is sent along the auditory nerve. (Figure adapted from the House Ear Institute)

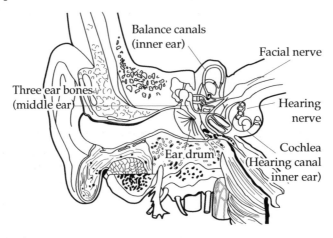

Sources of hearing loss

There are many sources of hearing loss and we will not attempt to cover them all here; suffice to say that viruses (such as cytomegalovirus, rubella, HIV, herpes), especially contracted prenatally, and other infections such as bacterial meningitis, as well as genetics and a host of birth defects, injury including birth injury, drug toxicity, and tumors are all possible sources of deafness. It is thought that about 68 percent of deafness arises from genetics and about 25 percent from cytomegalovirus.

Even **middle ear infections**, which are exceedingly common in young children, can result in transient hearing loss, which is worrisome especially if prolonged or recurrent, since these children are in their period of rapid language learning. Breast feeding, good hygiene to prevent infection at home and in daycare, and a smoke-free environment can assist in preventing ear infections in children.

True age-related hearing loss is called **presbycusis**, and current science suggests that it may have a genetic component. This hearing loss is gen-erally gradual and greater for higher frequency sounds. Various causes seem to be at play including disorders of the inner ear, auditory nerve, and/or

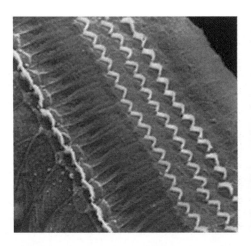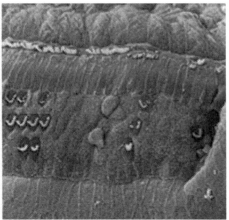

Figure 11.1   (left) Normal hair cells; (right) Hair cells damaged by noise. © 2008 House Ear Institute.

blood supply due to cardiovascular problems. Some hearing loss in older age is, however, not due strictly to presbycusis but is noise-induced hearing loss. About one in three adults between age 65 and 75 have a hearing loss and the number rises to one in two above 75. For these individuals, sounds often seem unclear or mumbled; conversations can be hard to understand.

Noise-induced hearing loss (NIHL) occurs when loud noises damage the hair cells in the inner ear. Figure 11.1 shows normal hair cells and hair cells damaged due to noise.

Noise-induced hearing loss can occur at any age and is permanent and irreversible. Dangerously, it is gradual and you can't feel it happening; you just painlessly, progressively, and unsuspectingly lose your hearing sensitivity. Eventually sounds become muffled and speech becomes difficult to understand. Persons with this type of hearing loss might report that they can hear you but not understand you. Warning signs might include a ringing or buzzing in the ears (called tinnitus), a fluctuating need to have sounds louder than they normally need to be, or difficulty hearing or understanding in noisy environments. Even when an individual is unaware of his or her hearing loss, it can be detected with a hearing test. Unfortunately, what can happen is that people with NIHL may simply increase the volume of the music and TV they are trying to listen to, not realizing how dangerously high the levels become.

Some current US statistics suggest that a shocking *12 percent* of *children* have some noise-induced hearing loss. Whatever the statistics or age, there is no reason not to take active steps to protect your own hearing and for society to make sensible decisions about noise exposure for both adults and children. If you are in a situation where you must raise your voice to

Table 11.1 Environmental Noise Levels. Adapted from American Speech-Language-Hearing Association, NIDCD, & the National Institute for Occupational Safety and Health

Decibel level	Example	Hazardous exposure times for unprotected ears
150	Firecracker, ammunition	Any unprotected exposure in
120	Ambulance siren	proximity is hazardous
130	Jackhammer, sporting events	< 1 minute
100–120	Rock concert, iPod at max volume	Regular exposure of more than several minutes
100	Wood shop, snowmobile	No more than 15 minutes
95	Motorcycle	1 hour
90	Power lawn mower	2 hours
85	Heavy city traffic	Prolonged exposure can cause gradual hearing loss
60	Normal conversation	
40	Refrigerator humming	
30	Whispering	

be heard, that should alert you to a potential hazard. Noises over 85 dB are considered dangerous and the amount of damage is a combination of both the loudness and the overall time of exposure. Noise levels from loud equipment (ranging from household lawn mowers to motor cycles to industrial engines) or from ammunition, from traffic, or from music players and concerts (of any genre of music) can all be brought to safer levels. Simple foam earplugs available at any drugstore are helpful, and more serious ear protection is available at most hardware and sporting goods stores. Musicians and others in this type of environment should take care not to place themselves directly in front of amplifiers and not to have extended practices at performance volumes. Children too young to protect their own ears should have someone taking responsibility for monitoring their exposure to loud toys, music, and other environmental noise sources. And in all noisy environments, take regular breaks from the noise, such as 15-minute quiet periods every hour. Note that earbuds are particularly worrisome as they send sound directly into the ear at boosted volumes, and young people tend to wear them for long periods.

Hearing management

Conductive hearing losses and mild to severe sensorineural hearing losses are usually managed by **hearing aids**, which are devices that make sounds louder. There are many different types of hearing aids, and a hearing test

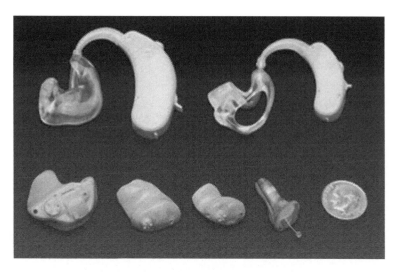

Figure 11.2   Various types of hearing aids for sensorineural hearing loss.
© 2008 House Ear Institute.

and audiologist can help determine optimal choices (but first a medical exam should be conducted to rule out medical conditions that might be present and impact hearing). Some hearing aids do little more than amplify; many are programmable and customizable to an individual's hearing profile. For example, they may convert sounds from a poorly heard frequency range into a better heard frequency range. Some hearing aids fit in and behind the outer ear while others sit inside the ear canal (see Figure 11.2).

Unfortunately, many people who could benefit from a hearing aid don't wear them. In addition to a lack of knowledge about the possible help the devices might provide, other reasons for not using a hearing aid can be because of inconvenience or issues concerning comfort, image, or finance.

Deafness generally refers to a profound hearing loss, but the term can be varied in its precise use. Some reserve the term "deaf" for those unable to hear normal conversation, while others include those with a lot of trouble hearing. For our purposes, the term **deaf** refers to the inability to hear well enough to rely on hearing for communication. About 3 in every 1,000 people in the US are functionally deaf, though fewer than 1 in 1,000 are deaf before age 18.

For a profound hearing loss in both ears, amplification may be of little or no benefit if too few of the hair cells in the inner ear are functional. A prosthetic device that is becoming more common among deaf children and adults is the **cochlear implant**. This is *not* amplification or a hearing aid. Rather, it is a surgically implanted device that transforms sound into electrical energy that directly stimulates the auditory nerve by using an electrode array permanently inserted in the cochlea, thereby substituting

There is substantial research underway to understand how hair cells in the inner ear might be regenerated, a process that does not occur normally in mammals. Various research groups are studying the genes that control hair cell development and proliferation in the hopes that gene therapy or regenerative medicine techniques might some day allow for functioning and correctly positioned hair cells to be reintroduced into the cochlea of a person with hearing loss.

for the nonfunctioning hair cells. Of course, this can only be used when the auditory nerve is intact and functioning. Here's how it works: an external microphone sends the sound to a digital signal processing device that manipulates it in a variety of ways. The signal is then transmitted through the skin on the head to the array of electrodes (these vary in number, but 8–24 channels is typical) that have been surgically wound through the cochlea. The electrodes stimulate the auditory nerve to send a sensory signal to the brain resulting in the sensation of hearing. Figures 11.3 and 11.4 show a cochlear implant.

This hearing is not like typical hearing, and it is very hard to compare the two directly. It is, however, usable sensory information.

In individuals who are born deaf, it is very important that the implant be done as early as possible, ideally between one and three and a half years of age, because the brain must learn to process sound and, specifically, spoken language. After age three and a half, the brain seems to be less

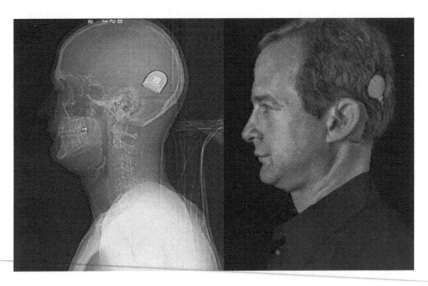

Figure 11.3 A depiction of a cochlear implant showing the processor and transmitter externally (on the right) and the receiver under the scalp internally (on the left). Used by permission from Michael Chorost; Credit: Matt Hoyle, Photographer.

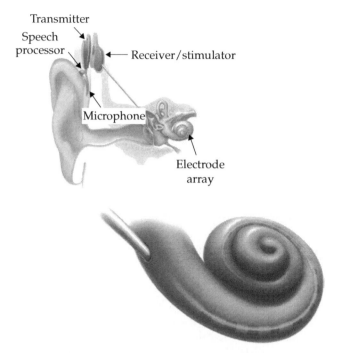

Figure 11.4 A depiction of a cochlear implant showing the processor behind the ear, transmitter and receiver on the side of the head, and the electrode array wound into the cochlea (zoomed in inset) (Medical illustrations by NIH, Medical Arts & Photography Branch).

malleable in its ability to learn these skills, and after age seven it is no longer very malleable at all. Success with using spoken language for children and congenitally deaf adults implanted later is more variable. For young children though, many using cochlear implants, receiving intensive aural training, and growing up in an environment rich in spoken language learn to use and understand speech. Importantly, the development of spoken language following implantation also

There are a number of interesting cochlear implant audio demonstrations hosted at the website of the House Ear Institute. That will give you a sense of the quality of speech captured by an implant for a user: *http://www.hei.org/research/aip/audiodemos.htm* Ⓦ

aids in education of deaf individuals as spoken language ability improves reading ability dramatically, since, as we'll see in the final chapter, reading depends heavily on phonological mapping from orthography to speech. Learning to read well is extremely challenging for profoundly deaf individuals who have hearing parents and who do not become fluent in spoken language.

When the cochlear implant was first introduced, the Deaf community did not welcome it and saw it as a threat to Deaf culture and language and an intrusion by the medical and hearing community viewing deafness as a medical disorder to be ameliorated. Now that the cochlear implant is becoming fairly common and is fairly successful, outright rejection of it is

Some reserve the term Deaf (capital D) for those individuals who view themselves as integrally connected to the Deaf community's culture and who (in the US) use American Sign Language.

no longer the mainstream prevailing view within the Deaf community. However, deciding on a cochlear implant for a deaf child is a family decision, and each family has its own priorities. Families in the Deaf community must make a decision balancing the importance of communication with a wide and diverse group outside the Deaf community against close ties with and integration into a cohesive familial and cultural identity. Many of these families are finding, however, that their children with cochlear implants move with ease back and forth between using ASL with the Deaf community and using spoken language with the hearing community. Regardless of the decision about whether to give a child a cochlear implant, early and rich exposure to language – spoken or signed – is of course of critical importance in a child's development.

The NIDCD reports that since the 1970s over 188,000 people have received cochlear implants, including nearly 25,500 children and 41,500 adults in the US. Although a cochlear implant doesn't cure deafness or create normal hearing, it can give a deaf person the ability to make use of spoken language and an auditory understanding of his or her environment.

Voice Disorders

Voice disorders are more common in older individuals but can occur at any age and are particularly problematic for professional speakers and singers. A person may be considered to have a voice problem if there is pain or discomfort in the larynx or pharynx during speech or if the pitch, loudness, or quality of voicing sounds sufficiently atypical to be noteworthy or impair communication with others. There are a wide variety of causes of voice disorders. Screaming too loud and long at a concert or ball game the night before might cause a temporary voice problem. But long-term misuse or overuse of the voice can also lead to problems for a speaker. Politicians "on the stump" can find this happening to them, as can teachers who give frequent lectures. In addition to being sensitive to overuse, infection, and inflammation, normal vibration of the delicate vocal folds can also be impaired by acid reflux from the digestive system, allergies, hypothyroidism, caffeine and alcohol (which are dehydrating), and other drugs. Even the distinctive hoarseness characterizing some children's voices can be a result of vocal abuse.

Laryngitis is an inflammation or swelling of the vocal folds that keeps them from vibrating normally. Laryngitis can arise for a variety of reasons including overuse, infections, or irritants that could be inhaled (e.g., chemicals or smoke) or encountered from internal sources (e.g., gastric acid). Someone with laryngitis may sound breathy, raspy, or hoarse. Resting the voice (no whispering) and/or removal of the irritant usually eases this temporary voice problem.

Another type of voice problem might result from small benign (noncancerous) growths or sores on the vocal folds. These are called vocal nodules (or nodes), vocal polyps, or contact ulcers. **Vocal nodules**, which are somewhat like calluses that develop from repeated pressure, are among the most common voice disorders and may be found, for example in professional voice users such as singers. Vocal nodules are most frequent in young and middle-aged adult women. **Vocal polyps** are more like a blister and are more likely to be on only one vocal fold. They are often associated with long-term smoking. The voice of a person with vocal nodules or polyps may sound hoarse, low pitched, and slightly breathy. **Contact ulcers** are a less common disorder and are caused when excessive forces or acid reflux creates sores on the vocal tissue or cartilages. Unlike nodes and polyps, these may be painful.

More traumatic damage to the vocal folds can occur due to an injury to the nerves that causes a **paralysis** of one or both vocal folds, disorders that affect the muscular innervation of the folds, or diseases such as cancer that present tumors in this area that must be treated and/or removed. It needs to be emphasized that smoking is likely to cause long-term voice problems and, ultimately, to cause death from cancer. Smoking is an enormous risk that is likely to contribute to much grief later in life. Impairment of vocal fold movement can lead to a person not being able to speak loudly, or quickly running out of air due to the glottal opening being excessively wide. Certain surgical approaches can improve the positioning of the vocal folds for voice production.

Dysphonia is a different source of voicing loss in which the vocal folds are not paralyzed but in which their muscular control is impaired and may spasm. It occurs mainly in women and mainly in middle age. People with dysphonia can have a voice that sounds weak, breathless, strained, or strangled; it may also tremor. Treatment of dysphonia symptoms is challenging, but a specialist can offer some, often temporary, treatment possibilities such as the expert injection of tiny amounts of botox into particular laryngeal muscles for certain cases.

Of course the most dire voice disorder is the potentially fatal disease of **laryngeal cancer**. The American Cancer Society estimates that in 2009 about 12,290 people in the United States will be newly diagnosed with laryngeal cancer and about 3,660 people will die of this disease. Nearly all of these cases are attributable to smoking. In order to prolong their lives, patients often must choose to have their larynx surgically removed; this operation is called a **laryngectomy**. There are about 50,000 people

You can hear examples of speech after laryngectomy at ⓦ: http://www.webwhispers.org/library/talking-again.asp

without larynxes living in the United States. Although they will never be able to speak normally again, in order to be able to produce some intelligible speech, these people have a few choices. An electronic device – called an **electrolarynx** – that creates a vibrating buzz sound can be held up to the throat to create a sound source to excite the resonant properties (formants) of the moving vocal tract while the person articulates. Another substitute voicing strategy that demands great practice is the use of **esophageal speech**. This is a technique that some patients have learned after a laryngectomy to swallow air into the esophagus and "belch" it back up in a way that sets tissue of the walls of the esophagus into vibration as a sound source that substitutes for vocal fold vibration. With much practice, some individuals become quite talented at producing this type of speech. Finally, esophageal speech can be aided by surgery that puts in place a tracheoesophageal puncture and prosthesis that allows air to move from the trachea to the esophagus rather than being swallowed into the esophagus. Unfortunately, all these techniques for replacing the vocal fold sound source offer little in the way of pitch control, making natural sounding intonation and prosody impossible for these speakers.

Apraxia: A speech production disorder

Apraxia of speech is a disorder in which people have problems producing the normal speech movements coordinated in an appropriate way. This is not a problem with the muscles that are important in articulation but rather in the successful deployment and execution of the phonological gestures of speech. The severity of apraxia can range from rather mild to quite severe. In this chapter we focus on **acquired apraxia of speech**. This problem in speaking is generally consequent to a stroke or trauma affecting the frontal region of the left cerebral hemisphere, which can also cause problems with a wide variety of language-related abilities (specifically, refer to our discussion of Broca's aphasia in Chapter 10). Some recovery in articulation often occurs right after the stroke or injury, but recovery tends to taper off. The speech problems of people with apraxia are pronunciation errors in which sounds of words appear to be omitted,

Developmental apraxia of speech occurs in children, more often boys, and is distinct from acquired apraxia. Rather than just being the delayed development of speech, it is a long-term difficulty in speaking related to overall language development. We don't know what causes this communication disorder, and it is very difficult to have a strong positive impact on remedying it.

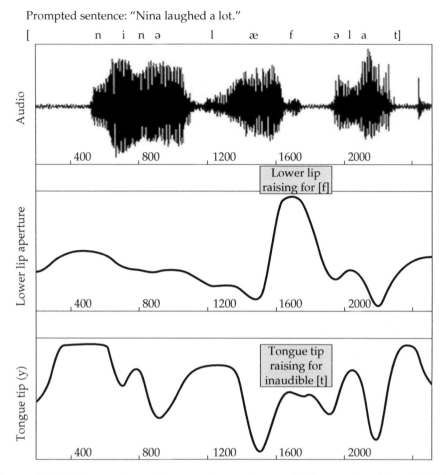

Prompted sentence: "Nina laughed a lot."

Figure 11.5 This speaker with apraxia was transcribed as saying "laugh" [læf] instead of "laughed" [læft], but when we examine the movement of the tongue tip inside the mouth we see that the gesture for the [t] is not in fact deleted; it is still present but is not of sufficient magnitude to yield the perception of a stop consonant. The fact that the consonant was not deleted but misproduced means that the phonological representation of the word was intact for the speaker but that the execution was impaired. It also exemplifies a pitfall inherent in relying on phonetic transcription for an accurate and complete account of speech disorders. [from Byrd and Harris]

added, or pronounced incorrectly, particularly in long or complex words; even the way a particular word is misarticulated will vary from one utterance to the next. In recent years, we've been able to use instruments to study the actual articulation of people with apraxia and have noticed that sounds that appear to be missing or misproduced can definitely be present in the articulation but may be obscured or altered because they are not being coordinated in time properly (see Figure 11.5). Thus phonetic transcription alone is not sufficient to characterize the articulatory problems of apraxia, and may even be incorrect or misleading regarding the articulatory events that are occurring.

The articulation difficulties of apraxia are highly variable both within and across individuals, and speech-language pathologists work with each individual generally over an extended period of time.

Stuttering

Stuttering (or stammering) refers to a communication impairment when the normal flow of speech is disrupted by repetitions or prolongations of words or portions of words; this often co-occurs with difficulties in starting to say a word or unwanted silences and muscular tensions in the vocal tract. In some individuals, stuttering may be accompanied by tremors or facial grimaces or eye blinks. This is a type of communication disorder called a **fluency disorder** and occurs in about 1 percent of the general population.

The precise cause of stuttering is unknown, though there is a genetic predisposition thought to be at work in most cases. It is perfectly normal to hear typically developing preschool children stutter, but some small portion of these children continue to stutter beyond this early word learning period and into the time when longer sentences are produced and then possibly on into adulthood. This becomes a cause for concern. Stuttering is three to four times more common in boys than girls.

There is the misconception in some popular media that stuttering found across the general population is due to low intelligence or mental health problems or emotional states such as fearfulness – this is simply untrue. Of course, if individuals who stutter are criticized, stigmatized, or ostracized, this will no doubt lead to unhappiness and anxiety and low self-esteem. This is not the cause of the fluency disorder, but unfortunately, the stress of these feelings can certainly exacerbate stuttering and can isolate a person by causing them to avoid interpersonal contact and communication.

It is important to note that the character and severity of stuttering and the types of speaking situations that are challenging can vary widely from individual to individual and even in the same individual at different times. Stressful situations can certainly intensify stuttering. Some challenging situations include speaking on the phone or being "put on the spot." People who stutter can learn strategies and techniques to help manage these situations. Interestingly, other speaking situations such as singing or speaking in unison (choral speech or reading) are known to ease this fluency disorder.

Early professional intervention can prevent many children who have persistent problems with stuttering from continuing to stutter as adults. But there is *no cure* for stuttering in adults. Adults can control stuttering with consistent practice of management techniques. For this reason, it is extremely important that children who have *persistent* stuttering work with a speech language pathologist who is a recognized specialist in fluency (stuttering) disorders.

When you are participating in a conversation with a person who stutters, they are likely to prefer that you do not attempt to finish their sentences or words and that you wait patiently and naturally for them to finish speaking without interrupting. For children, it is particularly important not to rush the pace of conversation.

Summary

In this chapter, we have looked at some ways in which the language, speech, and hearing systems can fail to function optimally; and there are many other disorders of language and understanding that also affect the spoken language communication process. Given that humans have such a complex system for speaking and hearing, it is not surprising that there are many functions within the system that, when damaged, can lead to difficulties. What is impressive to realize, though, is that even when faced with enormous challenges to using language, humans still manage to leverage numerous strategies for engaging in successful communication and working with and around obstacles in speech, language, hearing, and understanding. This is a testament to the resources and plasticity of the human brain and to the rich social structures in which humans live. In addition to some sound factual information, we hope you take away from this chapter the knowledge that research on communication disorders and their treatment and/or management is a compelling area of study that allows scientists and clinicians to make impactful contributions to the quality of life for millions of people.

Further Reading and Resources

Chorost, Michael (2006). *Rebuilt: My Journey Back to the Hearing World*. Boston: Mariner Books.

Rice, Mabel L. (2000). Grammatical Symptoms of Specific Language Impairment. In D. V. M. Bishop and L. B. Leonard (Eds), *Speech and Language Impairments in Children: Causes, Characteristics, Intervention and Outcome* (pp. 17–34). Hove, UK: Psychology Press.

American Speech-Language-Hearing Association: *http://www.asha.org/public/*

National Information Center for Children and Youth with Disabilities (2004). Fact sheet number 11, Speech and Language Impairments: *www.nichcy.org/pubs/factshe/fs11txt.htm*

National Institute on Deafness and Other Communication Disorders: *http://www.nidcd.nih.gov/health/*

Occupational Health and Safety Administration, Safety and Health Topics, Noise and Hearing Conservation: *http://www.osha.gov/SLTC/noisehearingconservation/index.html*

Chapter 12
Reading and Dyslexia

Introduction

Print (or writing) is an extremely valuable cultural innovation. It allows us to convey ideas in language, without the presence of a speaker, which is a tremendously powerful tool. The reader's representation of *spoken* language, even though no speaker is involved, is critical for proficient reading. The reader's representation of how words *sound* has been shown to play a role in how skilled readers read and how children learn to read, and problems in this area have been linked to reading problems – dyslexia. In this chapter we will discuss the connections between reading and speech in these three domains. We will not discuss the aspects of reading that involve the purely visual processing – say, constructing a letter representation from squiggles on a page, though there are a host of interesting issues in that area. Our focus here is primarily on the interface between the printed word and spoken language. We begin by discussing how skilled readers read.

Skilled Reading

Defining the problem

By skilled reading we refer to the reading performance of adults who had no particular difficulty learning to read, and who read regularly. What are the mechanisms and processes by which they do so? Let's be a bit clearer on this question by first analyzing what reading is about, at a computational/functional level – how can we define the task of reading? We know that, at many levels, written language mirrors spoken language: there are written words in place of spoken words, written affixes in place of spoken affixes, and so on. The grammar of a spoken language is more or less identical to the grammar of the written form of the language. What differs is simply the *format* of the linguistic information: words are represented as marks on a page or screen. So the major task, then, that differentiates reading from comprehending spoken language is activating word meanings from **orthographic** (written) representations as compared to auditory representations. Therefore, when we discuss how skilled readers read, we will restrict ourselves to the question of how they activate words in the mental lexicon from text.

There are several important things to note about the **mapping**, or connection, between written words and their meaning. Perhaps the most important is that the mappings are *arbitrary*, just as the mappings from spoken words to their meaning (see Chapter 1). Just as there is nothing inherent in the sounds [dək] that correspond to duckness, there is no more so in the letter sequence "d," "u," "c," "k." Not only are the orthography-to-meaning mappings arbitrary, they are also **unsystematic**, just as sound-to-meaning mappings are. That is, the fact that *duck* and *luck* share three out of four letters does not mean that they have anything in common in their meaning. Similarly, the fact that there is a lot in common between the concepts *tiger* and *lion* doesn't imply that they are spelled similarly or sound similar. When you learned your native language, you learned a stunning number of arbitrary and unsystematic sound-to-meaning mappings – your vocabulary. Did you do the same thing for written words when you learned to read – did you have to learn a whole new set of arbitrary and unsystematic mappings? Do you regularly make use of these kinds of mappings as a skilled reader?

We'll refer to accessing meaning directly from the printed word as **direct access**. Of course, you probably realize that there are alternatives to direct access. Specifically, written words not only correspond to concepts, they also correspond to articulation and sound – the pronunciation of the words. Furthermore, and most importantly, while the mappings between written words and their pronunciation is arbitrary, it is **systematic**. That is, although there is nothing inherent about the visual form of a "b" and its pronunciation in English ([b]), the spelling-to-sound correspondence is extremely *regular*: the "b" on the page almost always corresponds to the sound [b] in a word. This should be no surprise, as **alphabetic writing systems** such as the Roman alphabet used to write English came into use precisely to represent the individual sounds of a word. The way the word is spelled, then, reflects how it is pronounced: alphabetic writing systems involve **systematic spelling-to-sound** correspondences.

An important consequence of the kind of systematicity found in alphabetic writing systems is that there are *fewer* mappings from orthography to sound than there are between orthography and meaning. In other

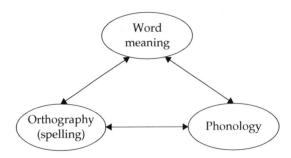

Figure 12.1 Ovals represent three types of representations involved in reading. Line represent links between different representations. Although the goal of reading is to activate meaning representations from orthography, the "phonological route" is implicated.

words, while each visual word form – that is, sequence of letters – would have a separate and usually unique mapping to a representation in the mental lexicon, there are far fewer mappings between letters (or letter sequences) and pronunciation. Figure 12.1 depicts what we'll call the **reading triangle**. The three ovals represent the three types of representations involved in recognizing spoken and written words, and the arrows represent all possible correspondences, or mappings, between different kinds of representations.

Although it is probably obvious to you, we emphasize that spelling-to-sound correspondences do not involve the representation of a word's meaning. However, accessing the pronunciation of a word *does* activate meaning. Once the pronunciation – the phonological form of the word – is accessed, the meaning of the word can be activated through the existing sound-to-meaning mappings involved in normal spoken word recognition. In summary, there are two logically possible routes to accessing meaning from print: the direct route, in which visual word forms directly activate the mental representation of the word's meaning (the Orthography to Meaning path on the left in Figure 12.1), and a **phonological route**, in which a visual word's pronunciation is activated from spelling-to-sound correspondences and that phonological representation in turn activates the meaning representation using the sound-to-meaning correspondences in place for spoken language (the Orthography to Phonology to Meaning path across the bottom and right side of Figure 12.1).

Which route or routes to reading do skilled readers use? Before examining the evidence that addresses this question, it's useful to think about the computational issues involving each route. Specifically, the direct route would seem to be more efficient from a processing perspective, in that there is basically one step from the activation of a visual word form and the corresponding meaning. On the other hand, from a *learning* perspective the direct route could be burdensome, as a new mapping must be learned for *every single word* you know! Not only would this constitute an enormous number of new associations to learn (duplicating much of what you already learned when learning a spoken vocabulary), but actually figuring out what meaning to connect with a brand new visual word form could be difficult. An advantage to the phonological route is that no new associations to meaning representations need to be formed (we already have the Phonology to Meaning path in place), and the spelling-to-sound correspondences that do need to be learned are far fewer in number than the new correspondences involved in the direct route. On the other hand, reading via the phonological route could be somewhat less efficient because there are more intermediate processes and representations involved before the word's meaning is activated.

With these issues in mind, we now discuss an experimental method developed by Guy van Orden that has provided important evidence about how skilled readers read. In these experiments, the subject is given information about a category, for example, *tool, furniture, insect*. Then a word is briefly flashed on a screen, and the subject has to press a button, as quickly as possible, indicating whether the flashed word was a member of the target category or not. For instance, if the category was *tool*, and the flashed word was "wrench," the subjects should press the YES button as quickly as possible. On the other hand, if the flashed word was "leaf," then the subject should press the NO button as quickly as possible. For each presentation the experimenters record reaction time (RT), and accuracy (whether the subject gives the right answer). The critical, informative test in these experiments is when the flashed word is not, in fact, a member of the target category but when it is a **homophone** with a word that is a member. Two words are homophones of each other if they have the same pronunciation, even if they are spelled differently, like "rows" and "rose." The experimenters were interested in how subjects behave when, for example, the category is *insect*, and the flashed word is "flee" (not "flea"). Why would this be informative? Could it differentiate between reading via the direct route versus the phonological route?

Figure 12.2 depicts two hypothetical scenarios of how homophones would be read using either direct access or the phonological route. Under direct access, each visual word form, "flee" and "flea," has an independent link to an associated meaning (shown here with a picture). The fact that the two words are pronounced the same is not represented anywhere in this direct-route scenario, and one would predict that subjects should be able to respond NO just as quickly and accurately to "flee" as to any other word. On the other hand, in the phonological route, the spelling-to-sound correspondences map the two distinct visual forms to an identical phonological form – depicted here with the IPA – which in turn is linked to two distinct meanings. Crucially, for these experiments, one of the

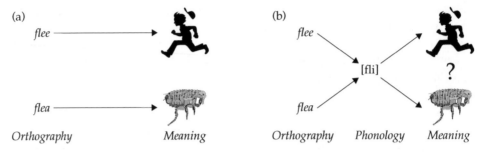

Figure 12.2   Depiction of two theories on how meanings are accessed from print. In (a) each word is directly associated with a meaning; the homophony between the two words could not have an affect on accessing meaning. In (b) visual word forms are mapped to phonological forms, which in turn activate meanings; homophones are represented by the same phonological code.

activated meanings (but *not* the one corresponding to the flashed word) is a member of the target category. If reading processes involve the phonological route and the sounds of words, then *both* meanings might become active, at least temporarily, and subjects might occasionally respond YES (incorrectly), and they might also take slightly longer to respond as they figure out which is the appropriate meaning. In fact, for pairs like *insect*–"flee," subjects indeed were more likely to respond YES, and they also took longer to respond even when they correctly responded NO. These results are consistent with an account of reading that involves the phonological route, but are hard to explain with a model that involves only the direct route.

The first experiments of this type provided strong evidence that the phonological route was implicated in skilled reading. But clearly something more is involved as well. Recall that many subjects, even if they were momentarily slowed down by the meaning confusion, ended up responding correctly; and even subjects who incorrectly responded YES quickly realized their mistake. How could they have done so? The only basis to make the correct meaning distinctions between homophones like *flee* and *flea* is to have some kind of direct link between the visual word form and the meaning. So, *in addition* to using phonological representations to read, skilled readers also seem to be able to use direct orthography-to-meaning correspondences.

> Of course, in normal reading context could also **disambiguate** – rule out conflicting alternatives – between the multiple meanings of homophones, but in these experiments there was no disambiguating context.

Similar experiments with homophones showed in a more direct way that the direct route is also used by skilled readers. If the homophones are very frequent words, then the rate of incorrect responses to the flea/flee task and the delay in reaction time is not observed. For example, if the category is *boy* and the flashed word is "sun," then subjects correctly reject the word as a member of the target category (whereas they would correctly say that "son" is a member). Because *sun* and *son* are very frequent in print, apparently direct mappings from the visual forms to meanings have been established and are used. This lends support to the notion that both the phonological and direct routes are active in skilled readers.

The picture that begins to emerge is one in which most words are initially read through the phonological route. Then gradually, as a word is encountered in text many times, the visual form and the meaning become directly associated through the coactivation of the visual word form and the activated meaning, and the strength of the association increases through exposure to that word in print. Eventually, the direct link can become so entrenched that it becomes very fast and efficient and, for those who are quite experienced readers, it becomes the dominant route for reading. One analogy is that the direct route starts out as a bunch of dirt roads – one for every word. But as a word is read frequently, the dirt road is paved and eventually becomes a superhighway. In other words, skilled reading may involve *dual routes* for accessing meaning from visual word forms: a direct route that is fast and efficient for processing more common words, and a phonological route in which word pronunciations are activated through spelling-to-sound correspondences and word meanings are retrieved from the established phonology-to-meaning mappings.

Reading in nonalphabetic systems

The value of the phonological route comes from the fact that there are systematic spelling-to-sound correspondences, something that is clearly true in an alphabetic writing system, like the Roman alphabet used in English and in many other languages. What about writing systems that are not alphabetic (or not syllabic), for example Chinese? Are there any advantages afforded by a phonological route? If sounds or articulation are not represented in the script, independent of meaning, then what advantage could there be in mapping the visual word first to a pronunciation-based representation?

As a matter of fact, even in written Chinese, in which a **logographic** orthography is used, there is still information in the scripts that relate to pronunciation. A logograph is a written symbol that has a meaning; for example, a red circle with a horizontal line across the middle is a logograph with the meaning *do not enter*. Written Chinese consists of many single-character logographs, called *simple characters*, as shown in the first two rows of Table 12.1. Many of these are historically derived from **pictographs** – symbols that depict in some way the concepts to which they

Table 12.1 Simple characters and complex characters. The first set of complex characters has a shared phonetic radical. The second set has a shared semantic radical.

Character	Pronunciation	Meaning
青	chin	green – like young grass
鸟	niao	bird
清	chin – level tone	clear
情	chin – rising tone	affection
请	chin – dipping tone	invite
晴	chin – rising tone	sunny
鹊	que	magpie
鸡	ji	chicken
鹅	er	goose
鹤	he	crane

refer – but have come to be more abstract (much like some gestures in a sign language originate as iconic representations but become abstract symbols as the language evolves). In addition, there are *compound characters* that are composed of two simple characters. Interestingly, in about 80–90 percent of the compound characters there is a component of the character that corresponds to pronunciation. This is because the pronunciation of the compound character often corresponds in some way to the pronunciation of one of the simple characters that make it up. The part of a compound character that corresponds to its pronunciation is called a **phonetic radical**; examples are given in the third to sixth rows of Table 12.1. As you can see, the words for *clear*, *affection*, *invite*, and *sunny* have the same pronunciation as the simple character *chin* that is part of the compound character for each word. (In these cases, the pronunciations consist of the same phonological sequence with different tones. Sometimes only the onset or rhyme might be shared between the different words.) Notice that these words don't overlap in meaning and have no meaning in common with the simple character. It is just the pronunciation corresponding to the phonetic radical that is common among the compound characters. Essentially, then, the prevalence of characters with phonetic radicals means that there *are* orthography-to-phonology regularities in Chinese, even though the writing system is not alphabetic.

In addition to phonetic radicals some compound signs have a **semantic radical**, which is a simple character that contributes something to the meaning of the compound. Examples are given in the last four rows of Table 12.1: *magpie*, *chicken*, *goose*, and *crane* all share a simple character that itself means *bird*. Note that these words are not pronounced similarly, despite their similarity in meaning (just as the English words for the same birds don't sound the same).

Experiments similar to the homophone experiment described above demonstrate that Chinese readers also rely on phonological representations when accessing meaning, when the character contains orthography-to-phonology correspondences in the phonetic radical. But experiments have also shown that Chinese readers rely more on direct access than readers in alphabetic systems. This turns out not simply to be due to less robust orthography-to-phonology correspondences but to the fact that in Chinese there are some orthography-to-meaning systematicities that are not present in alphabetic systems. Just as the phonetic radical marks shared pronunciations, the semantic radical marks shared meanings. This fact means that direct access could be accomplished with somewhat fewer direct mappings than in alphabetic systems because there is somewhat more systematicity between orthography and meaning.

The overall thrust of research on skilled reading is that the basic architecture is the same for any writing system: there are two potential paths for recovering meaning from print, one that is mediated through phonological representations, and one that is direct. Both routes are in place regardless of the writing system, but the relative prominence of one route over the other in skilled reading depends on the details of the structure of the correspondences in each language and its writing system.

Reading and orthographic depth

It appears, then, that Chinese and alphabetic writing systems are at opposite ends along the dimension of systematicity in orthography-to-phonology correspondences. However, even within alphabetic systems, some languages have more *transparent* correspondences than others. That is, some languages have fewer complexities, exceptions, and contingencies in how letters and letter sequences map onto sounds, than others. This idea has been given the technical term **orthographic depth**. The *deeper* the orthography of the writing system, the more complex and idiosyncratic the mappings from spelling to sound. Among Western European languages, English is orthographically deep, and Italian, Spanish, and Finnish, as just a few examples, are orthographically shallow. In Italian, for example, most letters are pronounced in only one way. Several letters have two pronunciations, depending on the letters with which they are combined. For example, "c" is pronounced [k] unless it precedes an "i" or an "e," when it becomes [tʃ]; but followed by an "h" (that is, the sequence "ch") is pronounced [k] again. There are a handful of other cases like this in Italian, and the rules are very general (that is, they apply across contexts). In contrast, a particular English letter sequence can take on different sounds in different words, for example "ea" is pronounced differently in *near*, *bear*, and *search*, and there is no straightforward generalization about which sound it should be (consider the nearly identical letter sequences in the vowel portions of *ear*, *earth*, *hearth*, and *hear*). In fact, of all Western European languages, English has the most orthographically deep written form. Ⓦ

Differences in orthographic depth among languages written in alphabetic systems means that there are different degrees of systematicity even within alphabetically written languages. As you will see below, these differences have consequences for early stages of learning to read.

Learning (and Teaching) to Read

Given the scientific evidence of how skilled readers read, what are the implications for learning how to read and for teaching reading in schools? We will focus in the beginning on alphabetic writing systems, but at the end you will see that the conclusions apply more broadly to other writing systems.

The logic of learning to read and the importance of phonology

We hinted above at the advantages that reading through the phonological route would confer on learning to read. Basically, at the age when they begin learning to read (at around age six in the United States), children already have a large spoken language vocabulary. This means that they have already learned a large number of arbitrary sound-to-meaning mappings, as part of the process of acquiring a language. Since the correspondences between spelling and sound involve many systematic generalizations, there are relatively few of these mappings to grasp in learning to read and they can ultimately be used to activate meanings by accessing how written words sound. (Here we use "relatively" in comparison to children learning as many new spelling-to-meaning mappings as the number of words they know – that is what a learner would have to do if learning to read involved learning to access meaning from print directly.) Clearly, then, the phonological route has advantages for learning in terms of the memory resources required, even in an orthographically deep writing system like English.

Importantly, the phonological route offers an additional advantage when encountering a word the novice has never seen before in print but may know in spoken form. By sounding out the letter sequences to access the phonological form, the meaning then comes for free. (Of course, this is true for skilled readers as well, but it's a more likely occurrence with novice readers.) Using phonological information rather than direct access means that beginning readers are far less hindered by their lack of experience in seeing words in print than if they couldn't retrieve the sound of the word from its spelling. In direct access, there is *no* way to determine the meaning of an unfamiliar written word other than by explicit instruction or if the context of a sentence is completely unambiguous as to what the word is.

In light of the importance of phonology and mastering spelling-to-sound correspondences, consider now the significance of orthographic depth. In orthographically shallow languages there is much more consistency, fewer exceptions, and generally simpler orthography-to-phonology mappings. One might then expect that beginning readers of orthographically shallow languages would be at an advantage compared to beginners learning to read in a deep orthography. This, indeed, turns out to be the case. For example, Philip Seymour and colleagues tested beginning readers' accuracy and speed at reading familiar and unfamiliar words. They found that children beginning to learn to read in languages with deep orthographies were one to two years behind beginning learners of shallow orthographies on those measures. They hypothesized that the problem was in efficiently decoding spelling to access phonology – the skills simply take longer to develop with deep orthographies because they are more complex.

It's important to stress that all readers, regardless of the language and orthography involved, can end up as skilled readers. However, the fact that orthographic depth is linked to differences in beginning reading is another indicator of the importance of phonological decoding in learning to read, as well as in proficient reading. An important consequence of all the scientific research we've reviewed so far is that successful learning should involve training in and mastery of the spelling-to-sound correspondences of the language.

Phonics

The teaching system called **phonics** aims to do just that. The term phonics covers a variety of specific curricula, but they all have in common the goal of teaching the link between letters (and letter sequences) and sounds. Phonics was the standard method of reading instruction in the United States until around the 1980s. At that time, some educators were becoming dissatisfied with phonics. For one thing, although we've been stressing the regularities in the mappings between spelling and sound, as we mentioned, there are many irregularities, ambiguities, and complexities in English spelling. Many of the exceptions and idiosyncrasies are encountered early in learning to read because they affect some of the most frequent words of English. For example, the letter sequence *–ave* in *have* is inconsistent with the regular [ev] pronunciation, as in words like *wave, save, rave, pave,* or *gave*. These complexities can lead to frustration early on in learning to read, and some educators thought it was an unnecessary impediment to early reading.

The whole language approach

Dissatisfaction with traditional phonics methods led to growth in an approach to teaching reading called **whole language**. One of the goals of the approach was to make learning to read more engaging early on by doing away with the phonics drills, and instead designing simple books and exercises that would allow children to start reading and writing, and being more active in the learning process. Instead of learning words by sounding them out and by learning the underlying pronunciation rules, children instead were taught directly what words meant. The assumption was that they would learn the pronunciations rules automatically, just as children learn to speak without explicit instruction. Some children did learn in this way, figuring out the correspondence rules on their own, but many did not. In particular, children who did not come from families that valued reading and who had minimal reading support at home had greater difficulty in whole language compared to traditional phonics methods. As a result, many children were not able to advance as quickly and attain the same level of performance as those with phonics training. These outcomes were not surprising given what science shows about the importance of understanding pronunciation rules in learning to read. Nevertheless, because of the early popularity and apparent success of the approach – children felt more confident and enthusiastic about reading early on and the problems don't surface until later – many school districts across the United States switched to these techniques, abandoning phonics.

As it became clear that children were not spontaneously learning spelling-to-sound correspondences, and as their reading skills suffered, schools began to shift back to phonics. Some of the refocusing was fueled by vocal psychologists and linguists who, from a scientific perspective, argued for the importance of phonics-based instruction. Now many instructors use a combined approach that allows children to engage in literature-based activities early on, but that also explicitly teaches the relationships between spelling and sound, knowledge which is fundamental to becoming a skilled reader. These combined approaches are proving to be the most effective in advancing children's reading skills.

Learning to read Chinese

The large-scale unfortunate "natural experiment" in the United States that resulted from a temporary switch away from phonics instruction clearly points to the importance of the phonological route in learning to read English. In our discussion of skilled reading, we said that skilled reading of Chinese is mediated by phonological representations, though not as much as in English. We also discussed the impact of orthographic depth on the earliest stages of learning to read. Given the reduced (but not absent) utility of phonological information in Chinese, it is natural to ask what factors influence *learning* to read Chinese?

In the late 1990s, Dominica So and Linda Siegel carried out a study with school children in Hong Kong, from first to fourth grade. They administered a range of tests, among which were tests of reading skills and **phonological awareness** – the ability to discriminate tones, rhymes, and other important units in Chinese orthography-to-phonology correspondences (see the "Dyslexia" section below). They found that phonological awareness correlated significantly with reading ability, suggesting a link between phonological skills and learning to read in Chinese, just as is seen for alphabetic readers. This finding was replicated in a number of studies. However, while the results clearly establish a link between phonological skills and reading skills, they only show a correlation; they do not show that phonological skills *predict* reading skills (as is the case in English; see "Phonological awareness" below). But they do establish that the two are related in youngsters learning to read Chinese.

Interestingly, it is common practice now in mainland China – but not Hong Kong where the study just discussed was carried out – that children first learn to read in an alphabetic representation of Chinese, called **pinyin**. Pinyin consists of Chinese words spelled with letters of the Roman alphabet, using consistent pronunciation rules. Learning pinyin early has been shown to improve phonological awareness, and results in better reading of the character-based system when children later learn it. It is not known precisely why reading of characters is improved. Perhaps the pinyin system heightens children's attention to the pronunciation regularities in any writing system, and in particular of the phonetic radicals of Chinese characters. It could also play a more general role in familiarizing children with the act of extracting meaning from print. In any case, the fact that it is so successful further underscores the importance of the phonological route in learning to read.

Dyslexia

Dyslexia is an impairment in the ability to read. Dyslexia, like aphasia, can be acquired in adulthood, as the result of some kind of trauma to the brain, but in this chapter, we will consider **developmental dyslexia**, which we define as: *a failure to acquire age-appropriate reading skills despite adequate intelligence and opportunity to learn.*

As you see from the definition, dyslexia is a *reading* impairment. A common misconception is that dyslexia involves reversing things (for example, left and right), or remembering or doing things in the wrong order. This may have to do with the fact that reading disabilities were once associated with reversing the orientation of letters, for example writing a "b" as a "d." Although many children with reading disabilities do reverse letters from time to time, it's also the case that children who learn to read without special difficulty also start out reversing letters when learning to read and write. While some forms of dyslexia may be associated with difficulty in processing print visually, a visual deficit is by no means a criterion for dyslexia and in fact is not a common underlying cause. So what are the symptoms and causes of dyslexia?

While there does not appear to be one underlying cause in all instances of developmental dyslexia, in the majority of individuals there is a fundamental problem with the ability to efficiently recover phonological representations from print. This goes hand in hand with impairments in the ability to consciously manipulate and reason about the sounds of a word, or **phonological awareness**. We used that term earlier in the chapter when we discussed learning to read Chinese. Below we take a closer look at phonological awareness in English, and in particular with respect to dyslexia.

There are, however, a smaller proportion of children with dyslexia who don't have severe impairments in phonological awareness and orthography-to-phonology decoding abilities. Nevertheless, these individuals are significantly behind in readings skills compared to their peers of the same age. Interestingly, individuals with minimal or no phonological problems perform similarly on a variety of reading tests as normally developing readers who are a few years younger. That is, they appear to be *delayed* relative to normal readers. In contrast, individuals with phonological problems show a characteristically different pattern of performance on a variety of tests and do not resemble normal readers of any age. This has led to some theories that there are two distinct subtypes of dyslexia, **phonological dyslexia** and **surface dyslexia** (a term borrowed from theories of adult-acquired dyslexia). Yet while there do seem to be consistent deficits underlying phonological dyslexia, the causes of dyslexia that resemble reading delay are not as well understood and seem to result from a range of different factors such as deficits in memory, low reading motivation, or limited exposure to print. In this chapter we will use "phonological dyslexia" to refer to the predominant form of dyslexia that is linked to underlying phonological impairments and "delay dyslexia" to refer to other forms. However, we stress that there does not appear to be a homogeneous *delay* subtype in terms of the underlying causes, and there are individual differences between children with phonological dyslexia in the severity of their symptoms and whether or not they have other additional sources of reading problems.

We now overview several types of tests that reveal the kinds of difficulties with reading and nonreading tasks experienced by children with phonological dyslexia. One of the advantages of the tasks that don't require reading is that children can be evaluated before they begin to learn to read. Children **at risk** for phonological dyslexia can be identified before they begin to have reading problems; as you will see, there are interventions that can be quite successful in improving reading outcomes for these individuals. The tests reveal a different pattern of difficulties for individuals with delay dyslexia, and different intervention methods can be used in those cases (although generally reading problems in these individuals become apparent only once they have begun to learn to read).

Phonological awareness

There are a variety of phonological awareness tests that probe different aspects of an individual's conscious access to the sounds of words. For example, a simple test might be the question, "How many sounds are there in the word *cat*?" or, "What's the first sound in the word *dog*?" or, "Say *split* without the 'puh' sound." These questions tap different aspects of an individual's awareness of the sounds of words: how many sounds, the sequence of sounds, the identity of sounds, imagining the results of manipulating the sounds, and so on. These questions are not directly related to reading or to print, but having the kind of awareness probed by these tests is important for having the tools to represent the pronunciation rules of written language. It turns out that children differ in their accuracy on phonological awareness tasks, and some children are quite poor. Children who perform poorly on these tasks are much more likely to have difficulty learning to read and to be diagnosed with dyslexia than children who do well. Children with dyslexia who have problem with phonological awareness would be considered to have phonological dyslexia.

The importance of phonological awareness for literacy skills makes sense given what we've established about learning to read: the spelling-to-sound correspondences are only useful if one has accurate awareness of the sounds of words, because the correspondences are systematic only given the appropriate representations of the way words sound. When awareness of the sounds of words is flawed, the phonological route no longer provides the same benefits. Note that impairments in phonological awareness do not imply difficulties with hearing spoken language. One's conscious awareness of sounds in a word seems to be relatively independent of speech processing.

One of the benefits of phonological awareness tests is that they can be administered to children before they learn to read, as a way of identifying children who may be at risk for dyslexia. Early identification before literacy training can be useful because there are methods of reading instruction that are specially tailored to this kind of problem that can be implemented as soon as learning to read commences.

Nonword reading tests

A more direct test of the ability to use spelling-to-sound correspondences is reading nonwords – letter sequences that do not make an actual English word, but are nonetheless a pronounceable sequence of letters. The nonwords are designed to vary in difficulty and test different rules of letter and letter sequences pronunciation. For example, the nonword *dee* is relatively simple, and assesses knowledge of the "ee"→[i] correspondence. The multisyllabic nonword *monglustamer* assesses knowledge of several consonant clusters, the "er" ending, and tests children's ability to map the letter sequences onto a long sequence of phonological segments in the correct order.

Performance on phonological awareness tests and nonword reading tests correlate with reading skill and with each other – that is, problems in one task predict problems in the other, and reading difficulties. Interestingly, there are some aspects of reading that phonological dyslexia does not appear to impair to such a degree. For instance, many readers with phonological dyslexia are relatively good spellers. It may seem counterintuitive that someone diagnosed with a reading disability would be a good speller; however, since the problem in phonological dyslexia is in the phonological route, readers have to rely more heavily on the direct spelling-to-meaning links in order to read. As a result, they tend to become more attuned to details of spelling, as minor differences could mean the difference between two words.

Spelling awareness tests

In fact, there are other reading tests that explicitly test spelling knowledge, called spelling awareness tests. A typical portion of the test might look like the example below, which is an orthographic choice test. It contains examples of test pairs that consist of two forms that are pronounced in the same way – in a sense they are homophones – but only one is a correctly spelled word. A child is presented a pair of words from one of the rows and is asked which one is spelled correctly.

rane	rain
soap	sope
brain	brane
teech	teach

In order to perform well on spelling awareness tests, readers have to have detailed knowledge of the particular letter sequences that correspond to a given word. Notice that proficiency in reading nonwords could actually lower performance in these tests, as one reason why the two-word pairs can be confusing is that they sound the same. If a reader does not have good phonological awareness and does not adequately access the phonological route, then the nonword homophone would not be misleading. In fact, readers with delay dyslexia perform poorly on spelling awareness tests but perform relatively well on phonological awareness tests and nonword reading. Conversely, children with phonological dyslexia who perform poorly on phonological awareness and nonword reading tests perform relatively well on spelling tests; better than those with delay dyslexia and better than normal readers who are matched for overall reading level. It should be emphasized that although there are individuals who have difficulties that uniquely fit the profile for phonological or delay types, some children have a mix of symptoms and perform relatively poorly on all the tasks we've mentioned so far.

Irregular words

A problem that is evident in all forms of developmental dyslexia is difficulty reading **irregular words**, also called **exception words**. These are words that don't follow the conventional spelling-to-sound correspondences. We mentioned the example of *have* earlier, but English is full of such exceptions. *Pint* is another example; it differs from the standard *lint, stint, mint, hint, glint*, and so on. Reading irregulars is particularly challenging because it involves overriding regular pronunciation rules. Identifying the visual word forms that are irregular requires accurate memorization. This kind of memorization seems to be one of the areas where readers with delay dyslexia are impaired, so knowing when to suppress the regular pronunciations rules may be one of the particular problems for readers with this form. On the other hand, readers with phonological dyslexia have difficulty reading all types of words, and their performance on reading irregular words is no better or worse than their (poor) overall performance.

As with spelling awareness, in reading irregular words, delay dyslexics perform similarly to normal readers who are matched for overall reading level, and who generally are a few years younger. Their profile of performance on all of these tasks looks like the performance profile for normal readers, but delayed. With increased exposure to print and tutoring, many of these children eventually can achieve reading performance within the normal range – in other words, they "catch up." In contrast, the underlying deficits in individuals with phonological dyslexia make their developmental profile different from that of normal readers, and their core deficits in phonological awareness and problems mapping from orthography to meaning pose considerable challenges for eventual attaining a normal reading level. Fortunately, however, there are interventions that target the specific problems encountered by children with phonological dyslexia that can dramatically improve reading proficiency.

Having dyslexia need not be a total obstacle to one's ability to be successful. Some very successful historical figures had symptoms of dyslexia, for example, the inventor Thomas Edison, and the artist Pablo Picasso. There are even individuals whose success is in the realm of literature and reading who had dyslexia. In 1923, poet and playwright William Butler Yeats won the Nobel Prize for literature. In his autobiography he described an aspect of his early childhood as follows: "Several of my uncles and aunts had tried to teach me to read, and because they could not, and because I was much older than children who read easily, had come to think, as I have learnt since, that I had not all my faculties."

Successful interventions

As you now know, study after study of skilled reading and reading disabilities highlights the importance of good phonological awareness and understanding of spelling-to-sound correspondences for skilled reading. Fortunately, for individuals who are at risk for reading difficulties because of impairments in these skills, there are relatively simple and inexpensive steps that can be taken to improve learning outcomes. This has been shown in one large-scale longitudinal study (a study that followed individual children for several years) in the North Vancouver school district, in British Columbia. Schools in that district serve children from a variety of socioeconomic, cultural, and language backgrounds. For a sizeable portion of students, English is a second language (ESL). That population in particular historically had lower reading scores and overall academic achievement than their native English-speaking peers.

In 1997, Linda Siegel and her colleagues undertook a large intervention program, targeting kindergarteners who were at risk for reading difficulties. (A full 37% percent of ESL students were identified as at risk for learning disabilities, compared to about 24% of native English speakers.) These children were then given specialized instruction in 20-minute periods, three to four times a week. These brief sessions included practice with phonological awareness, reading exercises, and targeted one-on-one help with problem areas in reading. By fourth grade, the vast majority of these individuals were reading normally, with ESL students slightly surpassing their native English peers. Similar kinds of targeted intervention – emphasizing phonological skills and sounding out words – has also been successfully used in Hong Kong to improve the reading skills of children with dyslexia.

Models of Reading and Learning to Read

Now that we have reviewed some of the scientific evidence about skilled reading and learning to read, we consider some concrete models of reading that attempt to explain the data and provide insights into the underlying mechanisms of reading.

In our discussion so far, and in the diagram in Figure 12.1, we have been talking in general terms about the various routes to accessing meaning: one via phonology, or the representation of the sounds of words, and one that directly links printed words to meanings. Michael Harm and Mark Seidenberg have implemented such a model of reading in a connectionist network. Its design is similar to the "reading triangle" in Figure 12.1: there is a set of units that represents orthography, another set that represents phonology, and a third set that represents meaning. The orthography units correspond to letters in different positions in a word. The phonology units correspond to phonetic features of phonological units in particular positions in a word. The meaning units correspond to features of a word's meaning: for example, *dog* was represented by activating the units corresponding to *canine, mammal, has-tail, has-snout,* and so on. The sets of units at each level were connected to sets of units at the other two levels so that, as in the TRACE model, activation of units at one level of representation would result in connected units at the other levels becoming active. The details of functioning of the units was somewhat different from the TRACE model, and this description simplifies somewhat the connections between levels, but the general idea of the model's operation is similar to TRACE: activation in one type of representation spread to the others via connections. Because of its architecture we will refer to this model as the **triangle model**.

An important aspect of the triangle model was that, unlike the TRACE model, the connections between levels of representation that allowed for the modeling of skilled behavior were learned, rather than hardwired in. First, the model was trained on sound–meaning correspondences: given representations of the sounds of words in the phonological units and the meanings of words in the semantic units, the model had to learn how to activate the correct pronunciation when the experimenter activated a word in the meaning units, and likewise it learned to activate the right meaning when the experimenter activated the representation of a word in the phonological units. The model did so by adjusting the strength of the connections between individual units at the meaning and phonological levels so that the representation it generated (either phonological after a meaning was activated or a meaning after the sounds were activated) was closer to the desired target (also given by the experimenter). This phase of training corresponds to the prereading stage in which children build associations between spoken words and meanings. It was not intended to provide a theory of word learning, but rather to build up sound and meaning representations that would efficiently activate each other and that could be employed in learning to read.

Next the model learned how to activate meanings from orthography. Units at the orthography level were activated by the experimenter, and the model was trained to produce the correct meaning and phonological representations in a similar way as the phonology-semantic training just described. This is akin to a child learning to pronounce a written word and access its meaning. Notice that the training procedure allowed both phonology and meaning to be activated by two routes. For example, meaning units are activated directly via the orthography–meaning connections, but also indirectly via phonology (just as in Figure 12.1). Likewise, phonology units were activated directly via orthography–phonology connections, but also indirectly via meaning. The result was that the model could use two routes to access meaning from print. Recall from our discussion of homophones that reading must involve the direct spelling–meaning route and also the spelling–sound–meaning route. Without the direct route, we would never be able to distinguish *flea* from *flee*. We also saw that for frequent words, experienced readers are not misled by homophones, as in the case of *son* and *sun*. Both facts require a direct orthography–meaning route, and the latter fact suggests that it may develop with exposure.

One of the questions of interest was whether the triangle model would naturally develop this kind of behavior. To test this the experimenters presented a homophone to the orthographic level (i.e., activated the relevant units). To simulate the experiments with humans, the orthographic input was presented to the model for just a brief period of time, and the study observed what meaning representations were active. The model's behavior paralleled the performance of human skilled readers: for low frequency homophones, the model activated representations for both meanings; whereas for high frequency homophones, only the correct meanings were activated. If the experimenters let the orthographic representations stay active longer, then the correct meaning representations eventually dominated. This means that the orthography–meaning connections were active in both high frequency and low frequency words, but they were more accurate and efficient in the high frequency case.

Aside from the model's ability to perform in similar ways as humans, what is particularly noteworthy is that the model developed its behavior naturally, as a result of its general architecture and the way it learns. Importantly, it was not "programmed" in any explicit way to treat high and low frequency homophones differently. Rather, because of the greater systematicity in the orthography–phonology compared to orthography–meaning mappings, learning the spelling–sound mappings was quite accurate in both low and high frequency cases. Learning to map *sun* or *flee* to its corresponding sounds could make use of the regularities learned from learning the mappings of, for example, *fun, run, gun,* or *bee, knee, spree*. This guaranteed that regardless of frequency, the activation from phonology to meaning would provide support for the meanings of both homophones since the phonological representations would be readily activated. Of course, the orthography–meaning connections would not be able to make use of any regularities, so opportunities to learn the appropriate connections only came along when the model was trained on the word in question. Since it (by definition) experienced the low frequency words less frequently, it simply had less opportunity to learn to make the direct connections as compared to with the high frequency words. As a result, the direct orthography–meaning connections were less accurate in activating the correct meaning. In this way, the difference in behavior with respect to low and high frequency homophones was a natural consequence of the general organization of the reading model and how it learned. In general, a theory or model in which a desired behavior arises from general properties is preferable to one in which the behavior has to be programmed in specifically.

The triangle model was run through a battery of tests to evaluate its performance compared to humans. For example, it was tested on its ability to read nonwords, on its ability to read exception words, and a variety of other tasks. The factors that influence humans, such as word frequency and consistency of the spelling–sound correspondences, affected the model in similar ways. It thus has withstood many attempts to falsify it, and it captures a variety of different behavioral phenomena of human readers. In addition, because it implements the activation of meaning directly and through a phonological route, it provides a ready means for modeling reading in languages other than English, such as orthographically more shallow languages and nonalphabetic writing systems like Chinese. Finally, by disrupting different components of the model – for example, the efficiency of the phonological representations and the number of connections from orthography units to meaning units – researchers have been able to cause the model to display various forms of dyslexia. The ability of the model to capture these phenomena lend further support to its value as a model of human reading. It also provides a framework for understanding the processes and representations that might be compromised in individuals with dyslexia.

Another prominent theory is concerned primarily with reading aloud – that is, how readers generate a pronunciation from print – as opposed to accessing meaning. The **dual-route model** of Max Coltheart and colleagues proposes that there are two different routes for activating phonological representations from print (without access meaning *per se*), one familiar one that we have been calling the phonological route (but is termed the **sublexical route** in the theory) uses orthography–phonology correspondence rules. A **lexical route** involves recognizing the visual word form and directly accessing its pronunciation. This can be viewed as similar to the orthography–meaning route in that the association is a stored link between a visual form and the pronunciation, without reference to spelling–sound correspondence rules. Proponents of the dual-route theory equated this process to looking up a word in a pronunciation dictionary: find the entry for the letter sequence and look up its pronunciation. One motivation for hypothesizing dual routes to pronunciation was to explain the ability to read irregular or exception words (like *pint*). It was argued that irregulars could not be processed using spelling–sound correspondence rules because the wrong pronunciation would be produced, so there had to be a special lexical entry for exceptions. In contrast, a route that relies on the correspondence rules is necessary to explain readers' ability to pronounce nonwords (like *nust*), as there can be no prior entry established for words that haven't previously been encountered. However, the triangle model shows that when more of the representations associated with reading are incorporated – meaning and its connections to orthography and phonology – then both types of processes can be carried out without building in an explicit distinction in the model.

Summary

In this chapter we have discussed the structure of skilled reading. We began with a speculative discussion of possible "routes to reading" – paths by which meaning could be activated from printed words. The overview of scientific research on reading demonstrated that while skilled readers can access meaning directly from orthography for frequent words, the phonological route is a critical pathway. We also established that accessing meaning through sound was critical in learning to read, and that problems in this domain lead to reading difficulties and dyslexia. The phonological route to reading plays a role in all writing systems, and in every language that has been studied. Improving children's phonological skills and knowledge of orthography-phonology regularities improves their success in learning to read. The sum of the research we overviewed in this chapter suggests that in a fundamental way, print is a visual substitute for spoken language, albeit one that requires explicit instruction, unlike spoken language.

Further Reading

Rayner, Keith, Barbara R. Foorman, and Charles A. Perfetti, David Pesetsky, and Mark Seidenberg (2002). How Should Reading Be Taught? *Scientific American,* March, pp. 84–91.

Snowling, Margaret J., and Charles Hulme (2005). *The Science of Reading: A Handbook.* Oxford: Wiley-Blackwell.

Sally E. Shaywitz (1996). "Dyslexia" *Scientific American,* November, pp. 98–104.

Appendix

THE INTERNATIONAL PHONETIC ALPHABET (revised to 2005)

CONSONANTS (PULMONIC)

© 2005 IPA

	Bilabial	Labiodental	Dental	Alveolar	Post alveolar	Retroflex	Palatal	Velar	Uvular	Pharyngeal	Glottal
Plosive	p b			t d		ʈ ɖ	c ɟ	k g	q ɢ		ʔ
Nasal	m	ɱ		n		ɳ	ɲ	ŋ	N		
Trill	ʙ			r					R		
Tap or Flap		ⱱ		ɾ		ɽ					
Fricative	ɸ β	f v	θ ð	s z	ʃ ʒ	ʂ ʐ	ç ʝ	x ɣ	χ ʁ	ħ ʕ	h ɦ
Lateral fricative				ɬ ɮ							
Approximant		ʋ		ɹ		ɻ	j	ɰ			
Lateral approximant				l		ɭ	ʎ	L			

Where symbols appear in pairs, the one to the right represents a voiced consonant. Shaded areas denote articulations judged impossible.

CONSONANTS (NON-PULMONIC)

Clicks	Voiced implosives	Ejectives
ʘ Bilabial	ɓ Bilabial	' Examples:
ǀ Dental	ɗ Dental/alveolar	p' Bilabial
ǃ (Post)alveolar	ʄ Palatal	t' Dental/alveolar
ǂ Palatoalveolar	ɠ Velar	k' Velar
ǁ Alveolar lateral	ʛ Uvular	s' Alveolar fricative

OTHER SYMBOLS

- ʍ Voiceless labial-velar fricative
- w Voiced labial-velar approximant
- ɥ Voiced labial-palatal approximant
- ʜ Voiceless epiglottal fricative
- ʢ Voiced epiglottal fricative
- ʡ Epiglottal plosive

- ɕ ʑ Alveolo-palatal fricatives
- ɺ Voiced alveolar lateral flap
- ɧ Simultaneous ʃ and x

Affricates and double articulations can be represented by two symbols joined by a tie bar if necessary. k͡p t͡s

VOWELS

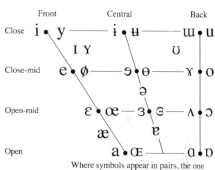

Where symbols appear in pairs, the one to the right represents a rounded vowel.

SUPRASEGMENTALS

ˈ	Primary stress
ˌ	Secondary stress ˌfoʊnəˈtɪʃən
ː	Long eː
ˑ	Half-long eˑ
˘	Extra-short ĕ
ǀ	Minor (foot) group
ǁ	Major (intonation) group
.	Syllable break ɹi.ækt
‿	Linking (absence of a break)

DIACRITICS

Diacritics may be placed above a symbol with a descender, e.g. ŋ̊

̥	Voiceless	n̥ d̥	̤	Breathy voiced	b̤ a̤	̪	Dental	t̪ d̪
̬	Voiced	s̬ t̬	̰	Creaky voiced	b̰ a̰	̺	Apical	t̺ d̺
ʰ	Aspirated	tʰ dʰ	̼	Linguolabial	t̼ d̼	̻	Laminal	t̻ d̻
̹	More rounded	ɔ̹	ʷ	Labialized	tʷ dʷ	̃	Nasalized	ẽ
̜	Less rounded	ɔ̜	ʲ	Palatalized	tʲ dʲ	ⁿ	Nasal release	dⁿ
̟	Advanced	u̟	ˠ	Velarized	tˠ dˠ	ˡ	Lateral release	dˡ
̠	Retracted	e̠	ˤ	Pharyngealized	tˤ dˤ	̚	No audible release	d̚
̈	Centralized	ë	̴	Velarized or pharyngealized ɫ			
̽	Mid-centralized	e̽	̝	Raised	e̝	(ɹ̝ = voiced alveolar fricative)	
̩	Syllabic	n̩	̞	Lowered	e̞	(β̞ = voiced bilabial approximant)	
̯	Non-syllabic	e̯	̘	Advanced Tongue Root	e̘		
˞	Rhoticity	ɚ a˞	̙	Retracted Tongue Root	e̙		

TONES AND WORD ACCENTS

LEVEL				CONTOUR		
e̋ or	˥	Extra high		ě or	˩˥	Rising
é	˦	High		ê	˥˩	Falling
ē	˧	Mid		e᷄	˦˥	High rising
è	˨	Low		e᷅	˩˨	Low rising
ȅ	˩	Extra low		e᷈	˧˦˨	Rising-falling
↓		Downstep		↗		Global rise
↑		Upstep		↘		Global fall

Index

Made in the USA
San Bernardino, CA
09 January 2020

62951827R00180